VALIANT.

Peter Cuneo
Chairman

Dinesh Shamdasani
CEO and Chief Creative Officer

Gavin Cuneo
CFO and Head of Strategic Development

Fred Pierce
Publisher

Warren Simons
VP Executive Editor

Walter Black
VP Operations

Hunter Gorinson
Director of Marketing, Communications
and Digital Media

Atom! Freeman
Sales Manager

Travis Escarfullery
Production and Design Manager

Alejandro Arbona
Associate Editor

Josh Johns
Assistant Editor

Peter Stern
Operations Coordinator

Ivan Cohen
Collection Editor

Steve Blackwell
Collection Designer

Rian Hughes/Device
Trade Dress and Book Design

Russell Brown
President, Consumer Products,
Promotions and Ad Sales

Jason Kothari
Vice Chairman

Shadowman®: Darque Recknoning. Published by Valiant
Entertainment, LLC. Office of Publication: 424 West 33rd Street,
New York, NY 10001. Compilation copyright ©2013 Valiant
Entertainment, Inc. All rights reserved. Contains materials originally
published in single magazine form as Shadowman® #5-9.
Copyright ©2013 Valiant Entertainment, Inc. All rights reserved. All
characters, their distinctive likeness and related indicia featured in
this publication are trademarks of Valiant Entertainment, Inc. The
stories, characters, and incidents featured in this publication are
entirely fictional. Valiant Entertainment does not read or accept
unsolicited submissions of ideas, stories, or artwork.
Printed in the U.S.A. First Printing.
ISBN: 9781939346056.

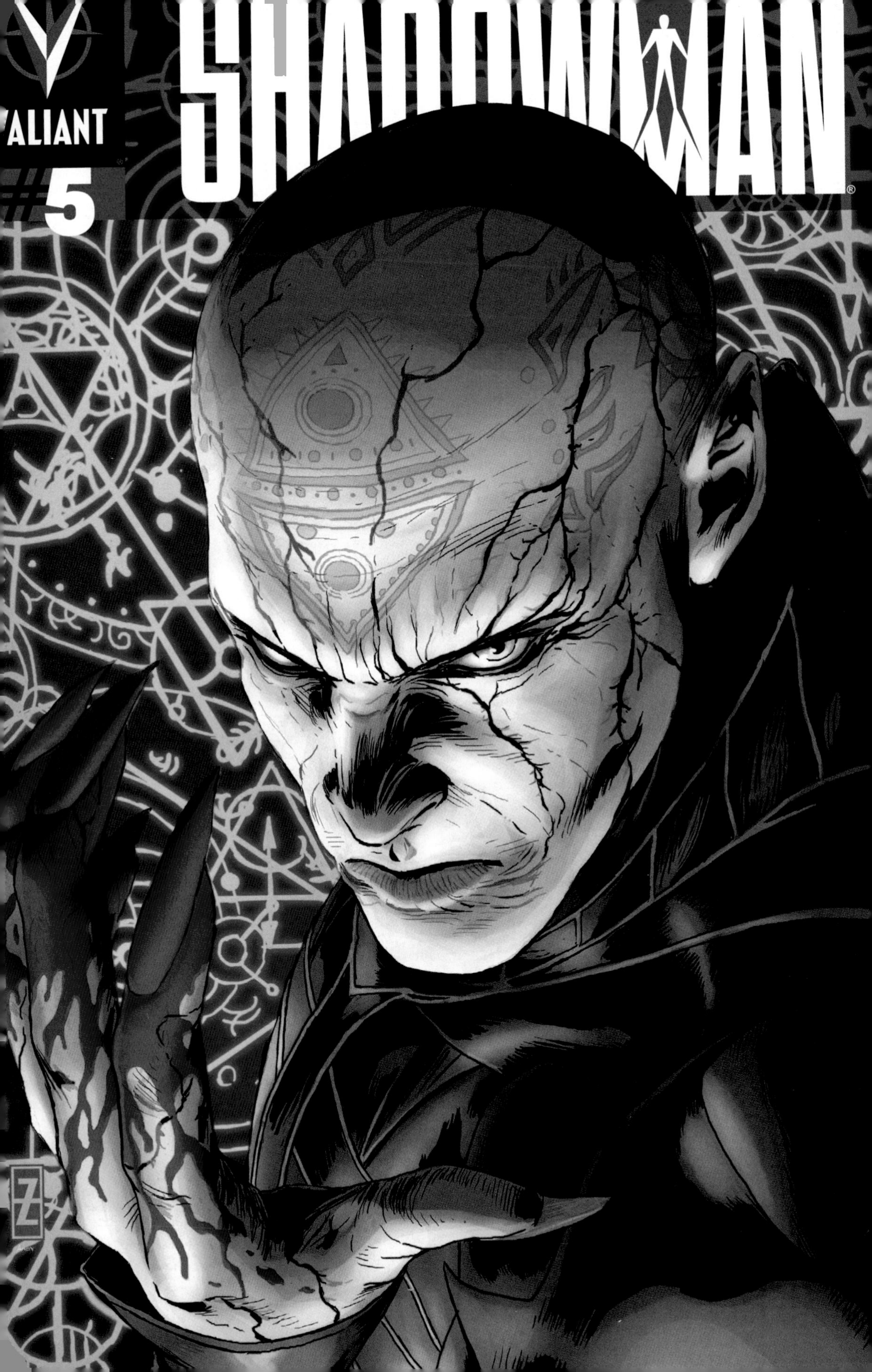
VALIANT
#5
SHADOWMAN

SHADOWMAN

Jack Boniface never met his father, and when he was 10-years-old, his mother, Helena LeBreton, died in a car accident, leaving him to the mercy of the state. Just before Helena died, she gave Jack a special amulet and made him promise that he'd always keep it with him. Years later, Jack returned to his childhood home of New Orleans to learn about his parents. When he learned they had long and violent criminal histories, Jack was enraged and threw his amulet away, rejecting his mother's final wishes.

What Jack couldn't have known is that his father, Josiah Boniface, was the hero known as Shadowman--the last line of defense between our world and the horrors of the nightmare parallel reality known as the Deadside. He also didn't realize that the amulet his mother gave him was protecting Jack from creatures that would kill him if they knew his legacy was to become the next Shadowman. With the amulet gone, Jack is transformed into Shadowman.

Confused and disoriented, Jack is taken in by two people named Dox and Alyssa who claim to be Abettors--individuals sworn to aid the Shadowman in his battle against the darkness. Before Jack can learn more, the group is attacked by a demon calling itself Mr. Twist who has been draining the souls of hundreds of victims in New Orleans in order to acquire necromantic energy. Once he has enough, he plans to use it to release the imprisoned sorcerer known as Master Darque into our reality. Should he succeed, the whole world could fall prey to Darque's necromantic energies.

Jack and Alyssa barely escaped from Twist by ducking into a portal to the Deadside. There Jack met Juanty, a talking monkey and inhabitant of the Deadside, who guided Jack to a ghostly visage that seemed to be Jack's father. His father offered him a choice: become the next Shadowman or return to his regular life. Knowing he would need the powers of Shadowman to save Alyssa, Jack accepted the Shadowman responsibility. Now, as thousands of lost souls swarm upon her, Jack races to save Alyssa before...

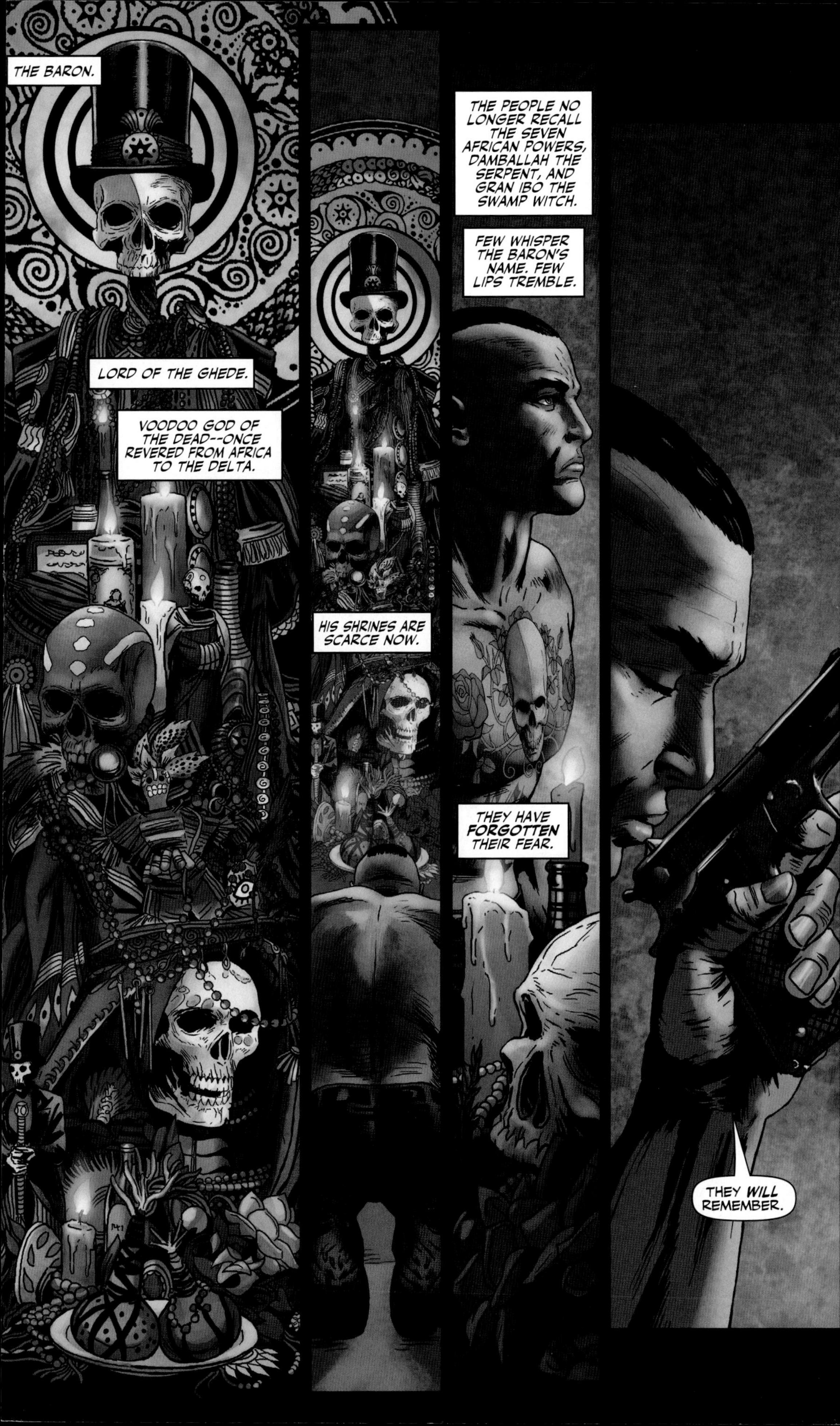
THE BARON.
LORD OF THE GHEDE.
VOODOO GOD OF THE DEAD--ONCE REVERED FROM AFRICA TO THE DELTA.
HIS SHRINES ARE SCARCE NOW.
THE PEOPLE NO LONGER RECALL THE SEVEN AFRICAN POWERS, DAMBALLAH THE SERPENT, AND GRAN IBO THE SWAMP WITCH.
FEW WHISPER THE BARON'S NAME. FEW LIPS TREMBLE.
THEY HAVE FORGOTTEN THEIR FEAR.
THEY WILL REMEMBER.

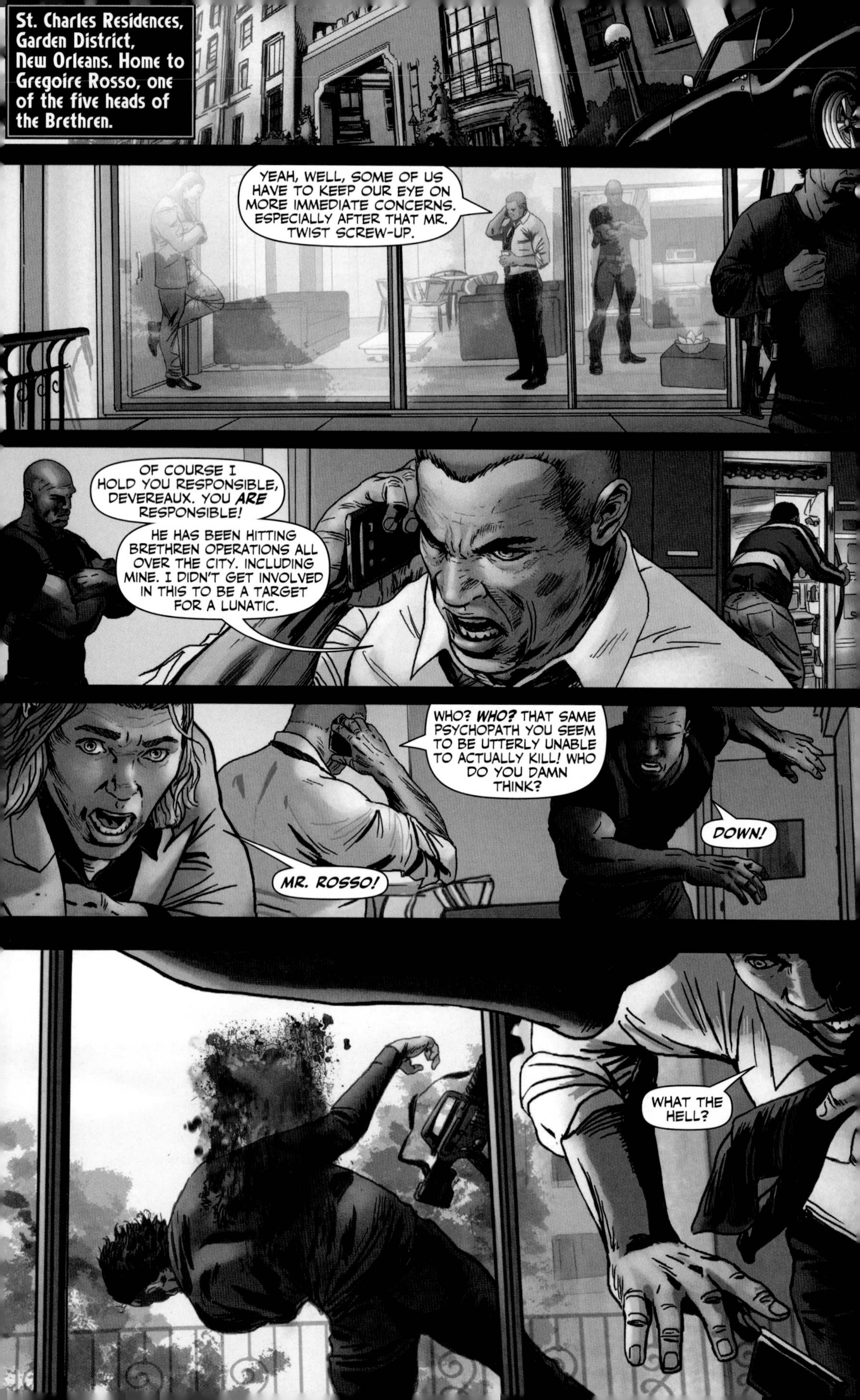
St. Charles Residences, Garden District, New Orleans. Home to Gregoire Rosso, one of the five heads of the Brethren.
YEAH, WELL, SOME OF US HAVE TO KEEP OUR EYE ON MORE IMMEDIATE CONCERNS. ESPECIALLY AFTER THAT MR. TWIST SCREW-UP.
OF COURSE I HOLD YOU RESPONSIBLE, DEVEREAUX. YOU ARE RESPONSIBLE!
HE HAS BEEN HITTING BRETHREN OPERATIONS ALL OVER THE CITY. INCLUDING MINE. I DIDN'T GET INVOLVED IN THIS TO BE A TARGET FOR A LUNATIC.
WHO? WHO? THAT SAME PSYCHOPATH YOU SEEM TO BE UTTERLY UNABLE TO ACTUALLY KILL! WHO DO YOU DAMN THINK?
MR. ROSSO!
DOWN!
WHAT THE HELL?

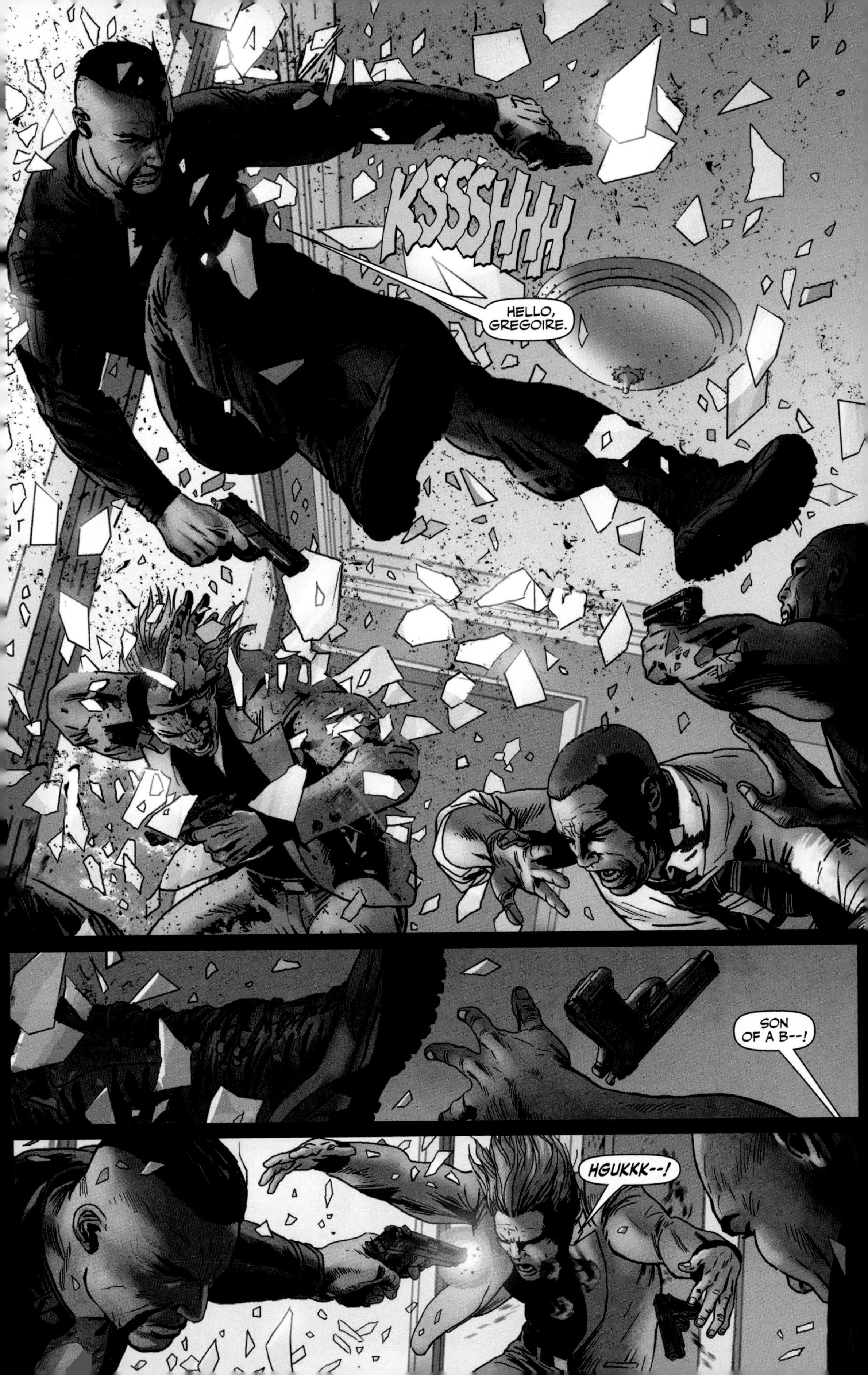
KSSSHHH
HELLO, GREGOIRE.
SON OF A B--!
HGUKKK--!

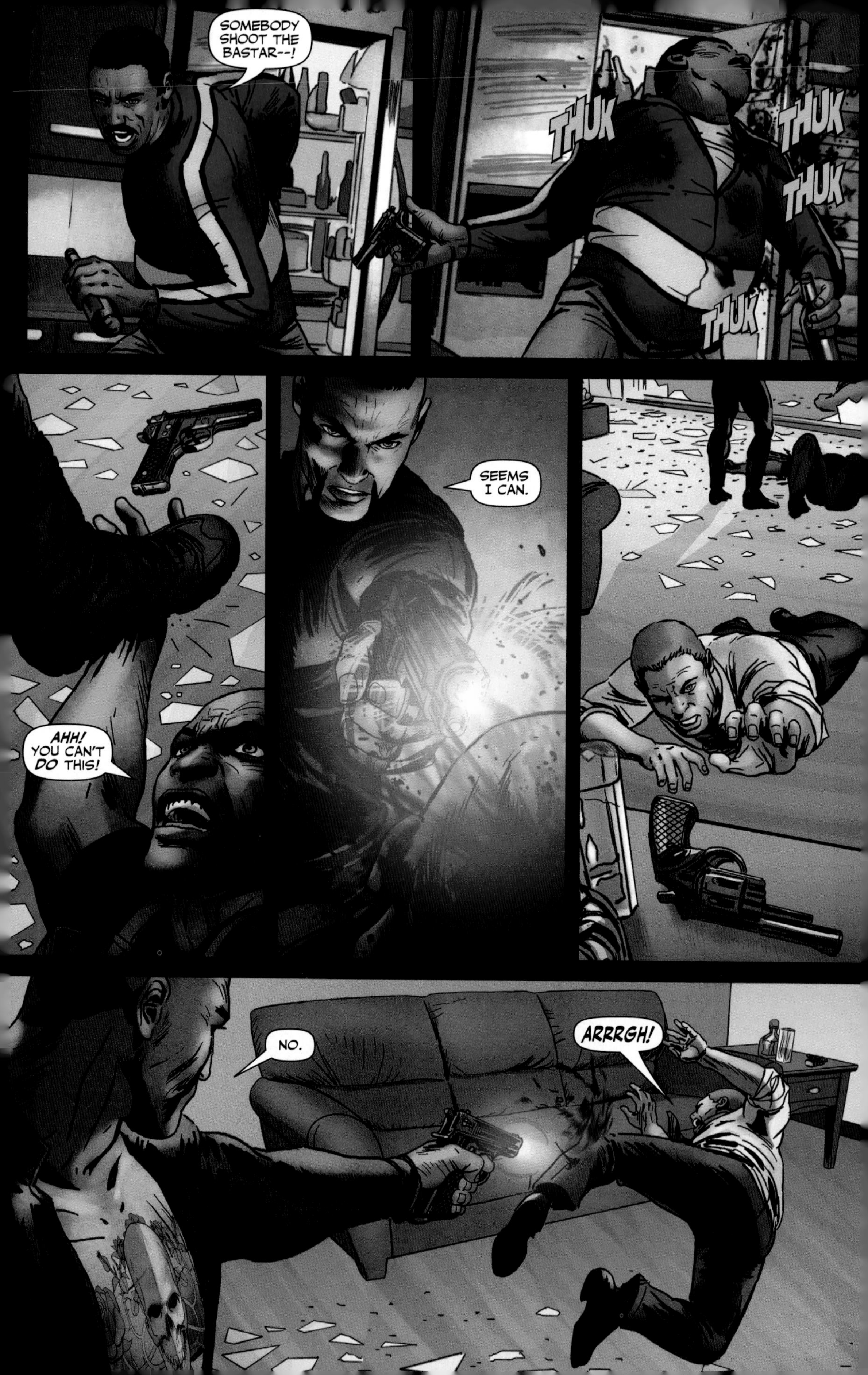
SOMEBODY SHOOT THE BASTAR--!
THUK
THUK
THUK
THUK
AHH! YOU CAN'T DO THIS!
SEEMS I CAN.
NO.
ARRRGH!

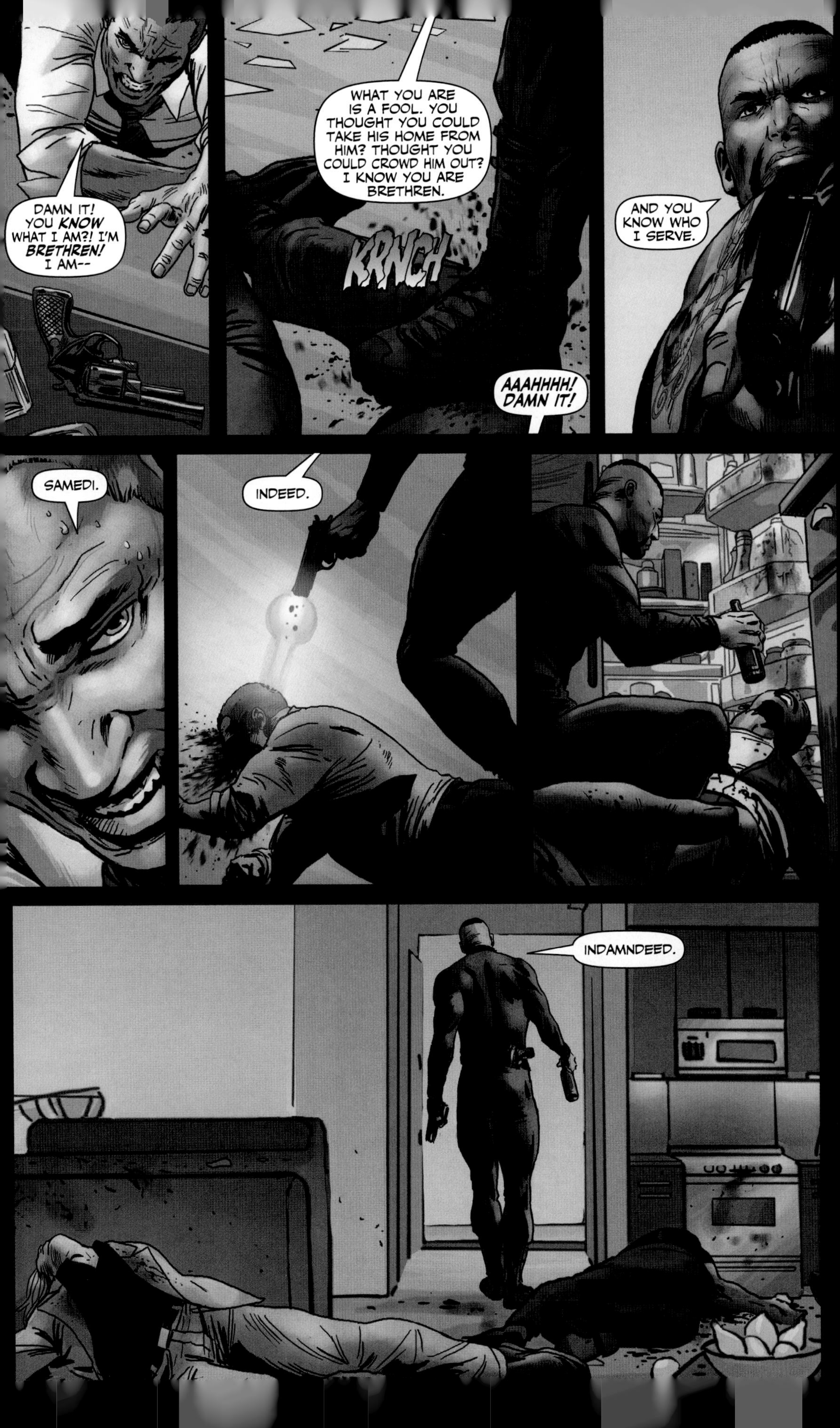
DAMN IT! YOU KNOW WHAT I AM?! I'M BRETHREN! I AM--
WHAT YOU ARE IS A FOOL. YOU THOUGHT YOU COULD TAKE HIS HOME FROM HIM? THOUGHT YOU COULD CROWD HIM OUT? I KNOW YOU ARE BRETHREN.
KRNCH
AAAHHHH! DAMN IT!
AND YOU KNOW WHO I SERVE.
SAMEDI.
INDEED.
INDAMNDEED.

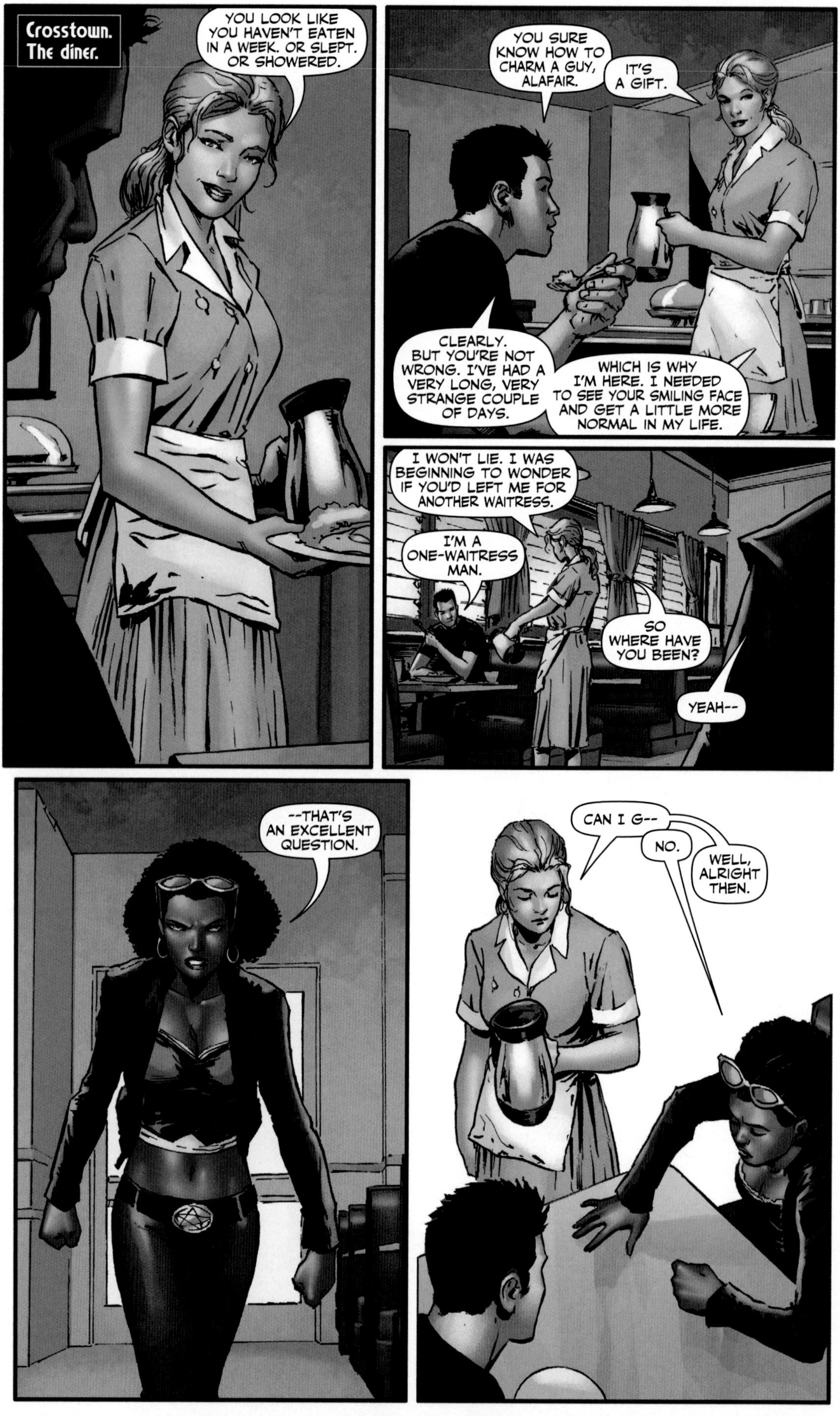
Crosstown. The diner.
YOU LOOK LIKE YOU HAVEN'T EATEN IN A WEEK. OR SLEPT. OR SHOWERED.
YOU SURE KNOW HOW TO CHARM A GUY, ALAFAIR.
IT'S A GIFT.
CLEARLY. BUT YOU'RE NOT WRONG. I'VE HAD A VERY LONG, VERY STRANGE COUPLE OF DAYS.
WHICH IS WHY I'M HERE. I NEEDED TO SEE YOUR SMILING FACE AND GET A LITTLE MORE NORMAL IN MY LIFE.
I WON'T LIE. I WAS BEGINNING TO WONDER IF YOU'D LEFT ME FOR ANOTHER WAITRESS.
I'M A ONE-WAITRESS MAN.
SO WHERE HAVE YOU BEEN?
YEAH--
--THAT'S AN EXCELLENT QUESTION.
CAN I G--
NO.
WELL, ALRIGHT THEN.

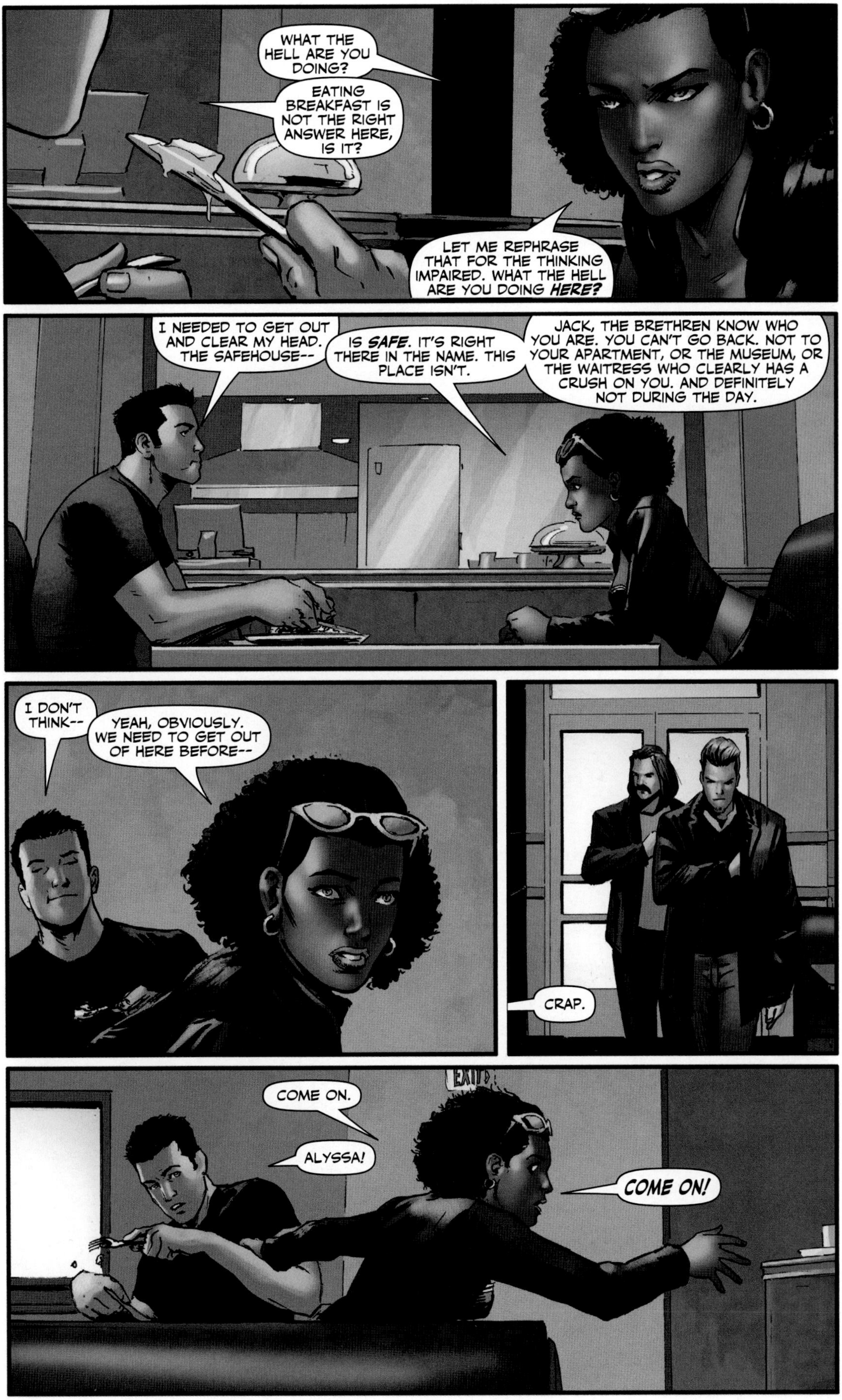
WHAT THE HELL ARE YOU DOING?
EATING BREAKFAST IS NOT THE RIGHT ANSWER HERE, IS IT?
LET ME REPHRASE THAT FOR THE THINKING IMPAIRED. WHAT THE HELL ARE YOU DOING *HERE?*
I NEEDED TO GET OUT AND CLEAR MY HEAD. THE SAFEHOUSE--
IS *SAFE*. IT'S RIGHT THERE IN THE NAME. THIS PLACE ISN'T.
JACK, THE BRETHREN KNOW WHO YOU ARE. YOU CAN'T GO BACK. NOT TO YOUR APARTMENT, OR THE MUSEUM, OR THE WAITRESS WHO CLEARLY HAS A CRUSH ON YOU. AND DEFINITELY NOT DURING THE DAY.
I DON'T THINK--
YEAH, OBVIOUSLY. WE NEED TO GET OUT OF HERE BEFORE--
CRAP.
COME ON.
ALYSSA!
COME ON!

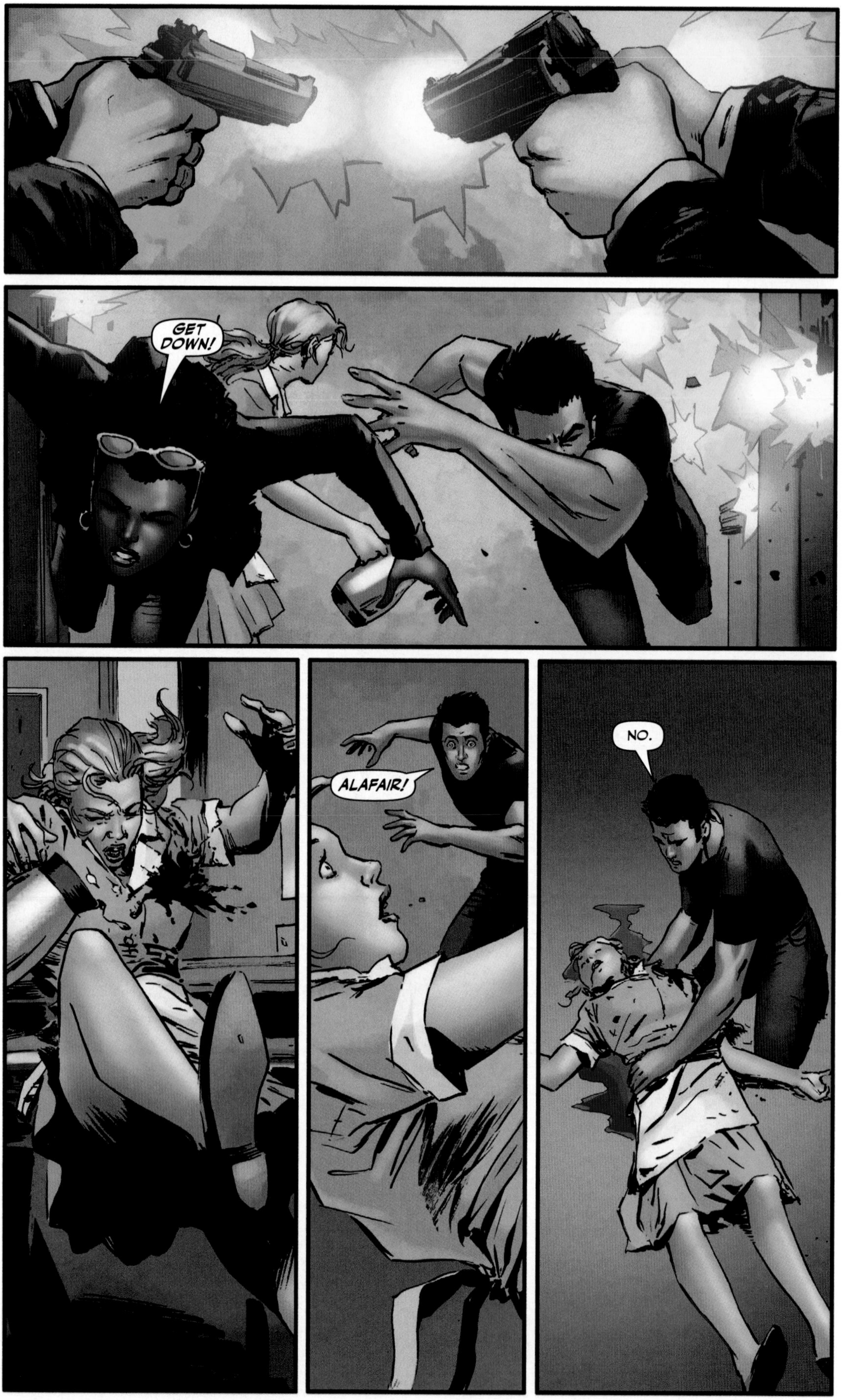
GET DOWN!
ALAFAIR!
NO.

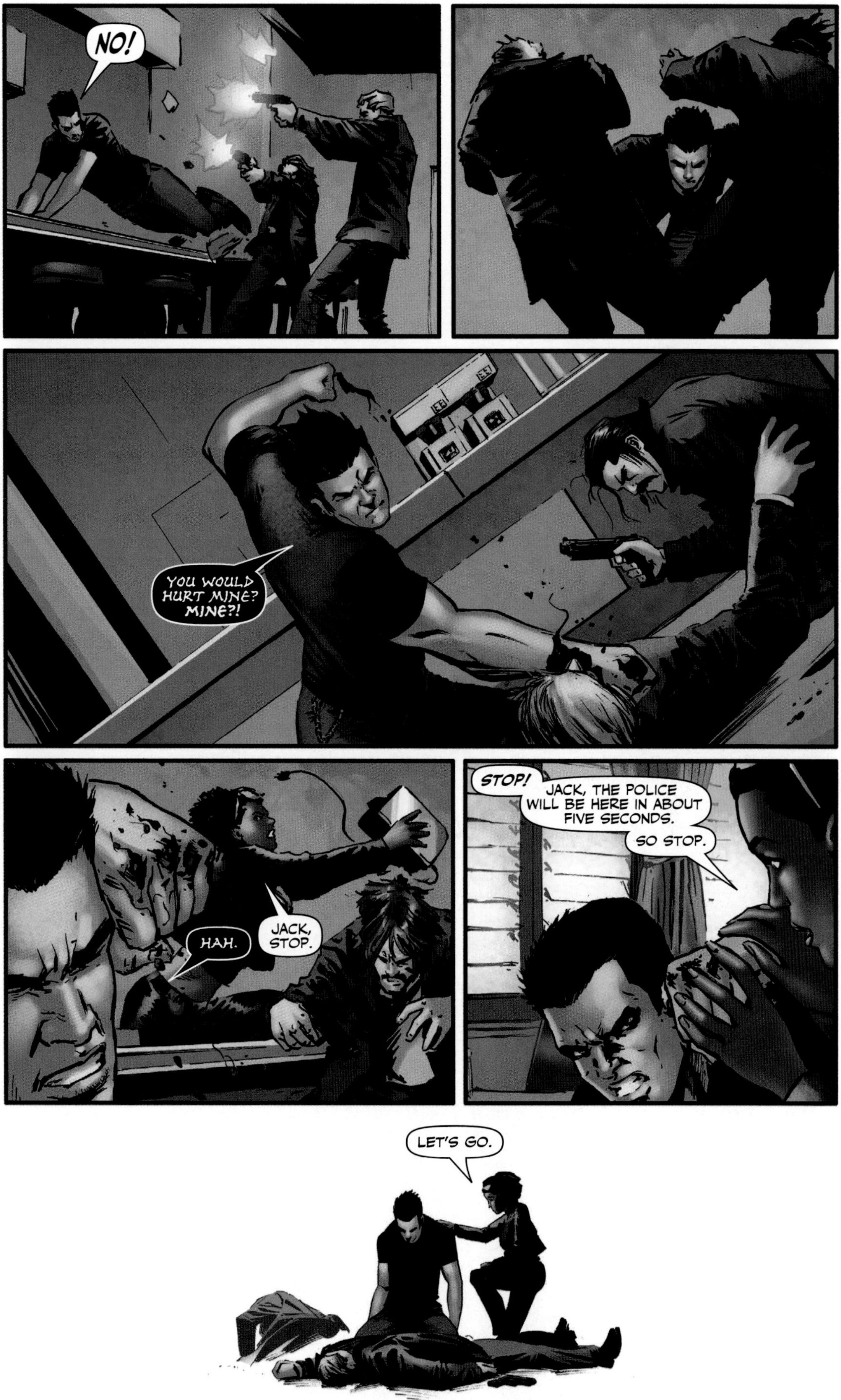
NO!
YOU WOULD HURT MINE? MINE?!
JACK, STOP.
HAH.
STOP!
JACK, THE POLICE WILL BE HERE IN ABOUT FIVE SECONDS.
SO STOP.
LET'S GO.

Men's Central Jail.

Los Angeles County, California.

WHAT ARE YOU? ONE OF THOSE DAMN CIRCUS PERFORMERS?

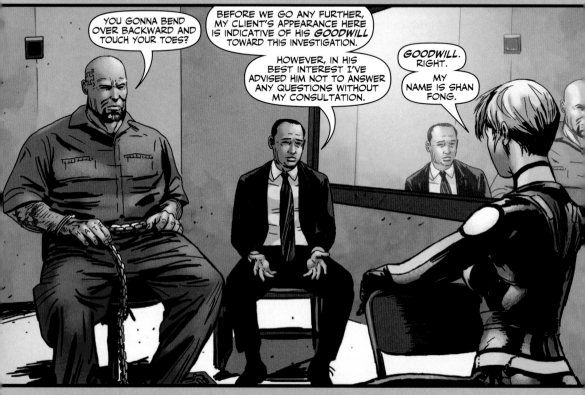

YOU GONNA BEND OVER BACKWARD AND TOUCH YOUR TOES?

BEFORE WE GO ANY FURTHER, MY CLIENT'S APPEARANCE HERE IS INDICATIVE OF HIS *GOODWILL* TOWARD THIS INVESTIGATION.

HOWEVER, IN HIS BEST INTEREST I'VE ADVISED HIM NOT TO ANSWER ANY QUESTIONS WITHOUT MY CONSULTATION.

GOODWILL. RIGHT. MY NAME IS SHAN FONG.

ACTUALLY, DR. SHAN FONG. BUT I'M PROBABLY BETTER KNOWN AS DR. MIRAGE, EVER SINCE THAT TELEVISION SHOW. IF YOU WANT TO GET TECHNICAL, I'M A PARANORMAL INVESTIGATOR.

THAT'S A LITTLE LIKE A PRIVATE INVESTIGATOR EXCEPT I DEAL WITH PSYCHIC PHENOMENA, THE SUPERNATURAL AND, FRANKLY, A LOT OF CRAZY PEOPLE WHO SHOULD PROBABLY GET OUT MORE.

AND EVERY ONCE IN A WHILE--IF A CLIENT LIKE THE L.A.P.D. IS DESPERATE ENOUGH--I DEAL WITH ORDINARY *HUMAN* MONSTERS LIKE YOUR CLIENT.

VISITOR
FONG, SHAN

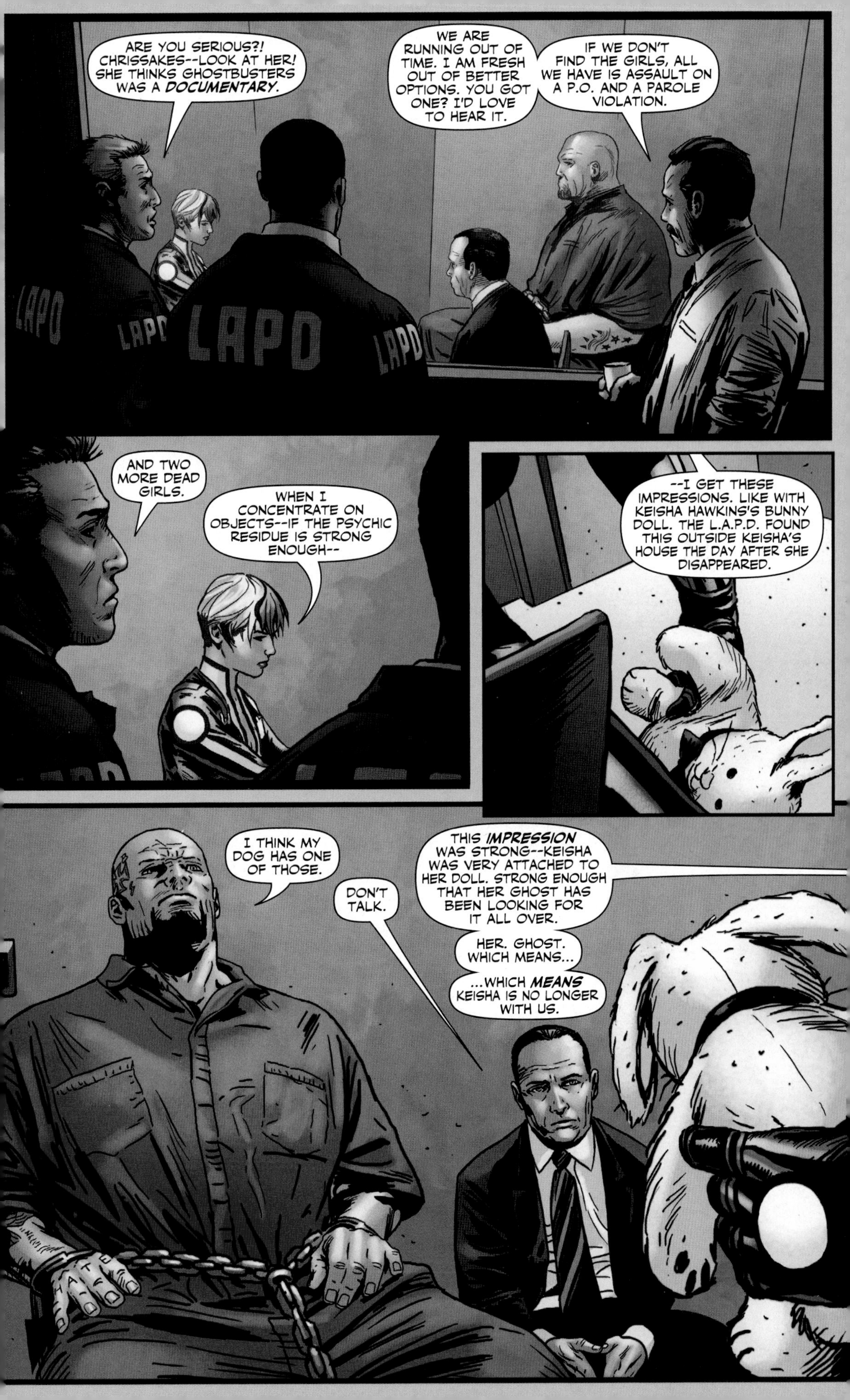
ARE YOU SERIOUS?! CHRISSAKES--LOOK AT HER! SHE THINKS GHOSTBUSTERS WAS A *DOCUMENTARY*.
WE ARE RUNNING OUT OF TIME. I AM FRESH OUT OF BETTER OPTIONS. YOU GOT ONE? I'D LOVE TO HEAR IT.
IF WE DON'T FIND THE GIRLS, ALL WE HAVE IS ASSAULT ON A P.O. AND A PAROLE VIOLATION.
LAPD
LAPD
LAPD
LAPD
AND TWO MORE DEAD GIRLS.
WHEN I CONCENTRATE ON OBJECTS--IF THE PSYCHIC RESIDUE IS STRONG ENOUGH--
--I GET THESE IMPRESSIONS. LIKE WITH KEISHA HAWKINS'S BUNNY DOLL. THE L.A.P.D. FOUND THIS OUTSIDE KEISHA'S HOUSE THE DAY AFTER SHE DISAPPEARED.
I THINK MY DOG HAS ONE OF THOSE.
DON'T TALK.
THIS *IMPRESSION* WAS STRONG--KEISHA WAS VERY ATTACHED TO HER DOLL. STRONG ENOUGH THAT HER GHOST HAS BEEN LOOKING FOR IT ALL OVER.
HER. GHOST. WHICH MEANS...
...WHICH *MEANS* KEISHA IS NO LONGER WITH US.

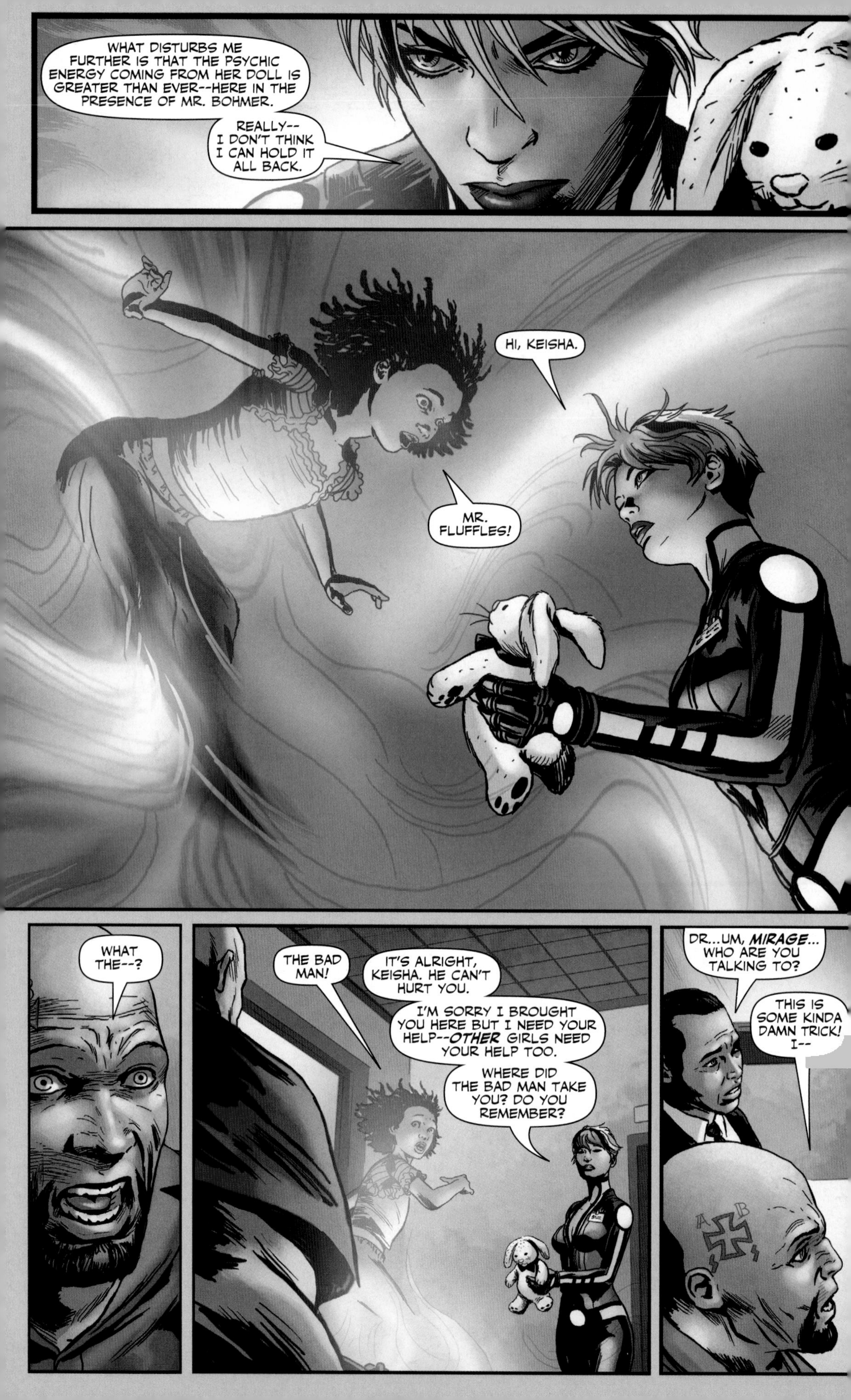
WHAT DISTURBS ME FURTHER IS THAT THE PSYCHIC ENERGY COMING FROM HER DOLL IS GREATER THAN EVER--HERE IN THE PRESENCE OF MR. BOHMER.
REALLY-- I DON'T THINK I CAN HOLD IT ALL BACK.
HI, KEISHA.
MR. FLUFFLES!
WHAT THE--?
THE BAD MAN!
IT'S ALRIGHT, KEISHA. HE CAN'T HURT YOU.
I'M SORRY I BROUGHT YOU HERE BUT I NEED YOUR HELP--*OTHER* GIRLS NEED YOUR HELP TOO.
WHERE DID THE BAD MAN TAKE YOU? DO YOU REMEMBER?
DR...UM, *MIRAGE*... WHO ARE YOU TALKING TO?
THIS IS SOME KINDA DAMN TRICK! I--

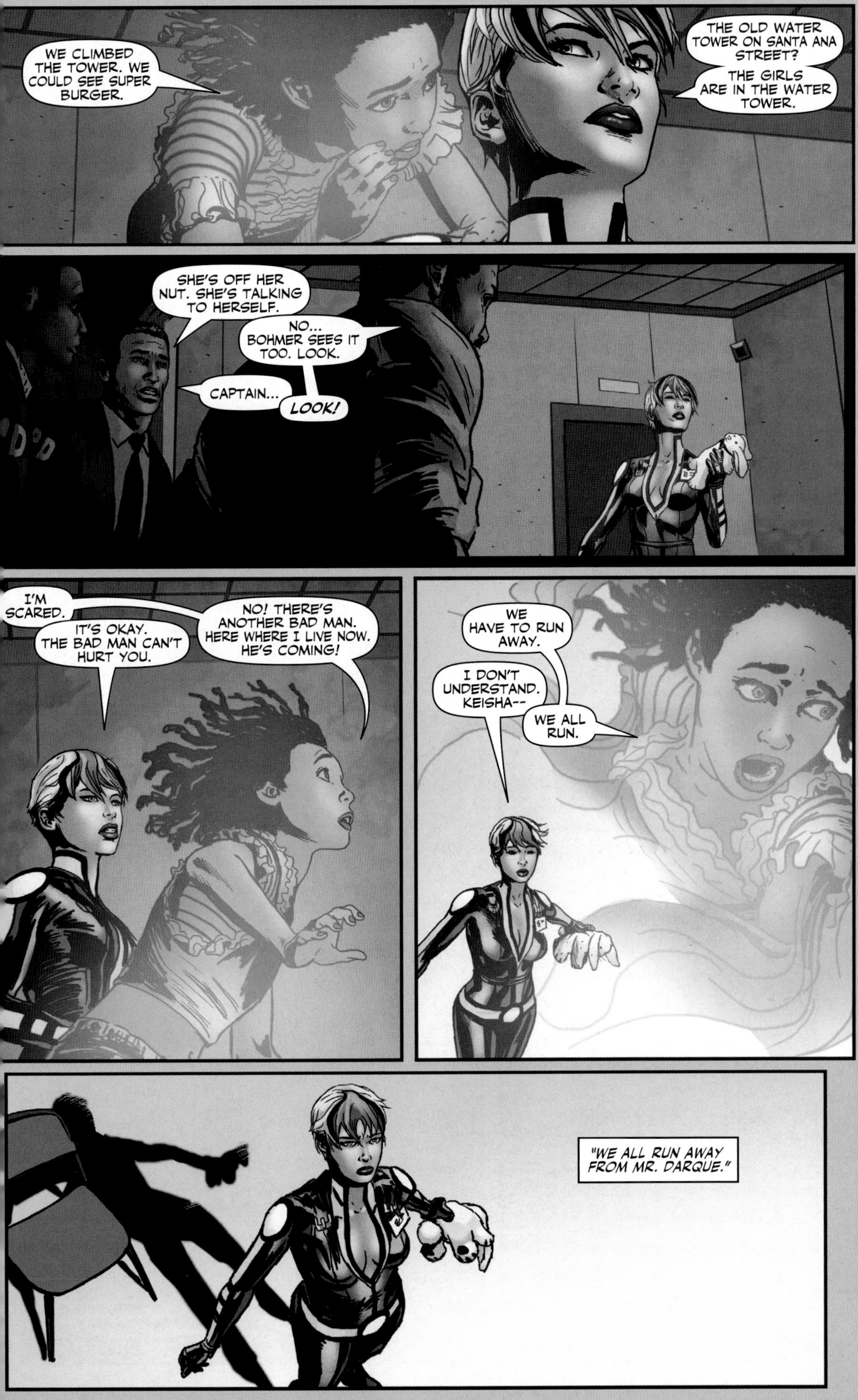
WE CLIMBED THE TOWER. WE COULD SEE SUPER BURGER.
THE OLD WATER TOWER ON SANTA ANA STREET?
THE GIRLS ARE IN THE WATER TOWER.
SHE'S OFF HER NUT. SHE'S TALKING TO HERSELF.
NO... BOHMER SEES IT TOO. LOOK.
CAPTAIN...
LOOK!
I'M SCARED.
IT'S OKAY. THE BAD MAN CAN'T HURT YOU.
NO! THERE'S ANOTHER BAD MAN. HERE WHERE I LIVE NOW. HE'S COMING!
WE HAVE TO RUN AWAY.
I DON'T UNDERSTAND. KEISHA--
WE ALL RUN.
"WE ALL RUN AWAY FROM MR. DARQUE."

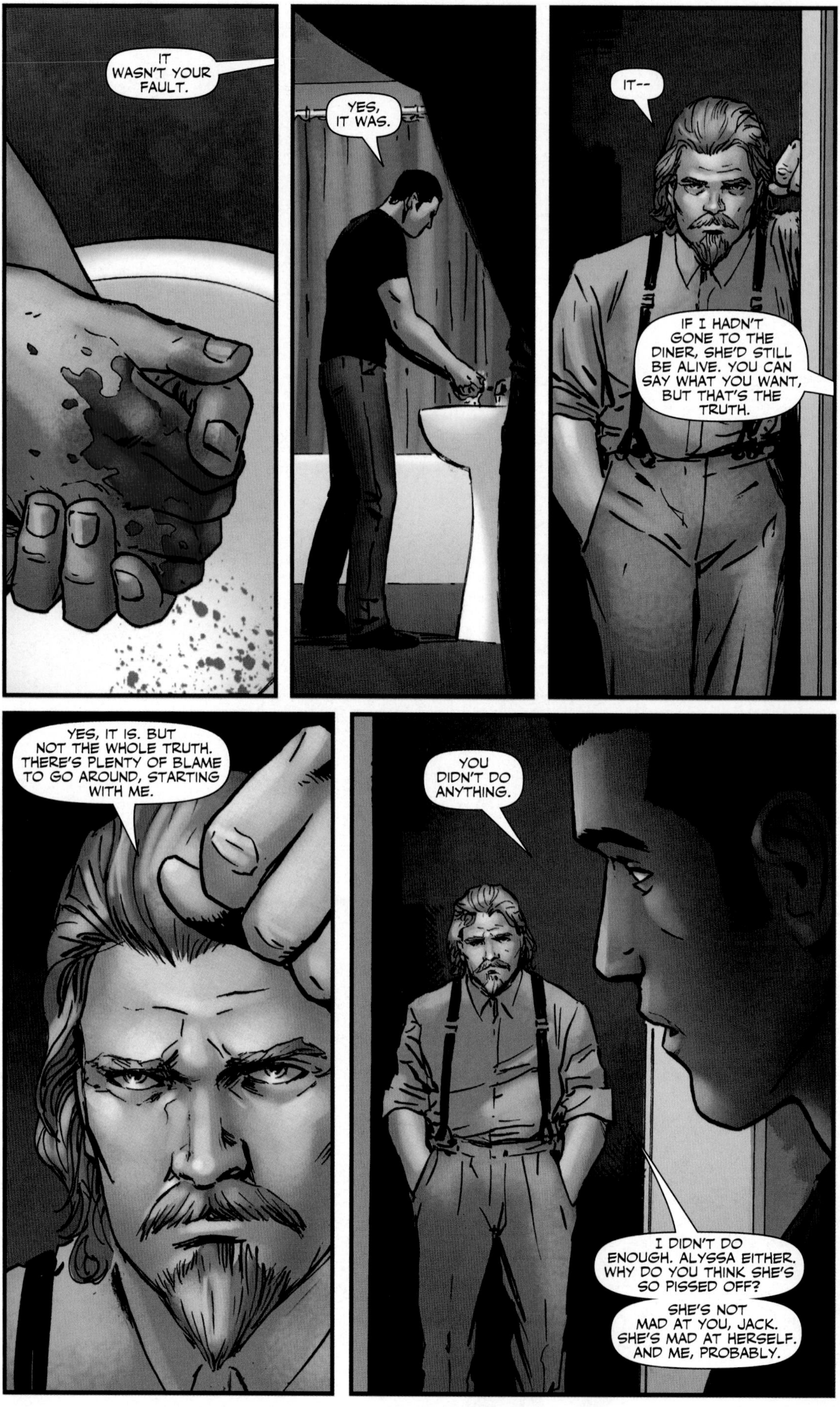
IT WASN'T YOUR FAULT.
YES, IT WAS.
IT--
IF I HADN'T GONE TO THE DINER, SHE'D STILL BE ALIVE. YOU CAN SAY WHAT YOU WANT, BUT THAT'S THE TRUTH.
YES, IT IS. BUT NOT THE WHOLE TRUTH. THERE'S PLENTY OF BLAME TO GO AROUND, STARTING WITH ME.
YOU DIDN'T DO ANYTHING.
I DIDN'T DO ENOUGH. ALYSSA EITHER. WHY DO YOU THINK SHE'S SO PISSED OFF?
SHE'S NOT MAD AT YOU, JACK. SHE'S MAD AT HERSELF. AND ME, PROBABLY.

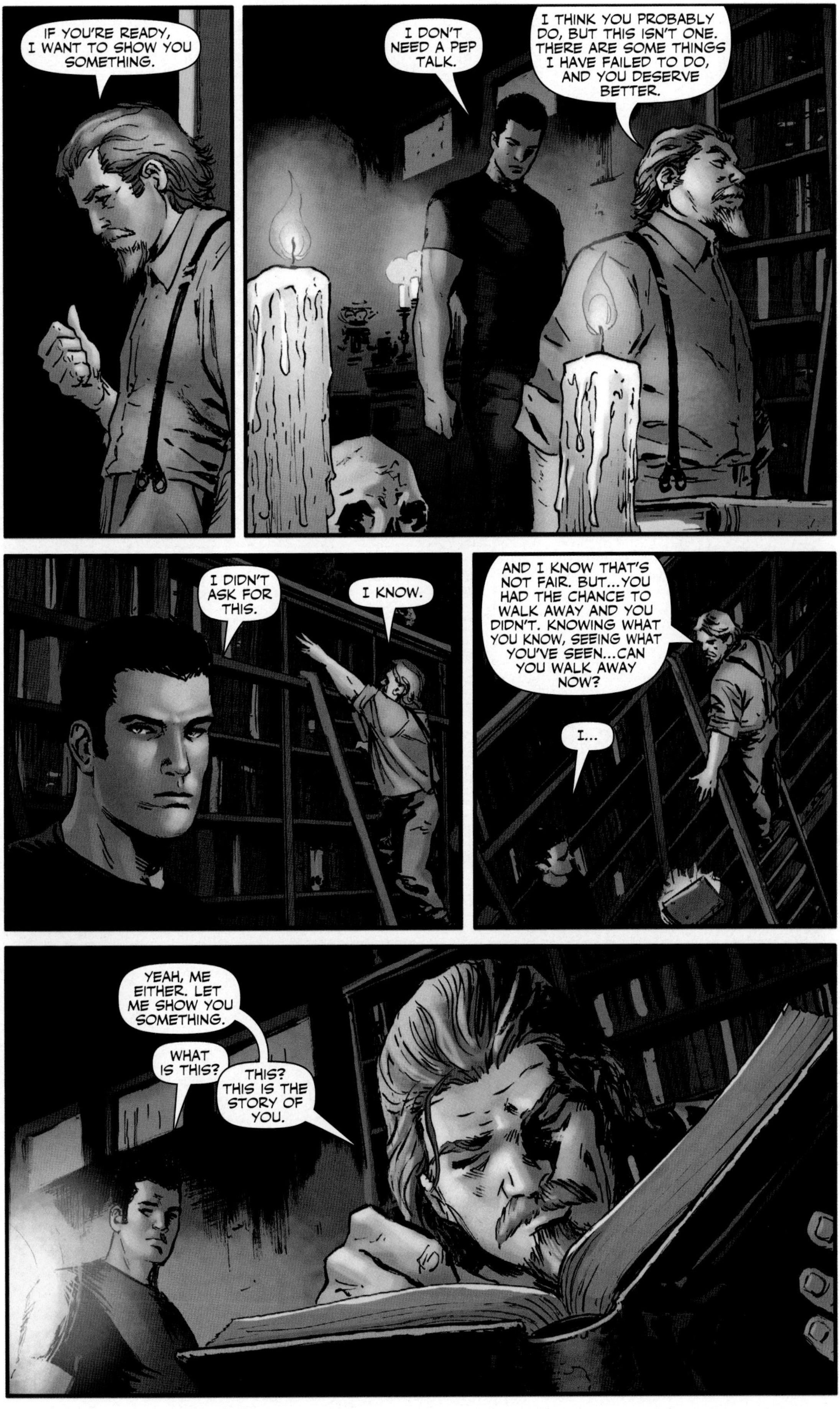
IF YOU'RE READY, I WANT TO SHOW YOU SOMETHING.
I DON'T NEED A PEP TALK.
I THINK YOU PROBABLY DO, BUT THIS ISN'T ONE. THERE ARE SOME THINGS I HAVE FAILED TO DO, AND YOU DESERVE BETTER.
I DIDN'T ASK FOR THIS.
I KNOW.
AND I KNOW THAT'S NOT FAIR. BUT...YOU HAD THE CHANCE TO WALK AWAY AND YOU DIDN'T. KNOWING WHAT YOU KNOW, SEEING WHAT YOU'VE SEEN...CAN YOU WALK AWAY NOW?
I...
YEAH, ME EITHER. LET ME SHOW YOU SOMETHING.
WHAT IS THIS?
THIS? THIS IS THE STORY OF YOU.

"THIS IS THE STORY OF THE SHADOWMAN.

"THE MANTLE, THE LOA, HAS PASSED DOWN FROM FATHER TO SON FOR GENERATIONS.

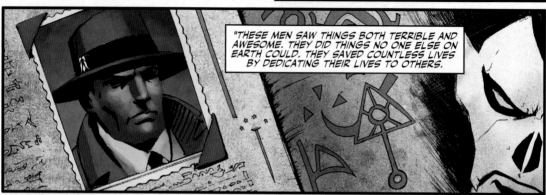

"THESE MEN SAW THINGS BOTH TERRIBLE AND AWESOME. THEY DID THINGS NO ONE ELSE ON EARTH COULD. THEY SAVED COUNTLESS LIVES BY DEDICATING THEIR LIVES TO OTHERS.

"AND MANY OF THEM DIED DOING IT."

NOW THAT RESPONSIBILITY FALLS ON YOU.

IS THERE A LESSON HERE?

YES, THERE IS.

THERE HAS NEVER BEEN A SHADOWMAN LIKE YOU, JACK. EVERY ONE OF THESE MEN, FROM MARIUS TO YOUR FATHER, WAS TRAINED FROM BIRTH TO BE WHAT THEY ARE.

I KNOW HOW TO FIX A LEAKY ROOF. I KNOW HOW TO READ LIBRARY OF CONGRESS CALL NUMBERS. I EVEN KNOW HOW TO FIX A CARBURETOR IF I NEED TO. BUT I DON'T KNOW HOW TO DO THIS.

NO. AND THAT'S A PROBLEM. I SHOULD HAVE DONE A BETTER JOB IMPRESSING ON YOU HOW DANGEROUS THIS LIFE IS. I SHOULD HAVE MADE SURE YOU KNEW.

AND I DIDN'T. THAT'S ON ME.

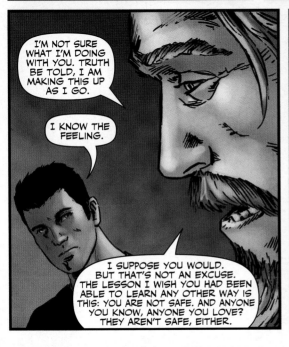

I'M NOT SURE WHAT I'M DOING WITH YOU. TRUTH BE TOLD, I AM MAKING THIS UP AS I GO.

I KNOW THE FEELING.

I SUPPOSE YOU WOULD. BUT THAT'S NOT AN EXCUSE. THE LESSON I WISH YOU HAD BEEN ABLE TO LEARN ANY OTHER WAY IS THIS: YOU ARE NOT SAFE. AND ANYONE YOU KNOW, ANYONE YOU LOVE? THEY AREN'T SAFE, EITHER.

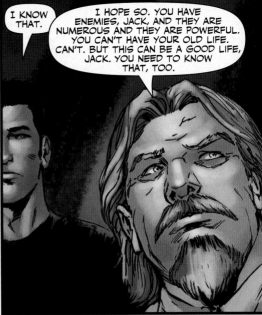

I KNOW THAT.

I HOPE SO. YOU HAVE ENEMIES, JACK, AND THEY ARE NUMEROUS AND THEY ARE POWERFUL. YOU CAN'T HAVE YOUR OLD LIFE. CAN'T. BUT THIS CAN BE A GOOD LIFE, JACK. YOU NEED TO KNOW THAT, TOO.

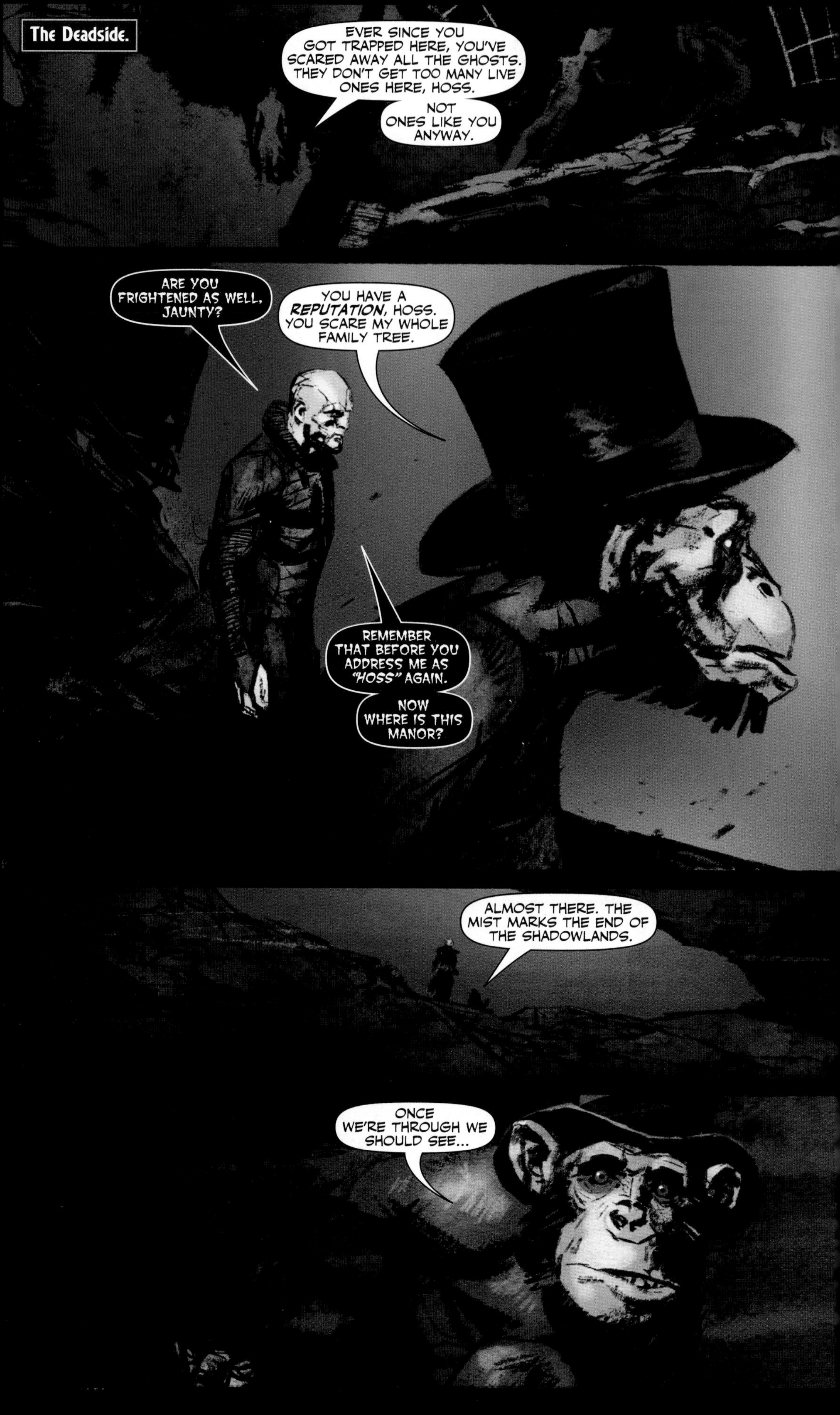
The Deadside.
EVER SINCE YOU GOT TRAPPED HERE, YOU'VE SCARED AWAY ALL THE GHOSTS. THEY DON'T GET TOO MANY LIVE ONES HERE, HOSS.
NOT ONES LIKE YOU ANYWAY.
ARE YOU FRIGHTENED AS WELL, JAUNTY?
YOU HAVE A *REPUTATION*, HOSS. YOU SCARE MY WHOLE FAMILY TREE.
REMEMBER THAT BEFORE YOU ADDRESS ME AS *"HOSS"* AGAIN.
NOW WHERE IS THIS MANOR?
ALMOST THERE. THE MIST MARKS THE END OF THE SHADOWLANDS.
ONCE WE'RE THROUGH WE SHOULD SEE...

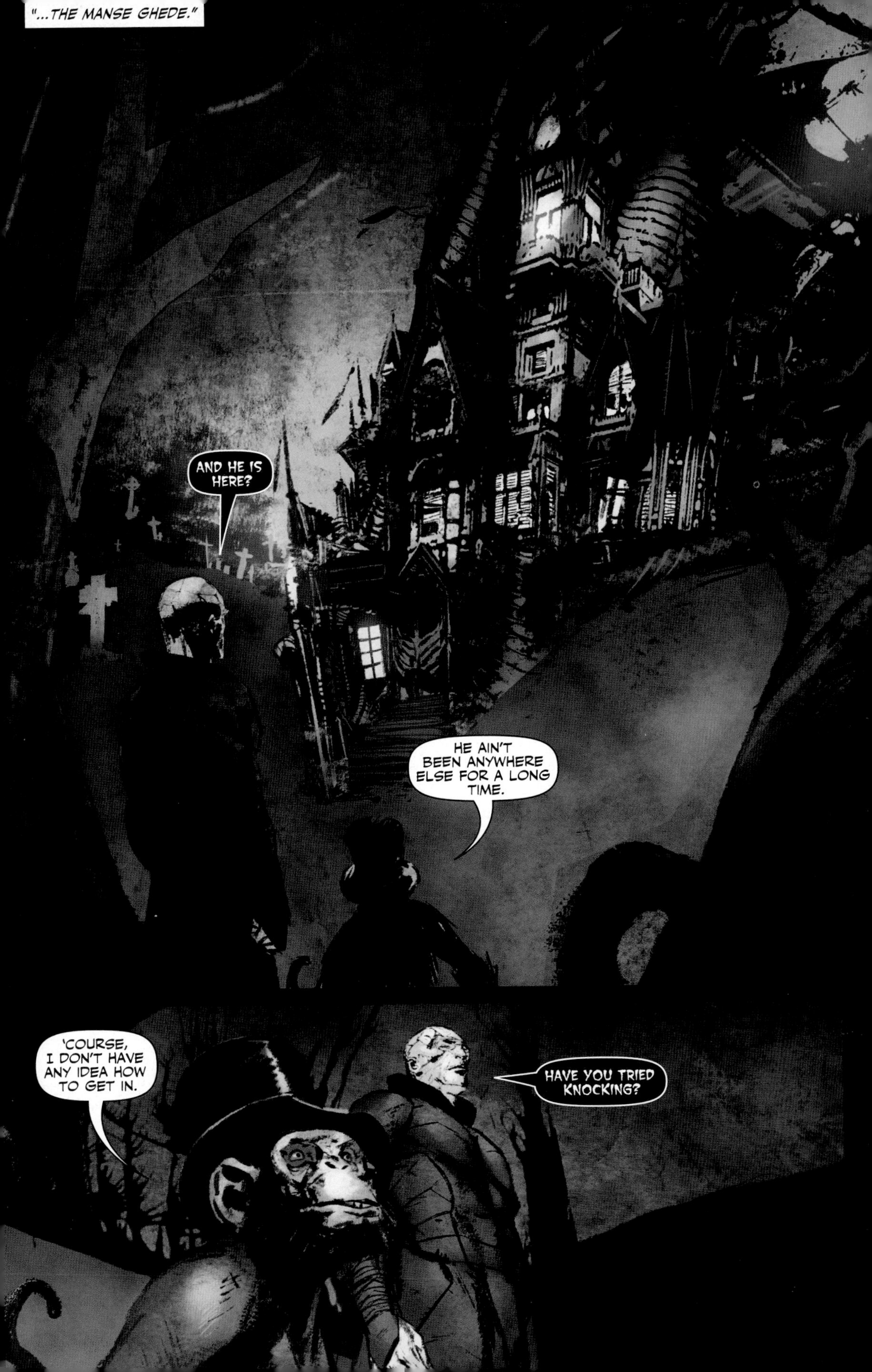
"...THE MANSE GHEDE."
AND HE IS HERE?
HE AIN'T BEEN ANYWHERE ELSE FOR A LONG TIME.
'COURSE, I DON'T HAVE ANY IDEA HOW TO GET IN.
HAVE YOU TRIED KNOCKING?

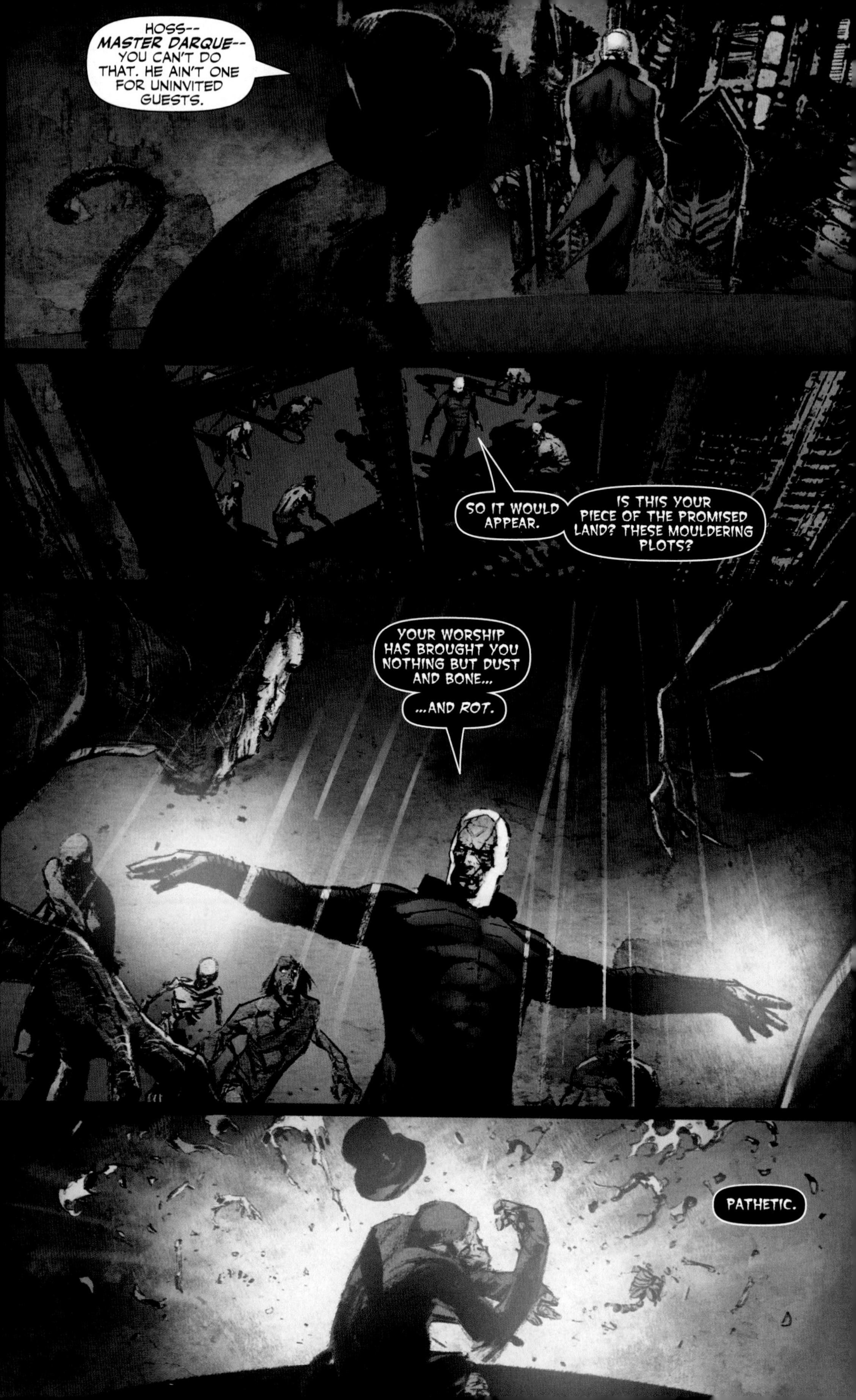
HOSS-- MASTER DARQUE-- YOU CAN'T DO THAT. HE AIN'T ONE FOR UNINVITED GUESTS.
SO IT WOULD APPEAR.
IS THIS YOUR PIECE OF THE PROMISED LAND? THESE MOULDERING PLOTS?
YOUR WORSHIP HAS BROUGHT YOU NOTHING BUT DUST AND BONE...
...AND ROT.
PATHETIC.

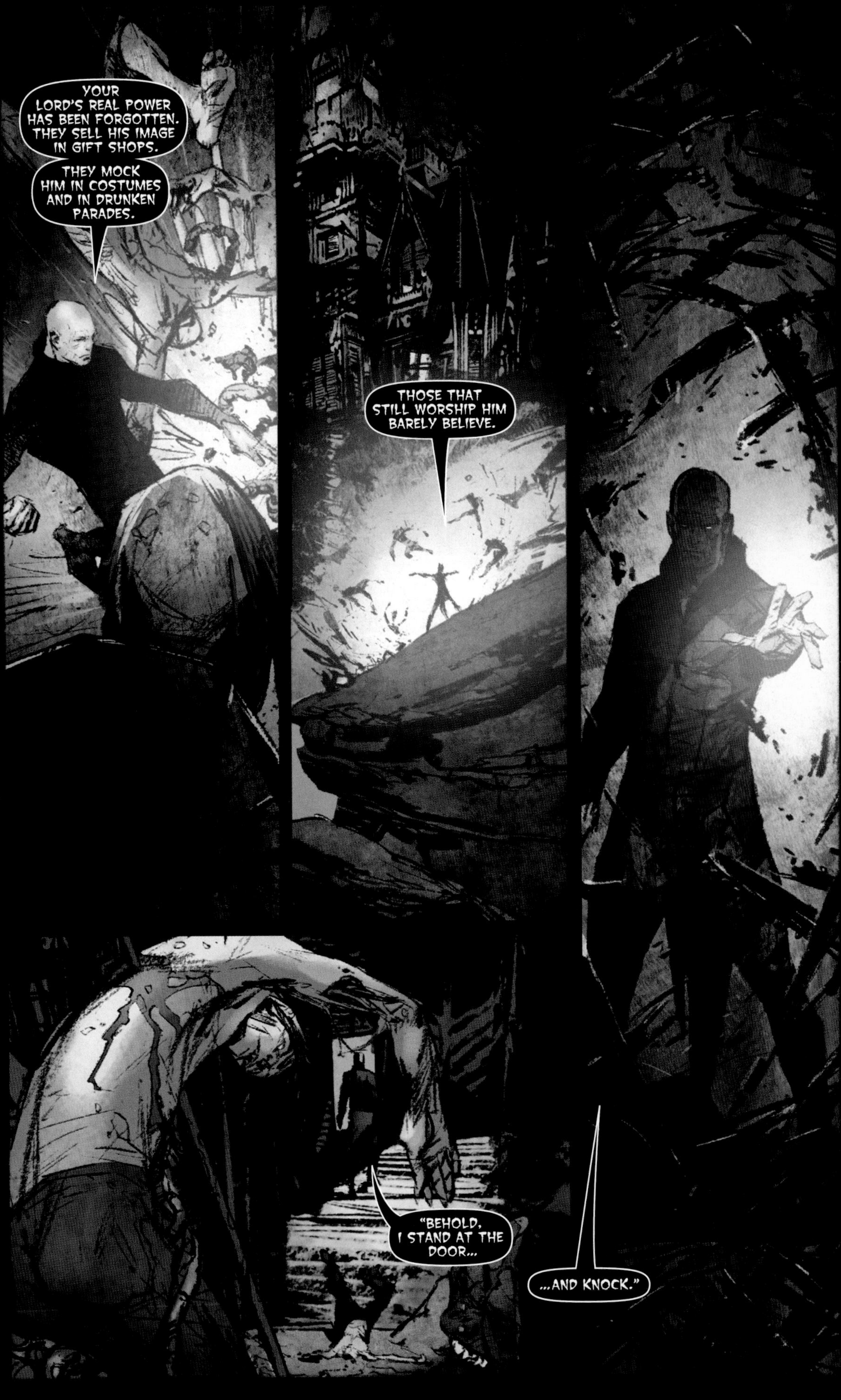
YOUR LORD'S REAL POWER HAS BEEN FORGOTTEN. THEY SELL HIS IMAGE IN GIFT SHOPS.
THEY MOCK HIM IN COSTUMES AND IN DRUNKEN PARADES.
THOSE THAT STILL WORSHIP HIM BARELY BELIEVE.
"BEHOLD, I STAND AT THE DOOR...
...AND KNOCK."

SO, THE DESTROYER HAS COME.
I KNOW WHAT YOU HAVE WROUGHT IN OTHER REALMS. HAVE YOU COME TO RAZE THIS PLACE AS WELL?
YOU HAVE BEEN TOO LONG IN THIS HOUSE. YOU ARE A LORD OF *DUST*-- LEFT HERE TO FADE INTO NOTHING.
BUT I HAVEN'T COME TO DESTROY YOU...
...I COME TO *RESTORE*.
I BELIEVE WE CAN HELP EACH OTHER-- *BARON SAMEDI*.

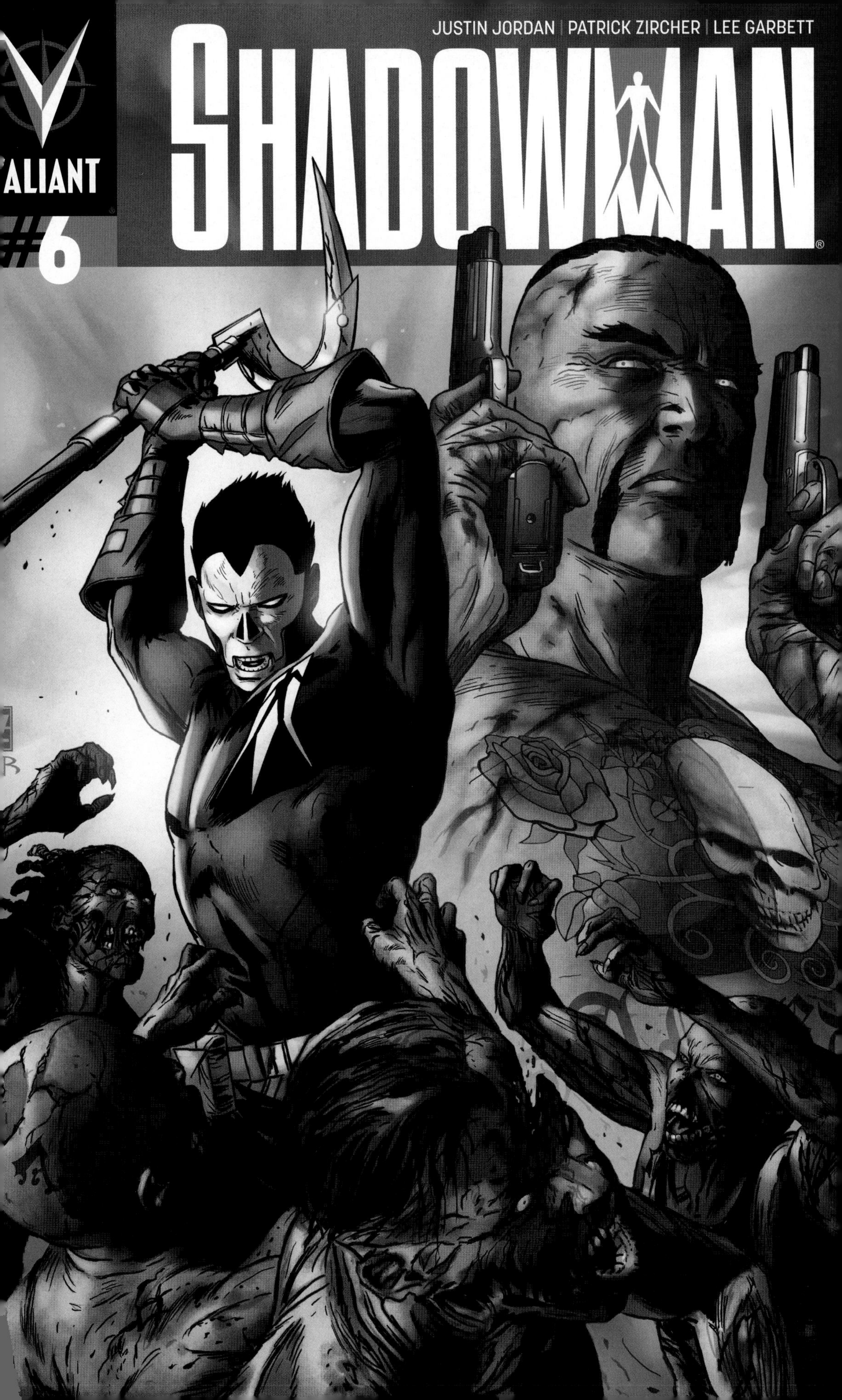

VALIANT
#6
JUSTIN JORDAN | PATRICK ZIRCHER | LEE GARBETT
SHADOWMAN

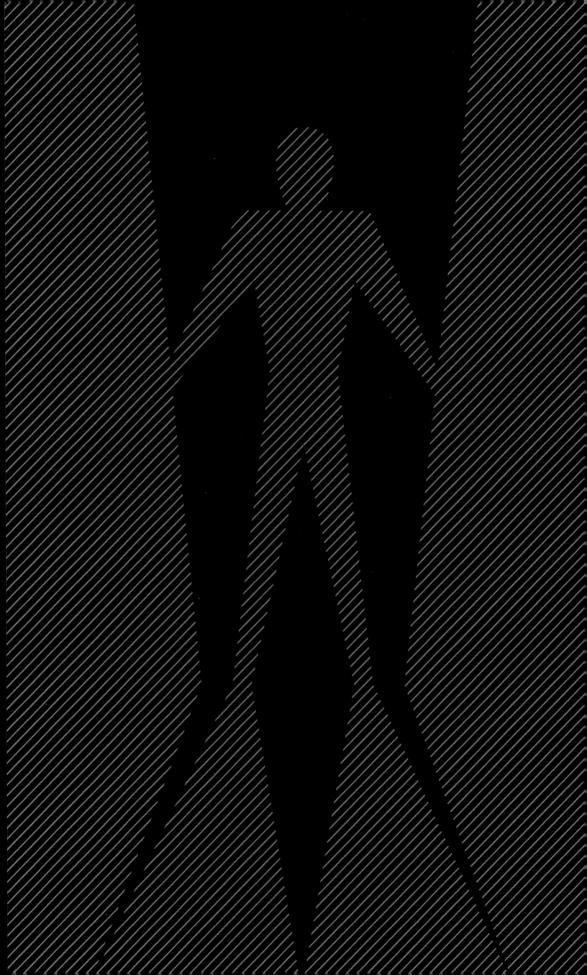

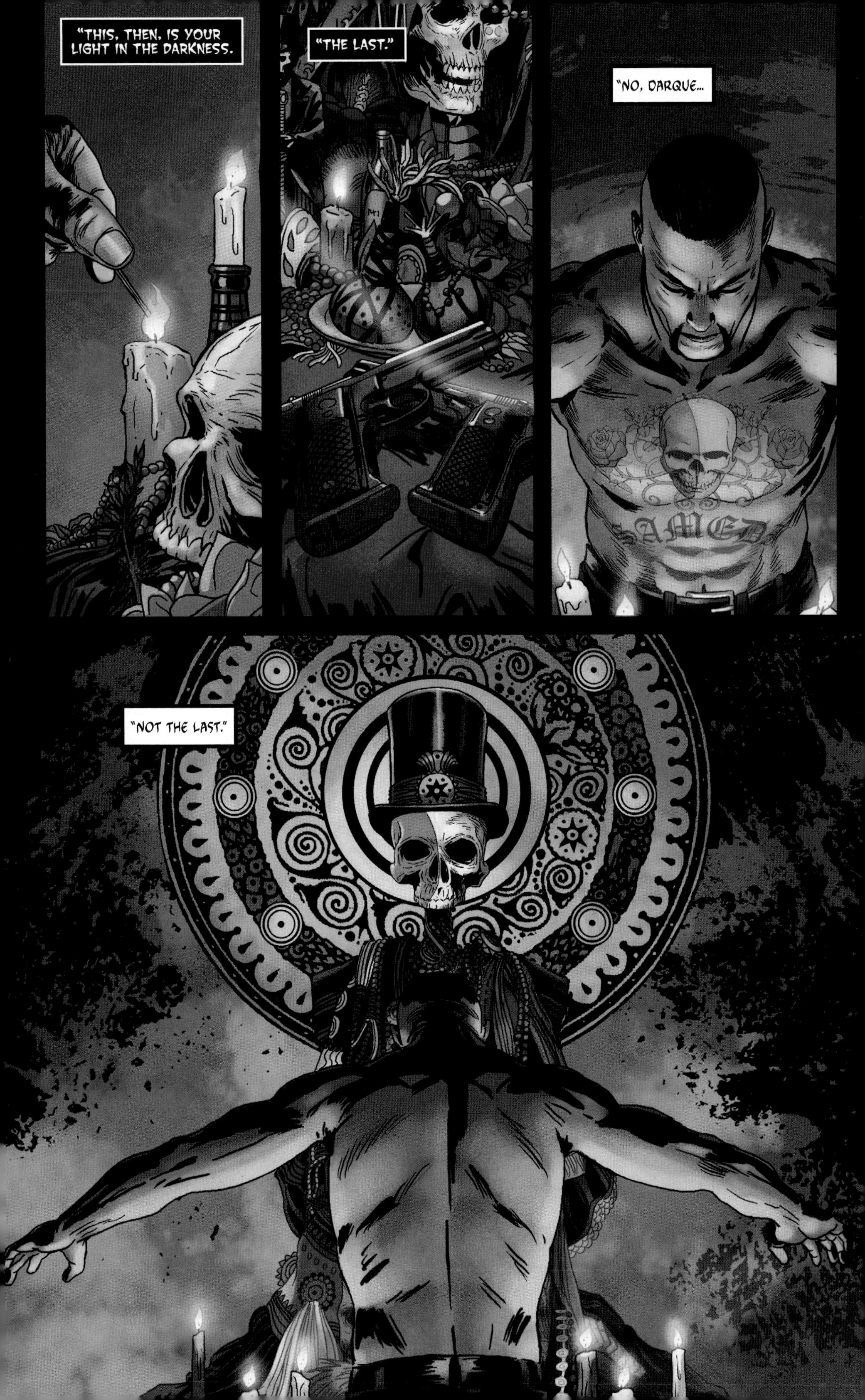
"THIS, THEN, IS YOUR LIGHT IN THE DARKNESS.
"THE LAST."
"NO, DARQUE...
SAMEDI
"NOT THE LAST."

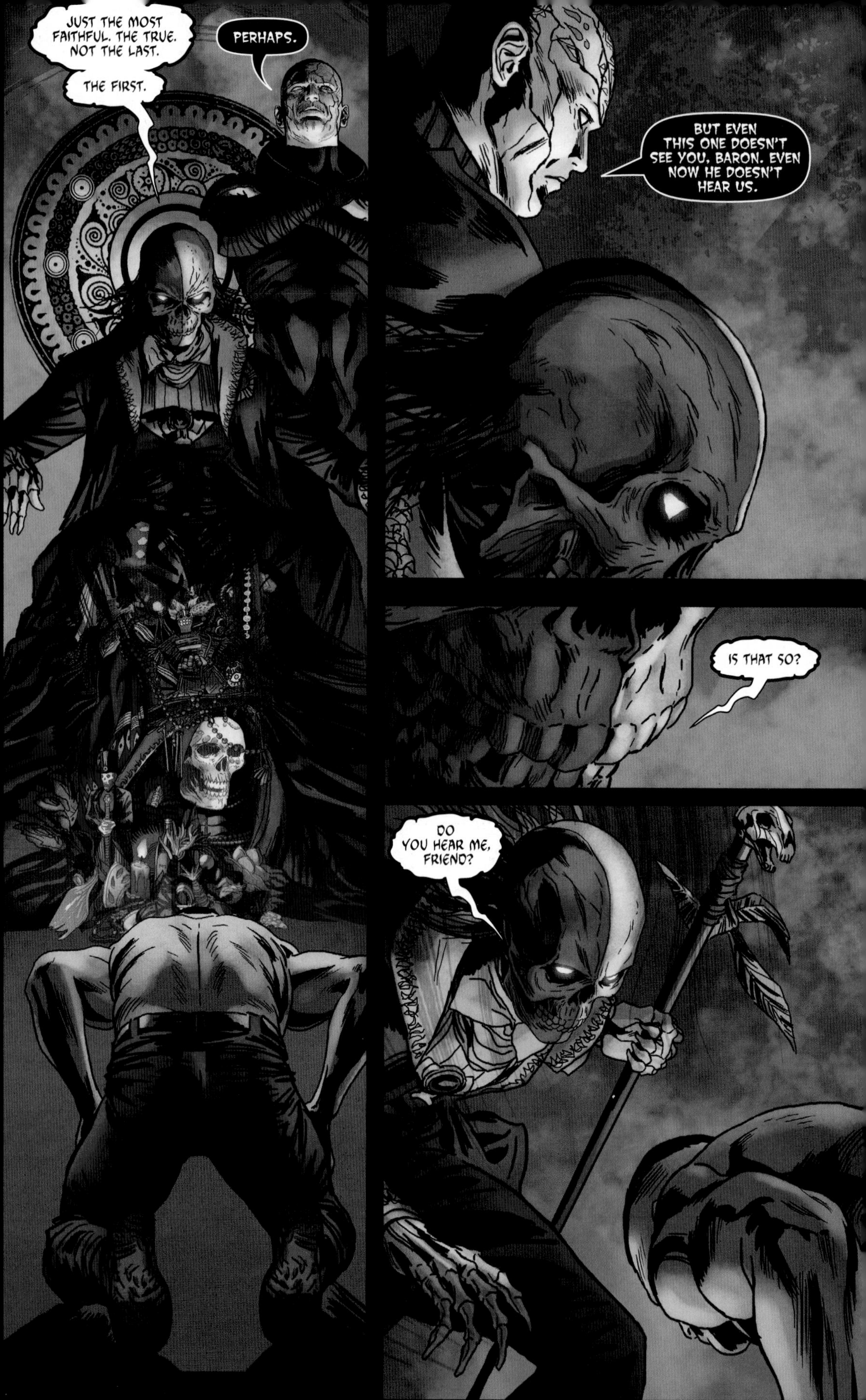
JUST THE MOST FAITHFUL. THE TRUE. NOT THE LAST.
THE FIRST.
PERHAPS.
BUT EVEN THIS ONE DOESN'T SEE YOU, BARON. EVEN NOW HE DOESN'T HEAR US.
IS THAT SO?
DO YOU HEAR ME, FRIEND?

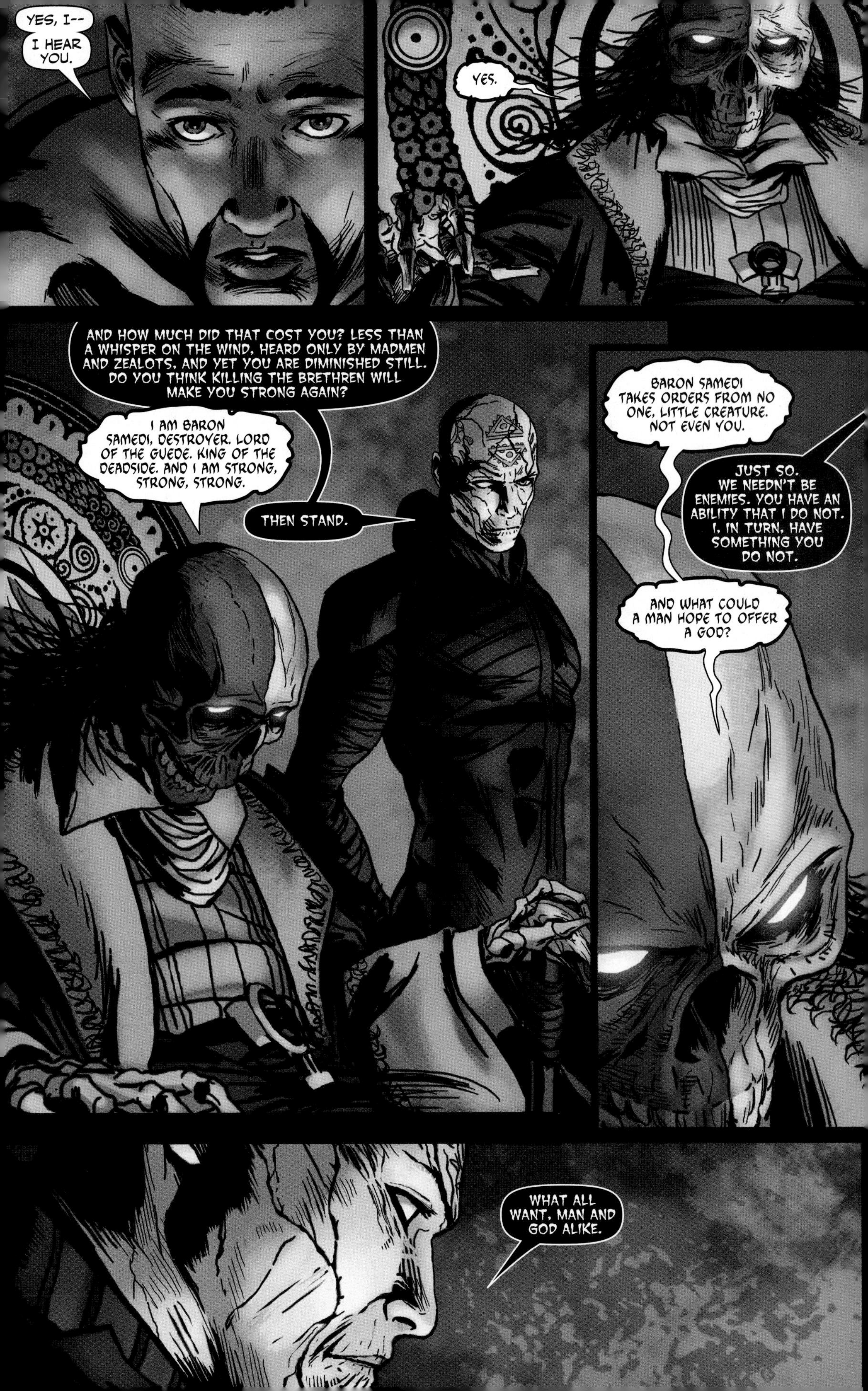
YES, I-- I HEAR YOU.
YES.
AND HOW MUCH DID THAT COST YOU? LESS THAN A WHISPER ON THE WIND, HEARD ONLY BY MADMEN AND ZEALOTS, AND YET YOU ARE DIMINISHED STILL. DO YOU THINK KILLING THE BRETHREN WILL MAKE YOU STRONG AGAIN?
I AM BARON SAMEDI, DESTROYER. LORD OF THE GUEDE. KING OF THE DEADSIDE. AND I AM STRONG, STRONG, STRONG.
THEN STAND.
BARON SAMEDI TAKES ORDERS FROM NO ONE, LITTLE CREATURE. NOT EVEN YOU.
JUST SO. WE NEEDN'T BE ENEMIES. YOU HAVE AN ABILITY THAT I DO NOT. I, IN TURN, HAVE SOMETHING YOU DO NOT.
AND WHAT COULD A MAN HOPE TO OFFER A GOD?
WHAT ALL WANT, MAN AND GOD ALIKE.

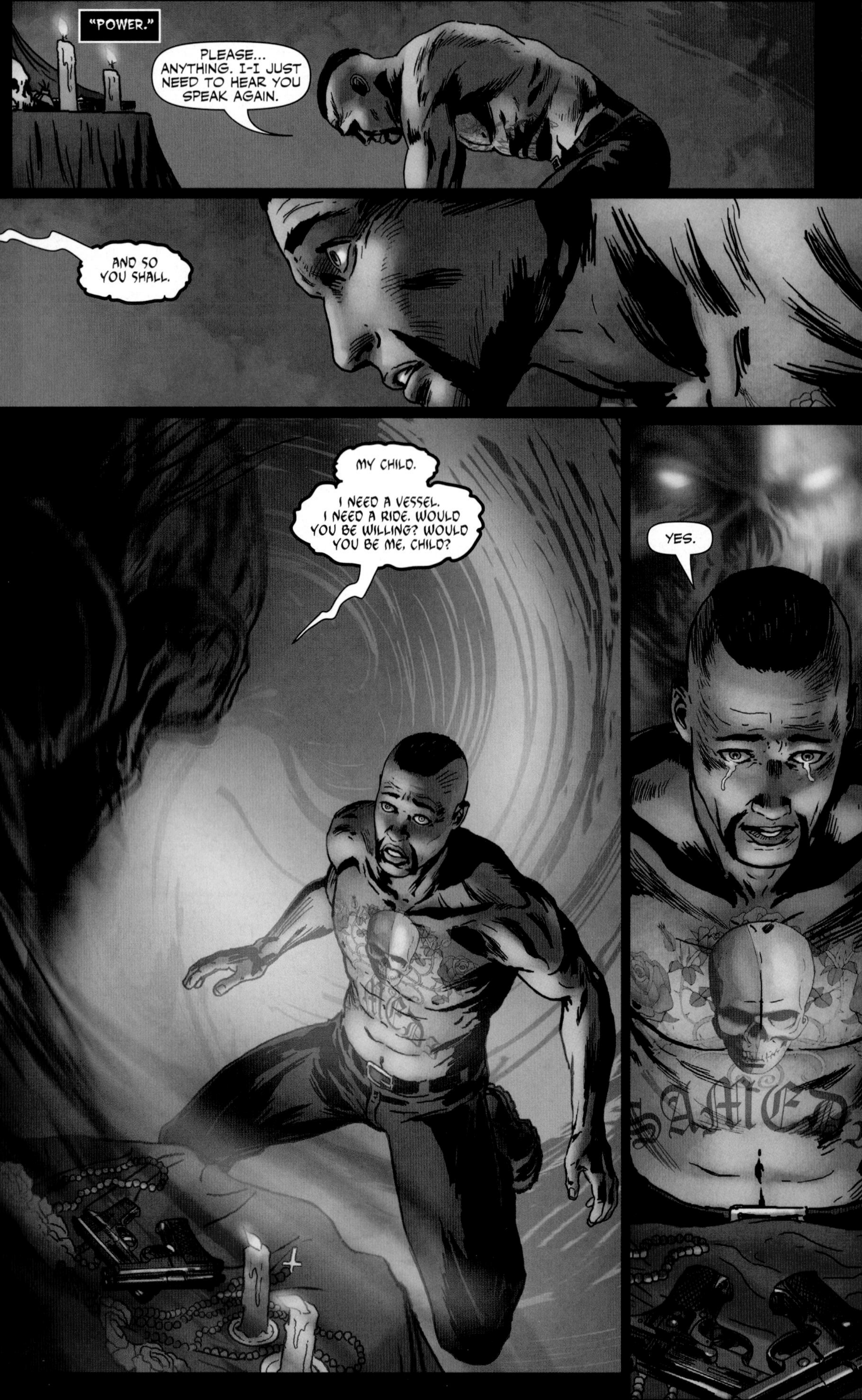
"POWER."
PLEASE... ANYTHING. I-I JUST NEED TO HEAR YOU SPEAK AGAIN.
AND SO YOU SHALL.
MY CHILD.
I NEED A VESSEL. I NEED A RIDE. WOULD YOU BE WILLING? WOULD YOU BE ME, CHILD?
YES.

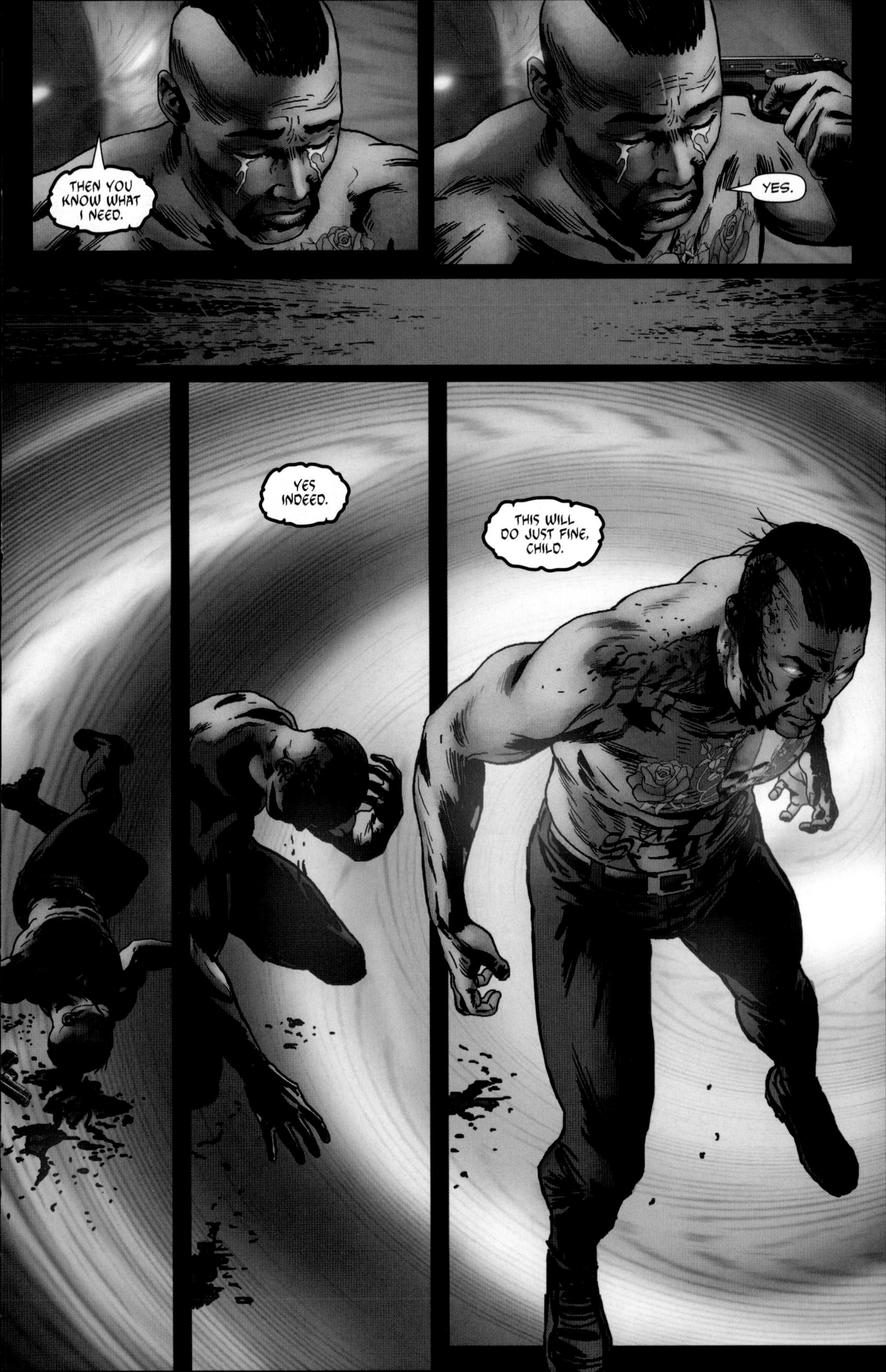
THEN YOU KNOW WHAT I NEED.
YES.
YES INDEED.
THIS WILL DO JUST FINE, CHILD.

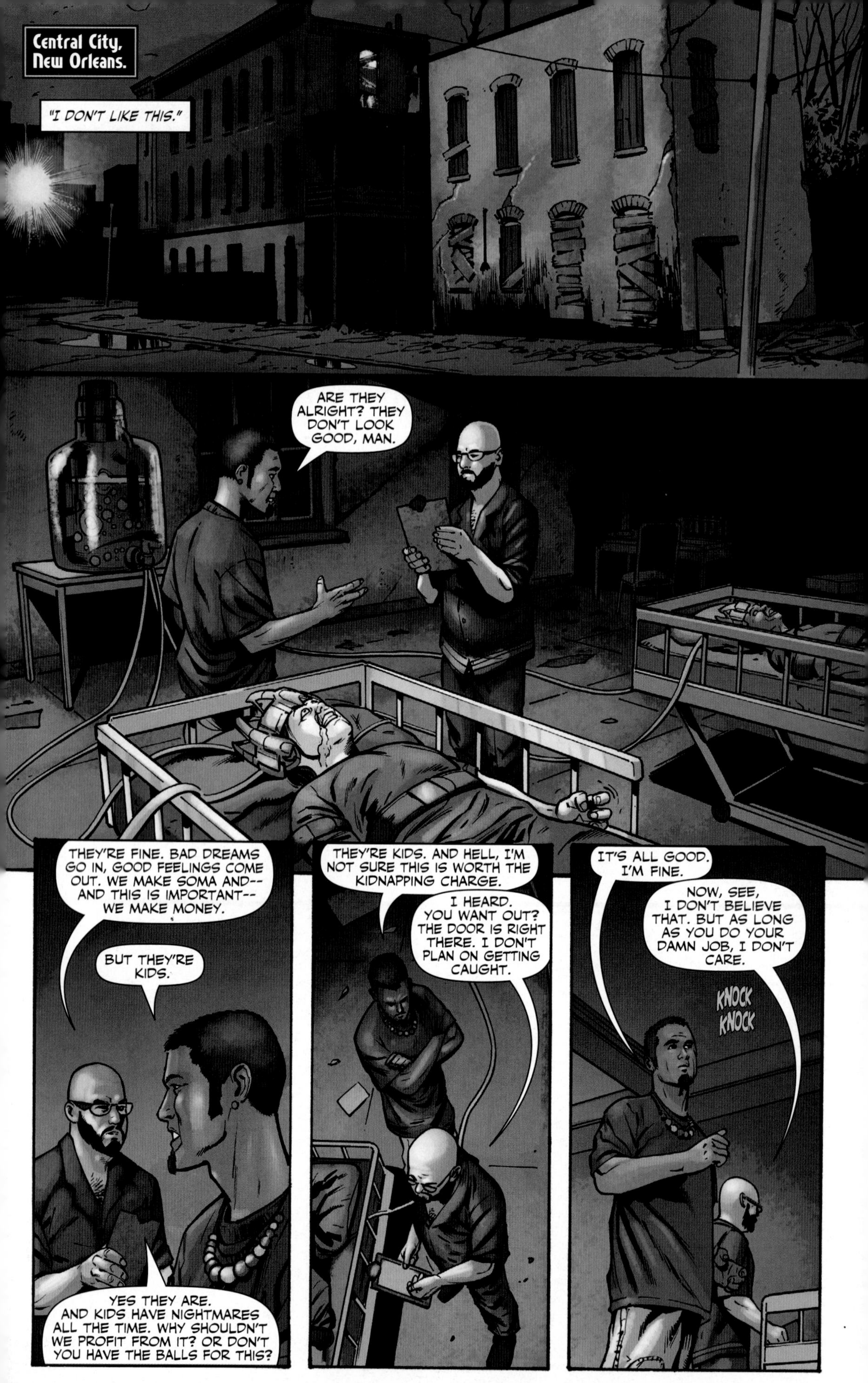
Central City, New Orleans.
"I DON'T LIKE THIS."
ARE THEY ALRIGHT? THEY DON'T LOOK GOOD, MAN.
THEY'RE FINE. BAD DREAMS GO IN, GOOD FEELINGS COME OUT. WE MAKE SOMA AND-- AND THIS IS IMPORTANT-- WE MAKE MONEY.
BUT THEY'RE KIDS.
YES THEY ARE. AND KIDS HAVE NIGHTMARES ALL THE TIME. WHY SHOULDN'T WE PROFIT FROM IT? OR DON'T YOU HAVE THE BALLS FOR THIS?
THEY'RE KIDS. AND HELL, I'M NOT SURE THIS IS WORTH THE KIDNAPPING CHARGE.
I HEARD. YOU WANT OUT? THE DOOR IS RIGHT THERE. I DON'T PLAN ON GETTING CAUGHT.
IT'S ALL GOOD. I'M FINE.
NOW, SEE, I DON'T BELIEVE THAT. BUT AS LONG AS YOU DO YOUR DAMN JOB, I DON'T CARE.
KNOCK KNOCK

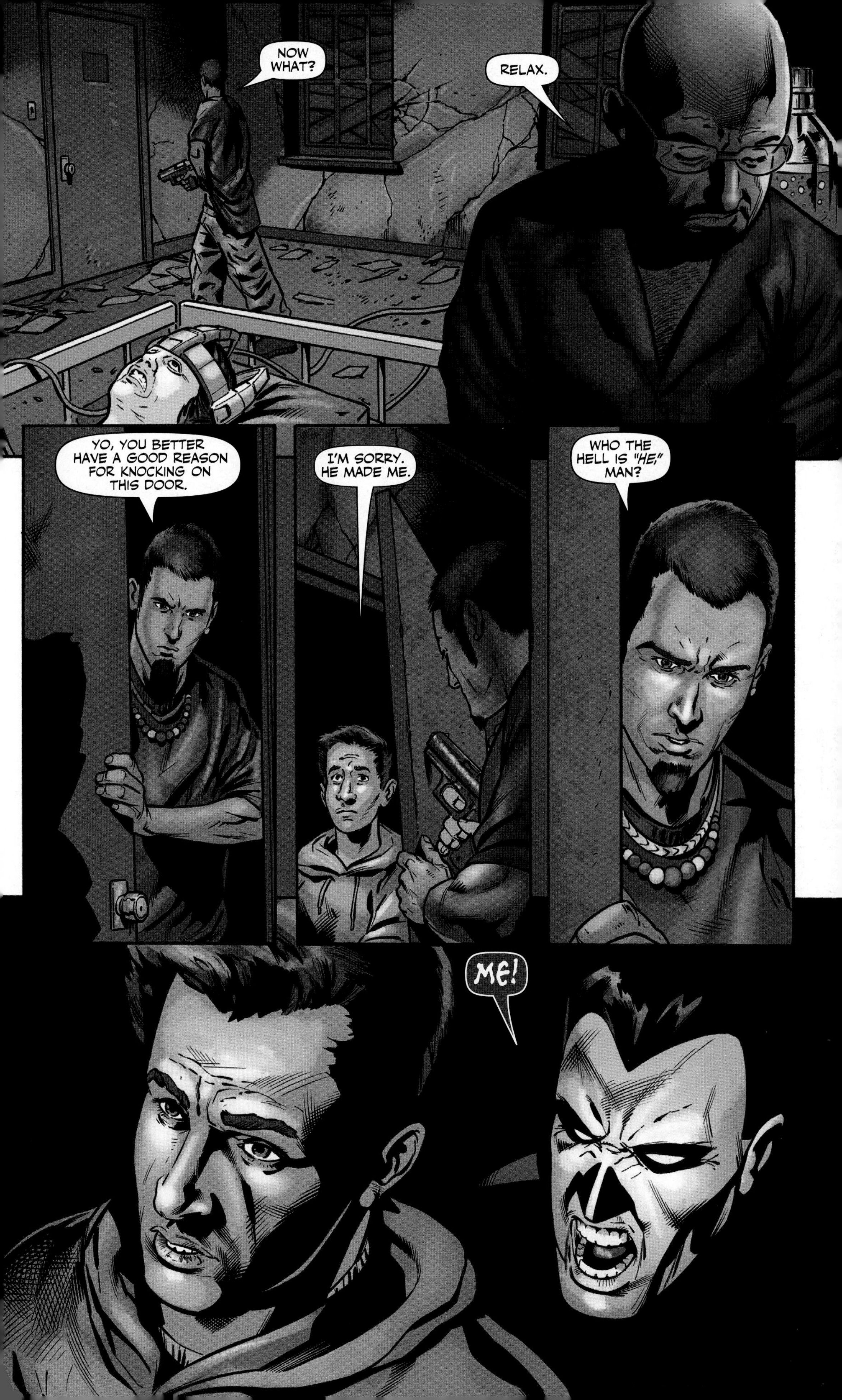
NOW WHAT?
RELAX.
YO, YOU BETTER HAVE A GOOD REASON FOR KNOCKING ON THIS DOOR.
I'M SORRY. HE MADE ME.
WHO THE HELL IS "HE," MAN?
ME!

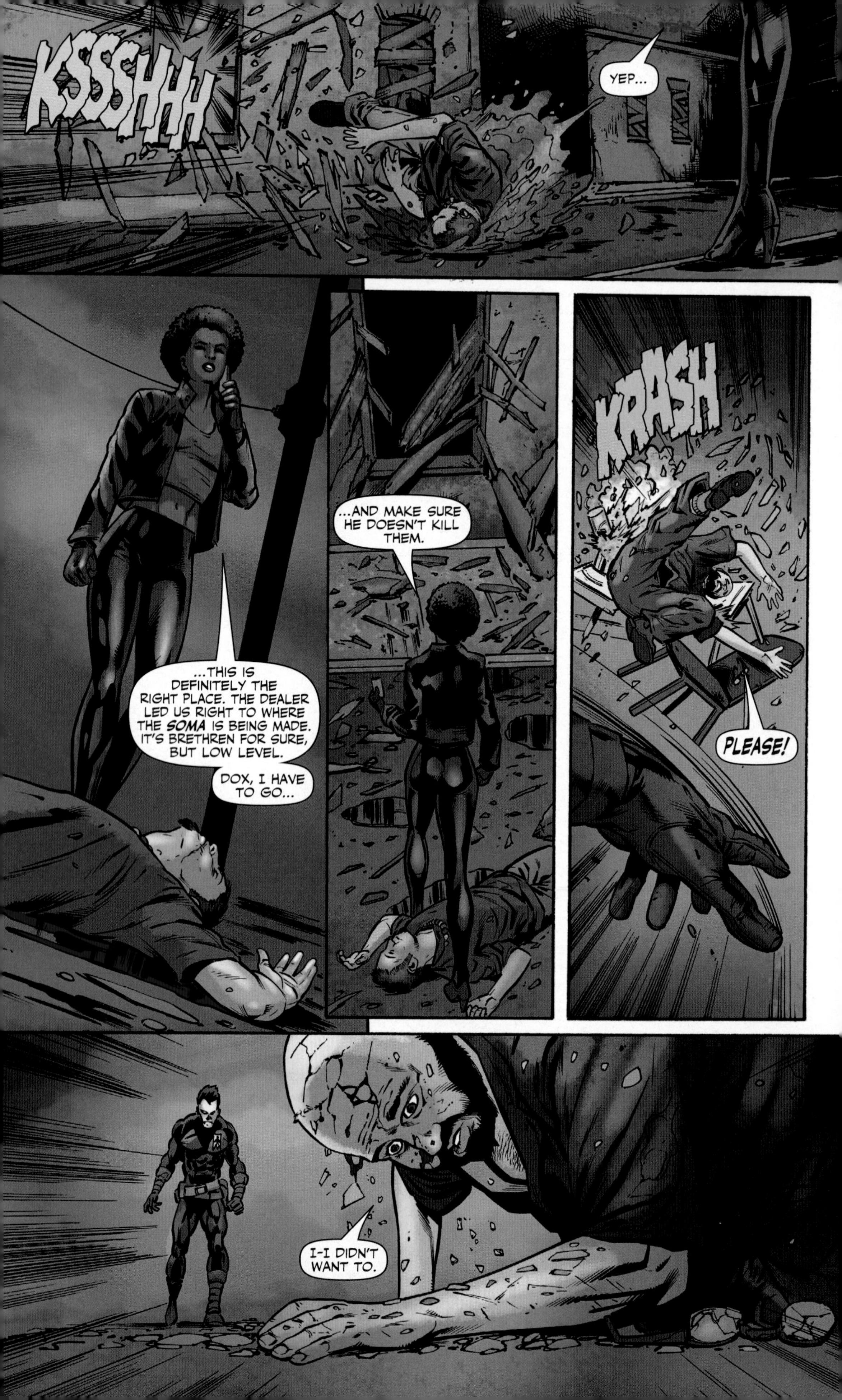
KSSSHHH
YEP...
...THIS IS DEFINITELY THE RIGHT PLACE. THE DEALER LED US RIGHT TO WHERE THE *SOMA* IS BEING MADE. IT'S BRETHREN FOR SURE, BUT LOW LEVEL.
DOX, I HAVE TO GO...
...AND MAKE SURE HE DOESN'T KILL THEM.
KRASH
PLEASE!
I-I DIDN'T WANT TO.

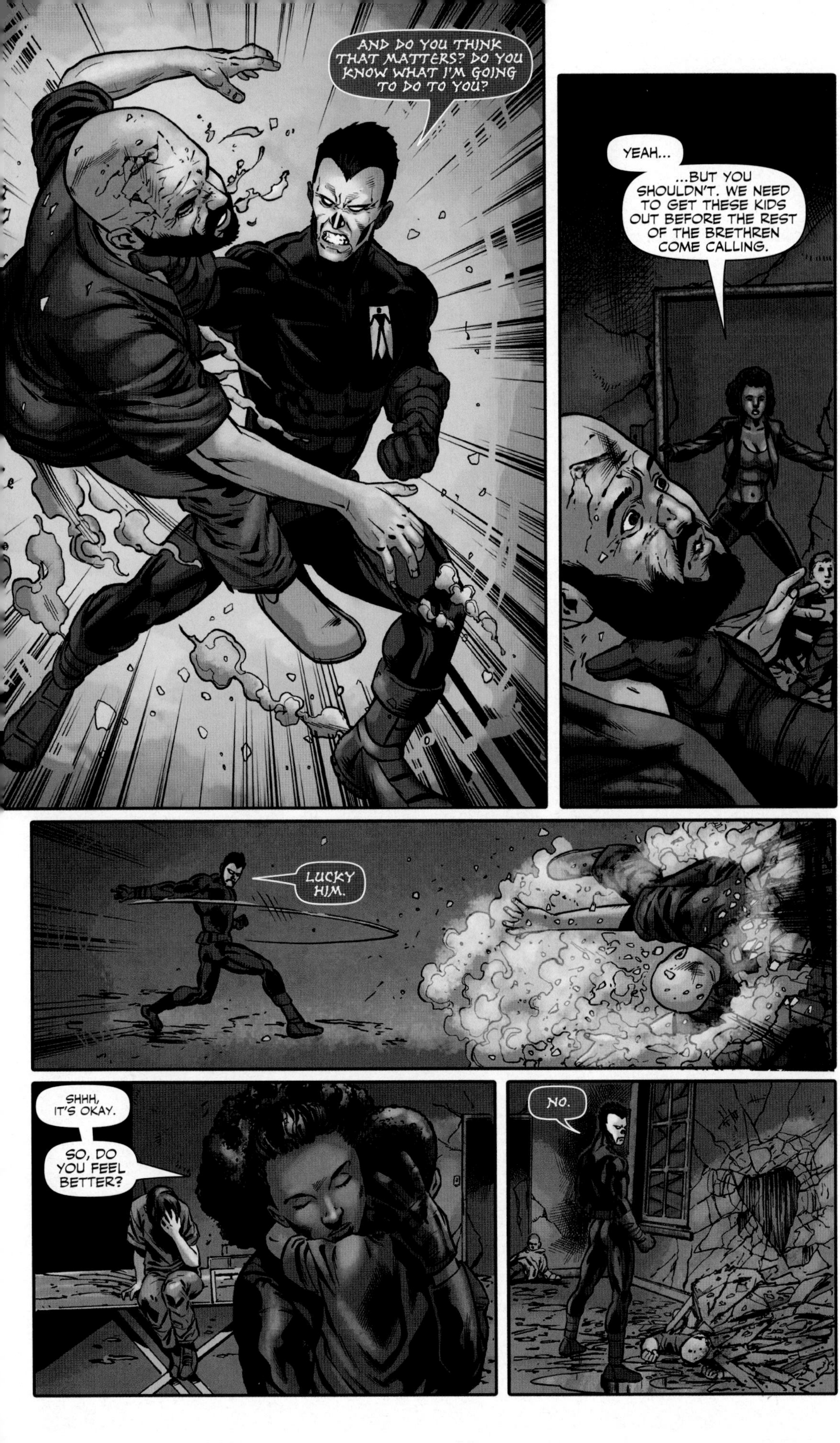
AND DO YOU THINK THAT MATTERS? DO YOU KNOW WHAT I'M GOING TO DO TO YOU?
YEAH...
...BUT YOU SHOULDN'T. WE NEED TO GET THESE KIDS OUT BEFORE THE REST OF THE BRETHREN COME CALLING.
LUCKY HIM.
SHHH, IT'S OKAY.
SO, DO YOU FEEL BETTER?
NO.

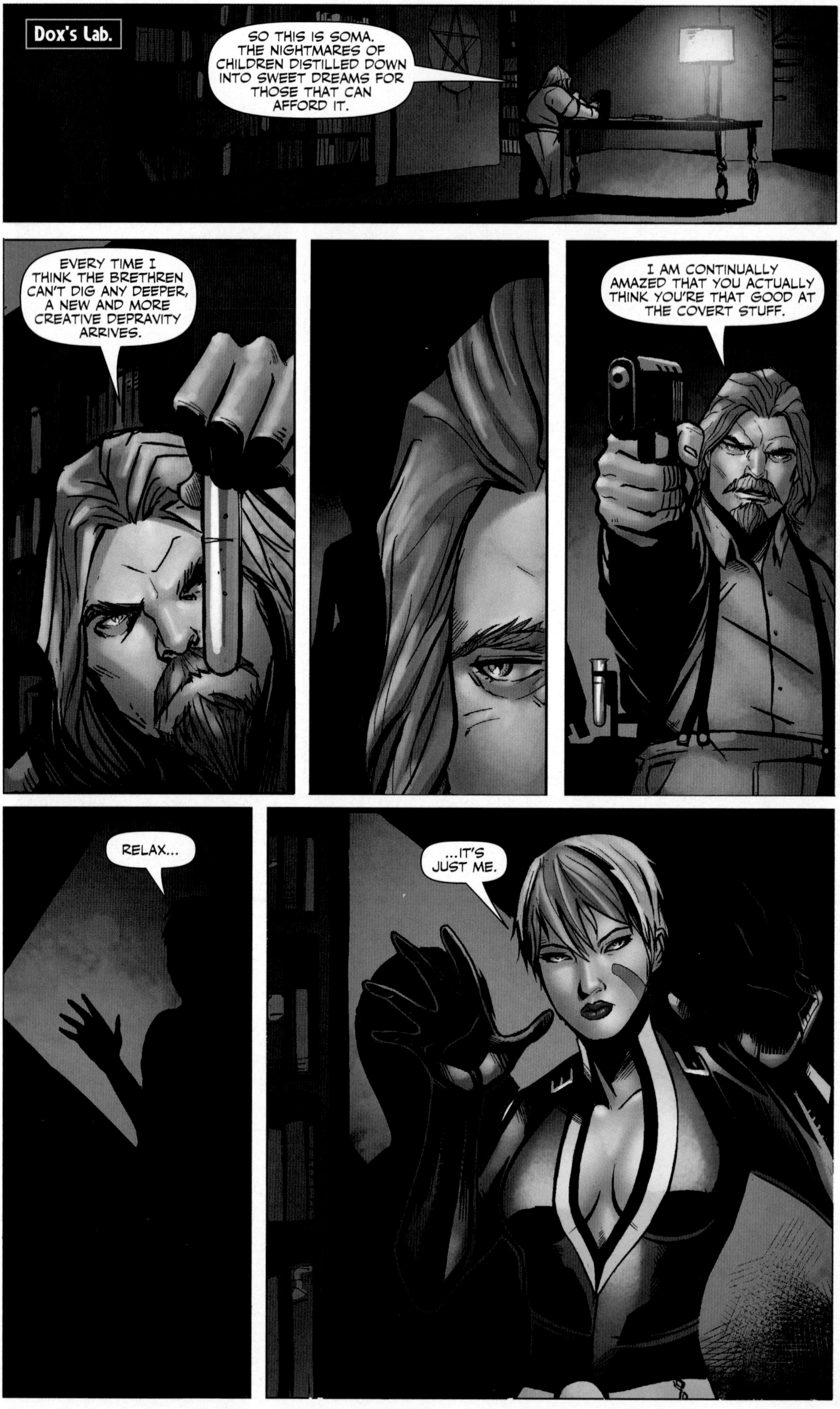
Dox's Lab.
SO THIS IS SOMA. THE NIGHTMARES OF CHILDREN DISTILLED DOWN INTO SWEET DREAMS FOR THOSE THAT CAN AFFORD IT.
EVERY TIME I THINK THE BRETHREN CAN'T DIG ANY DEEPER, A NEW AND MORE CREATIVE DEPRAVITY ARRIVES.
I AM CONTINUALLY AMAZED THAT YOU ACTUALLY THINK YOU'RE THAT GOOD AT THE COVERT STUFF.
RELAX...
...IT'S JUST ME.

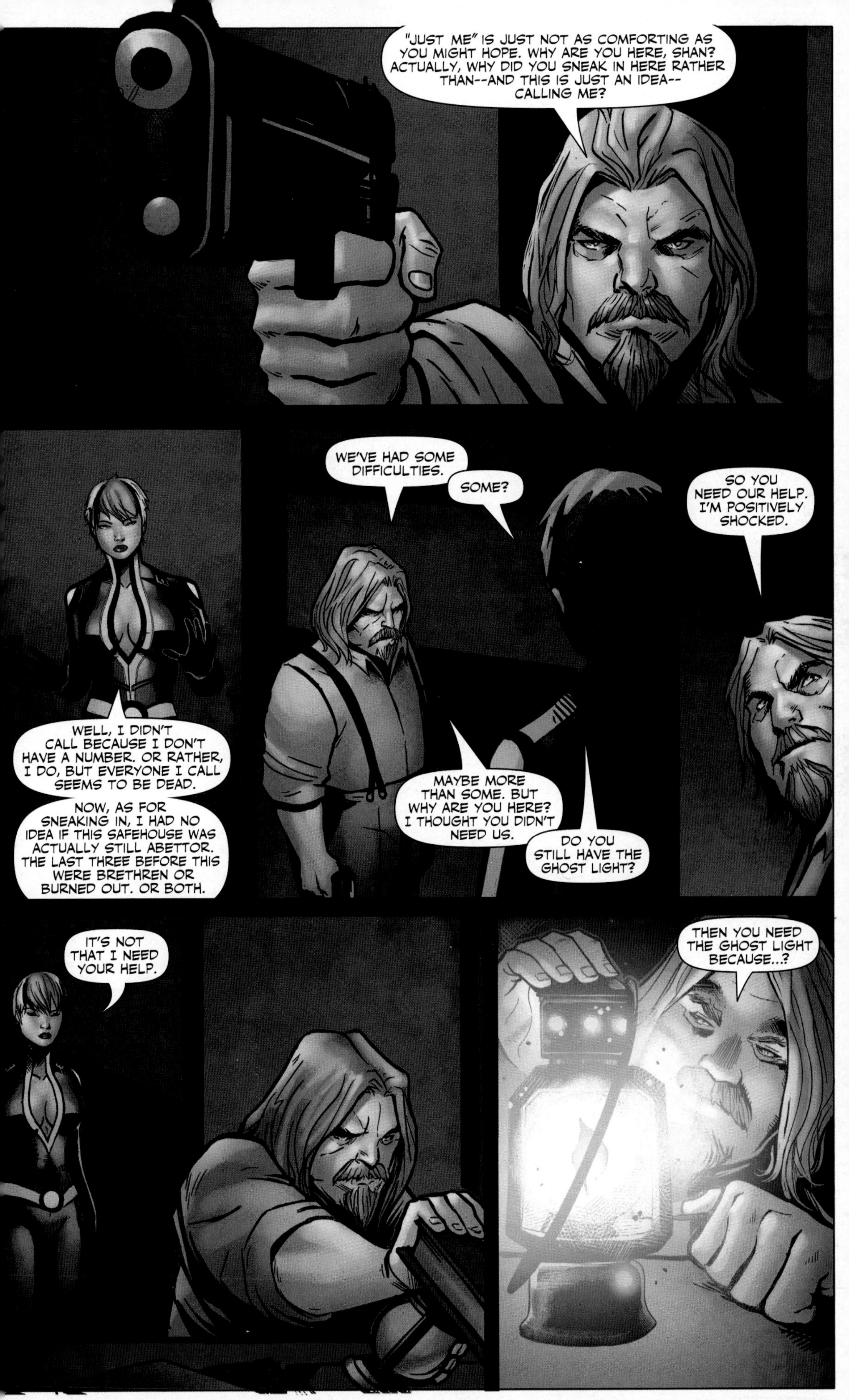

"JUST ME" IS JUST NOT AS COMFORTING AS YOU MIGHT HOPE. WHY ARE YOU HERE, SHAN? ACTUALLY, WHY DID YOU SNEAK IN HERE RATHER THAN--AND THIS IS JUST AN IDEA-- CALLING ME?
WELL, I DIDN'T CALL BECAUSE I DON'T HAVE A NUMBER. OR RATHER, I DO, BUT EVERYONE I CALL SEEMS TO BE DEAD.
NOW, AS FOR SNEAKING IN, I HAD NO IDEA IF THIS SAFEHOUSE WAS ACTUALLY STILL ABETTOR. THE LAST THREE BEFORE THIS WERE BRETHREN OR BURNED OUT. OR BOTH.
WE'VE HAD SOME DIFFICULTIES.
SOME?
MAYBE MORE THAN SOME. BUT WHY ARE YOU HERE? I THOUGHT YOU DIDN'T NEED US.
DO YOU STILL HAVE THE GHOST LIGHT?
SO YOU NEED OUR HELP. I'M POSITIVELY SHOCKED.
IT'S NOT THAT I NEED YOUR HELP.
THEN YOU NEED THE GHOST LIGHT BECAUSE...?

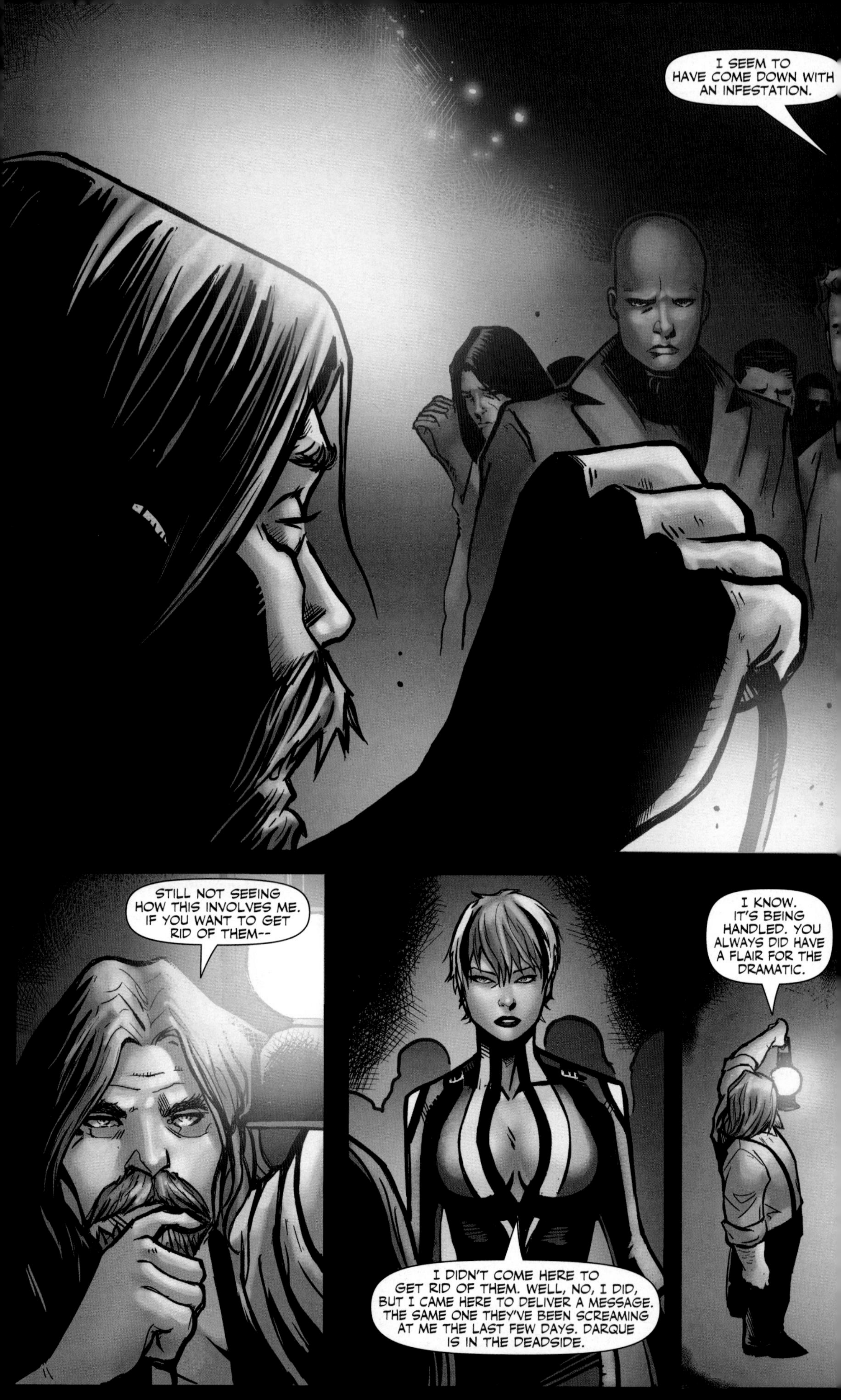
I SEEM TO HAVE COME DOWN WITH AN INFESTATION.
STILL NOT SEEING HOW THIS INVOLVES ME. IF YOU WANT TO GET RID OF THEM--
I DIDN'T COME HERE TO GET RID OF THEM. WELL, NO, I DID, BUT I CAME HERE TO DELIVER A MESSAGE. THE SAME ONE THEY'VE BEEN SCREAMING AT ME THE LAST FEW DAYS. DARQUE IS IN THE DEADSIDE.
I KNOW. IT'S BEING HANDLED. YOU ALWAYS DID HAVE A FLAIR FOR THE DRAMATIC.

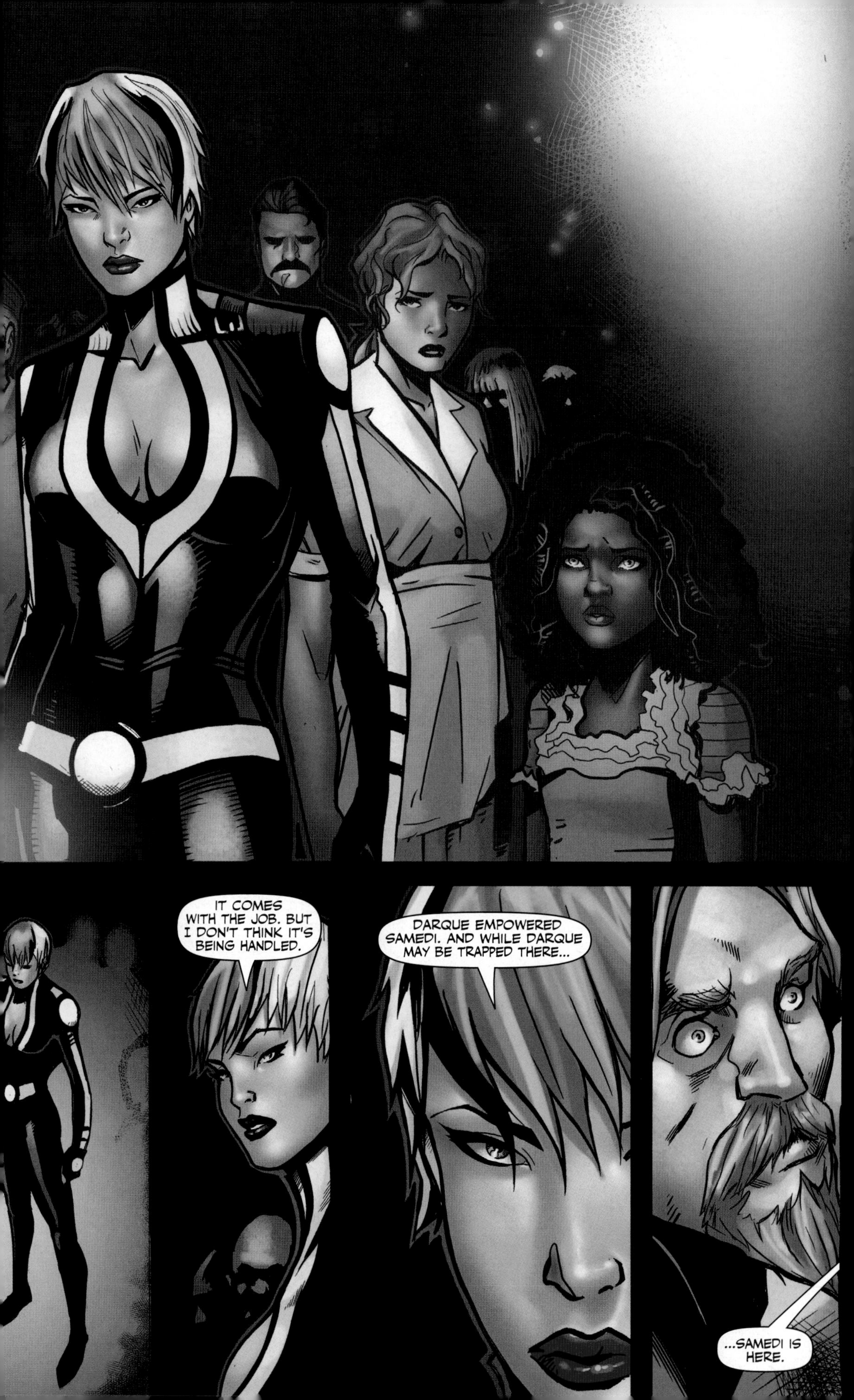
IT COMES WITH THE JOB. BUT I DON'T THINK IT'S BEING HANDLED.
DARQUE EMPOWERED SAMEDI. AND WHILE DARQUE MAY BE TRAPPED THERE...
...SAMEDI IS HERE.

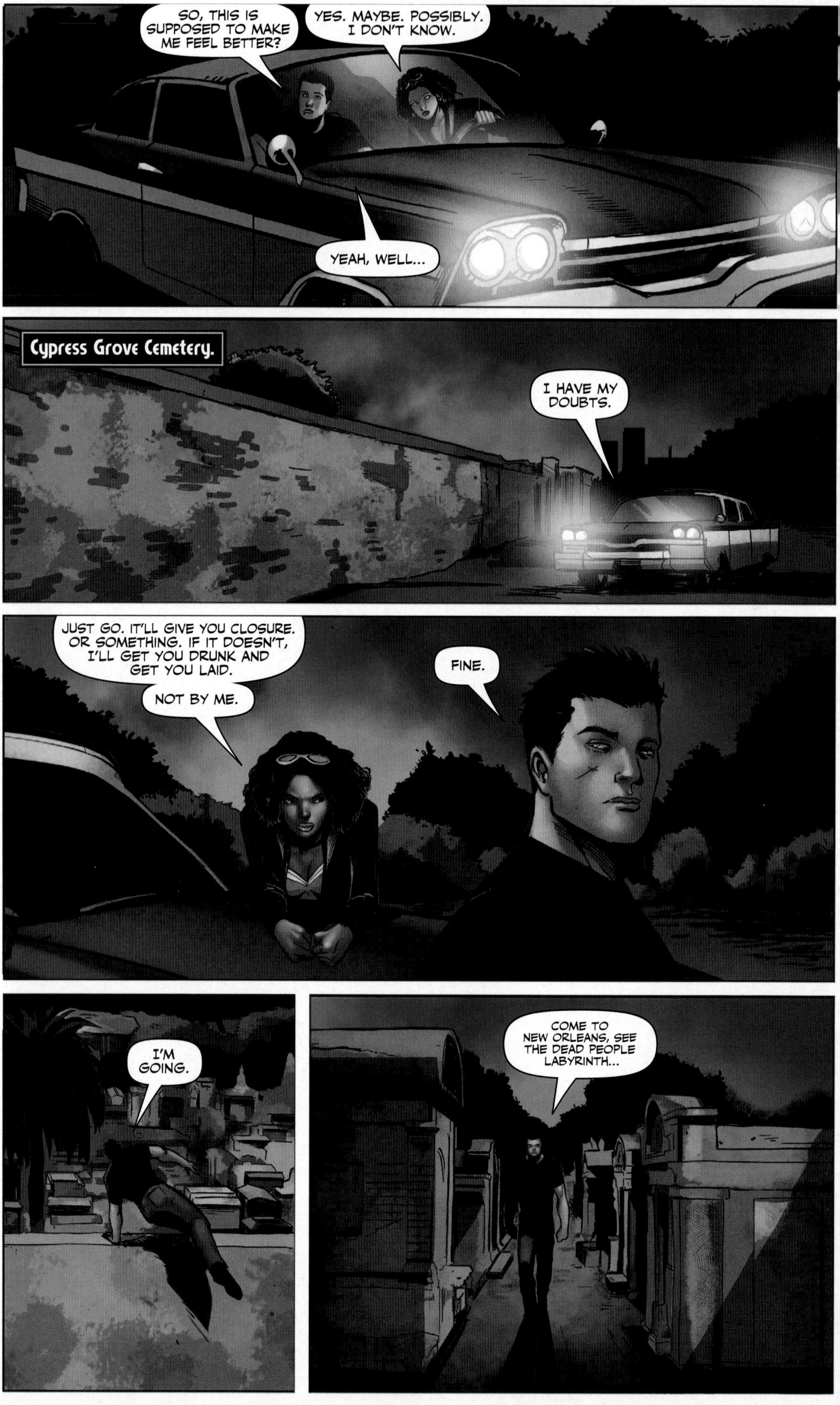
SO, THIS IS SUPPOSED TO MAKE ME FEEL BETTER?
YES. MAYBE. POSSIBLY. I DON'T KNOW.
YEAH, WELL...
Cypress Grove Cemetery.
I HAVE MY DOUBTS.
JUST GO. IT'LL GIVE YOU CLOSURE. OR SOMETHING. IF IT DOESN'T, I'LL GET YOU DRUNK AND GET YOU LAID.
NOT BY ME.
FINE.
I'M GOING.
COME TO NEW ORLEANS, SEE THE DEAD PEOPLE LABYRINTH...

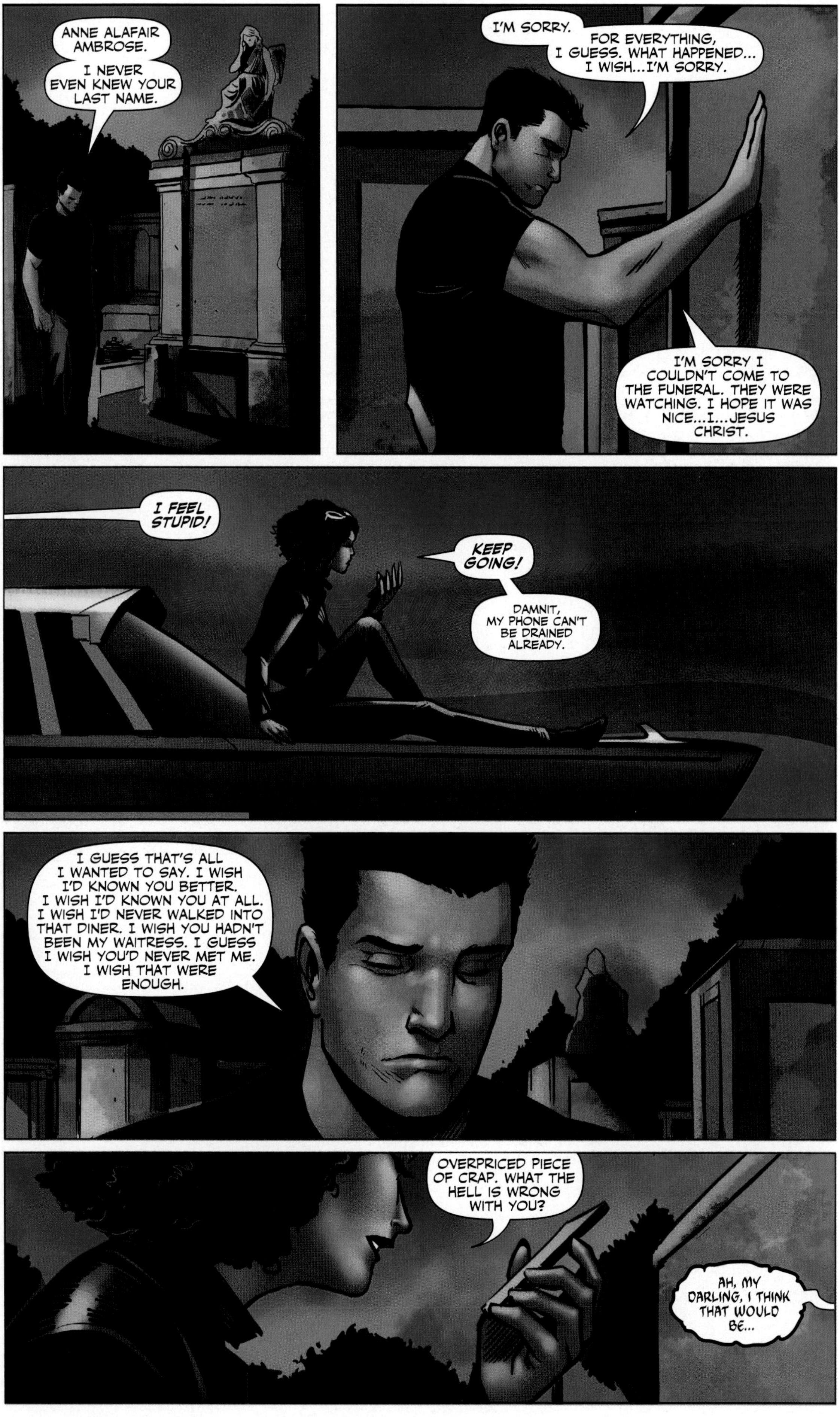
ANNE ALAFAIR AMBROSE.
I NEVER EVEN KNEW YOUR LAST NAME.
I'M SORRY.
FOR EVERYTHING, I GUESS. WHAT HAPPENED... I WISH...I'M SORRY.
I'M SORRY I COULDN'T COME TO THE FUNERAL. THEY WERE WATCHING. I HOPE IT WAS NICE...I...JESUS CHRIST.
I FEEL STUPID!
KEEP GOING!
DAMNIT, MY PHONE CAN'T BE DRAINED ALREADY.
I GUESS THAT'S ALL I WANTED TO SAY. I WISH I'D KNOWN YOU BETTER. I WISH I'D KNOWN YOU AT ALL. I WISH I'D NEVER WALKED INTO THAT DINER. I WISH YOU HADN'T BEEN MY WAITRESS. I GUESS I WISH YOU'D NEVER MET ME. I WISH THAT WERE ENOUGH.
OVERPRICED PIECE OF CRAP. WHAT THE HELL IS WRONG WITH YOU?
AH, MY DARLING, I THINK THAT WOULD BE...

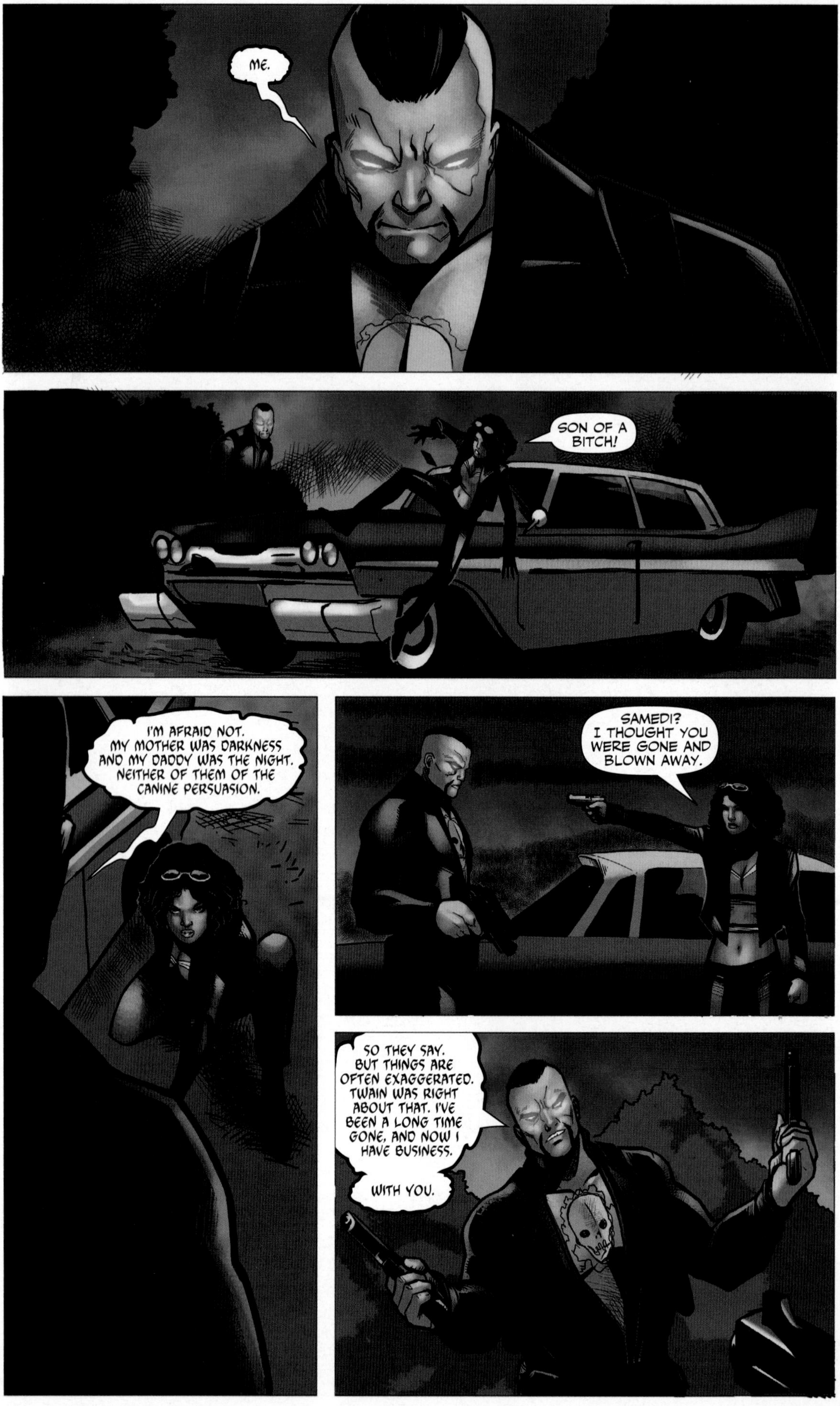
ME.
SON OF A BITCH!
I'M AFRAID NOT. MY MOTHER WAS DARKNESS AND MY DADDY WAS THE NIGHT. NEITHER OF THEM OF THE CANINE PERSUASION.
SAMEDI? I THOUGHT YOU WERE GONE AND BLOWN AWAY.
SO THEY SAY. BUT THINGS ARE OFTEN EXAGGERATED. TWAIN WAS RIGHT ABOUT THAT. I'VE BEEN A LONG TIME GONE, AND NOW I HAVE BUSINESS.
WITH YOU.

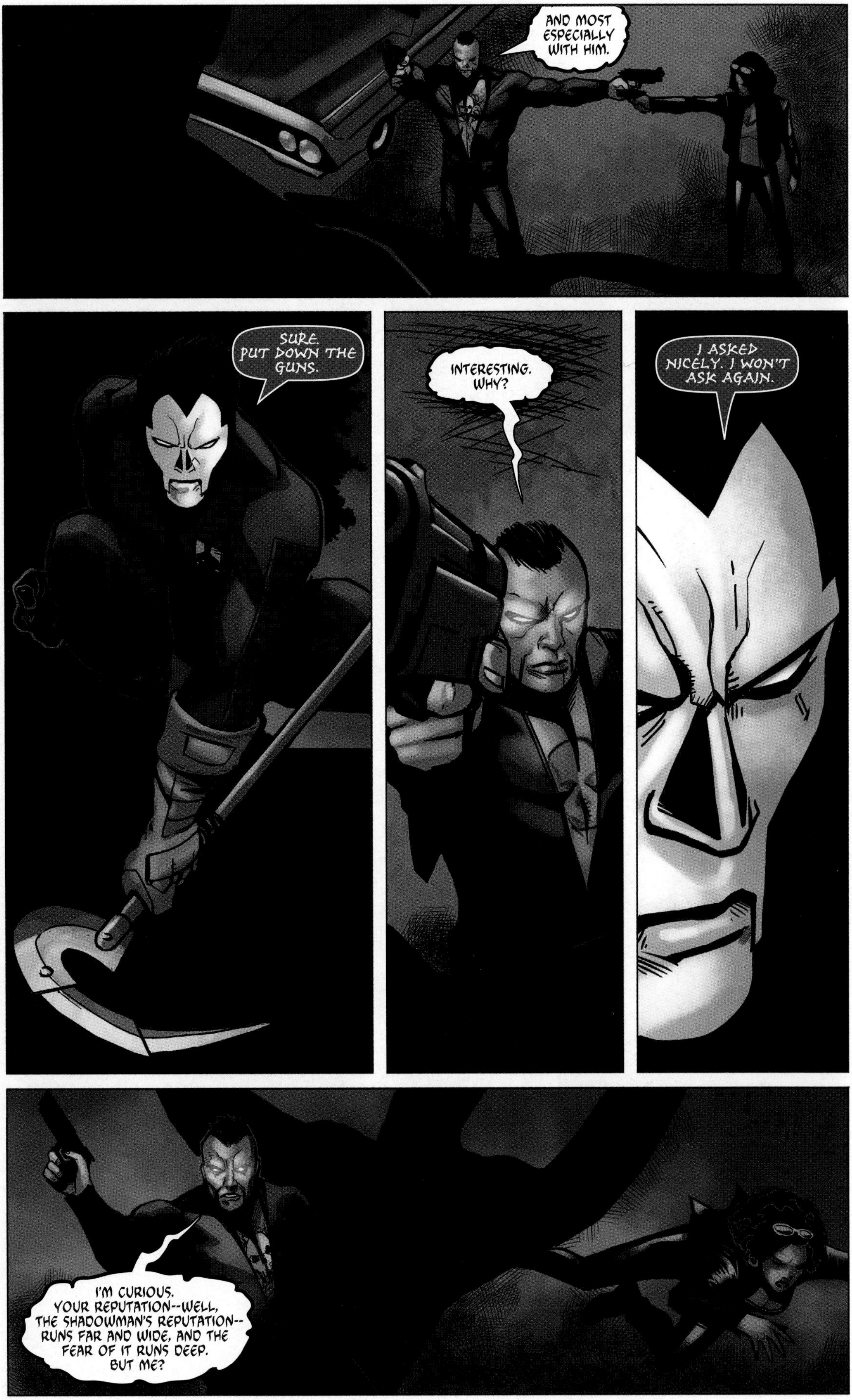
AND MOST ESPECIALLY WITH HIM.
SURE. PUT DOWN THE GUNS.
INTERESTING. WHY?
I ASKED NICELY. I WON'T ASK AGAIN.
I'M CURIOUS. YOUR REPUTATION--WELL, THE SHADOWMAN'S REPUTATION--RUNS FAR AND WIDE, AND THE FEAR OF IT RUNS DEEP. BUT ME?

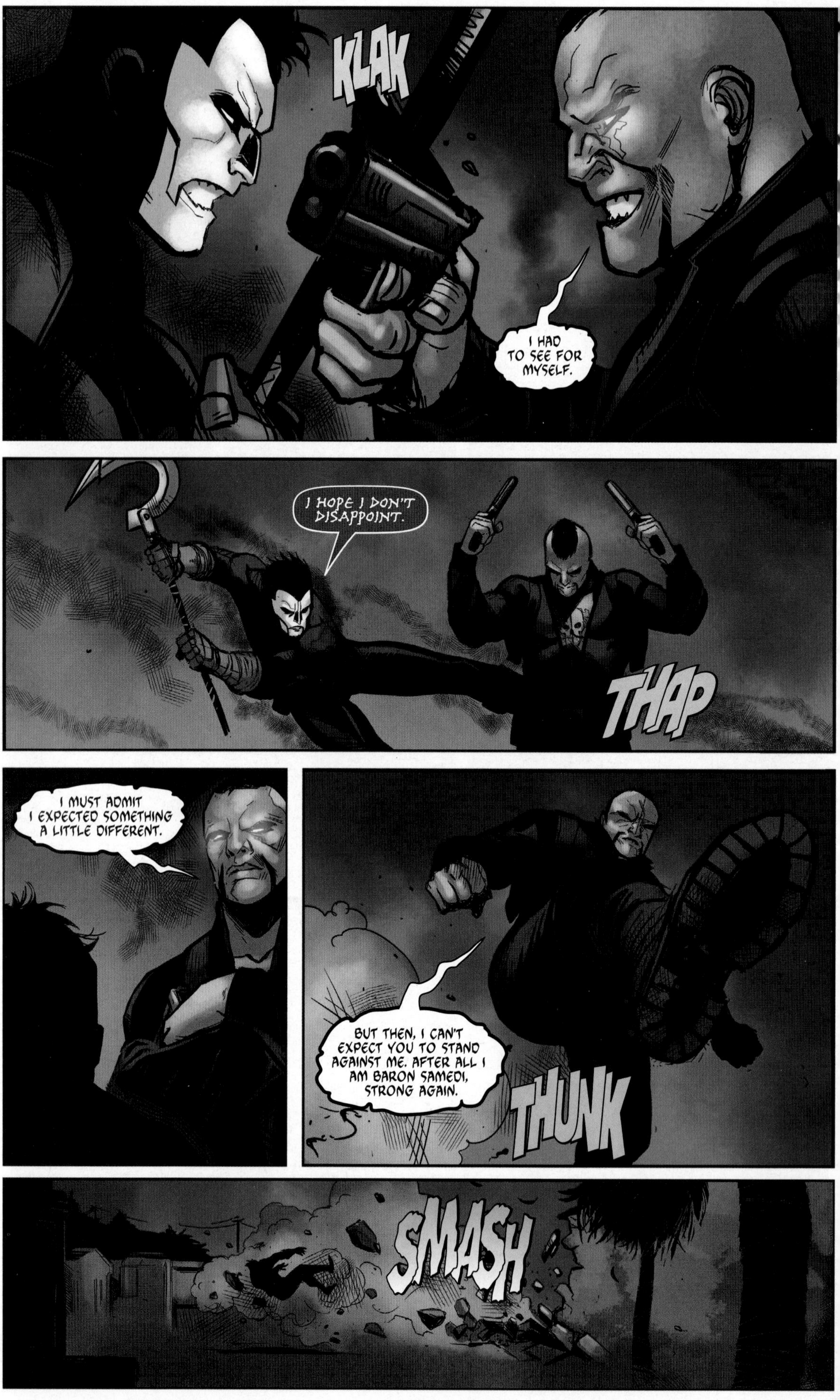
KLAK
I HAD TO SEE FOR MYSELF.
I HOPE I DON'T DISAPPOINT.
THAP
I MUST ADMIT I EXPECTED SOMETHING A LITTLE DIFFERENT.
BUT THEN, I CAN'T EXPECT YOU TO STAND AGAINST ME. AFTER ALL I AM BARON SAMEDI, STRONG AGAIN.
THUNK
SMASH

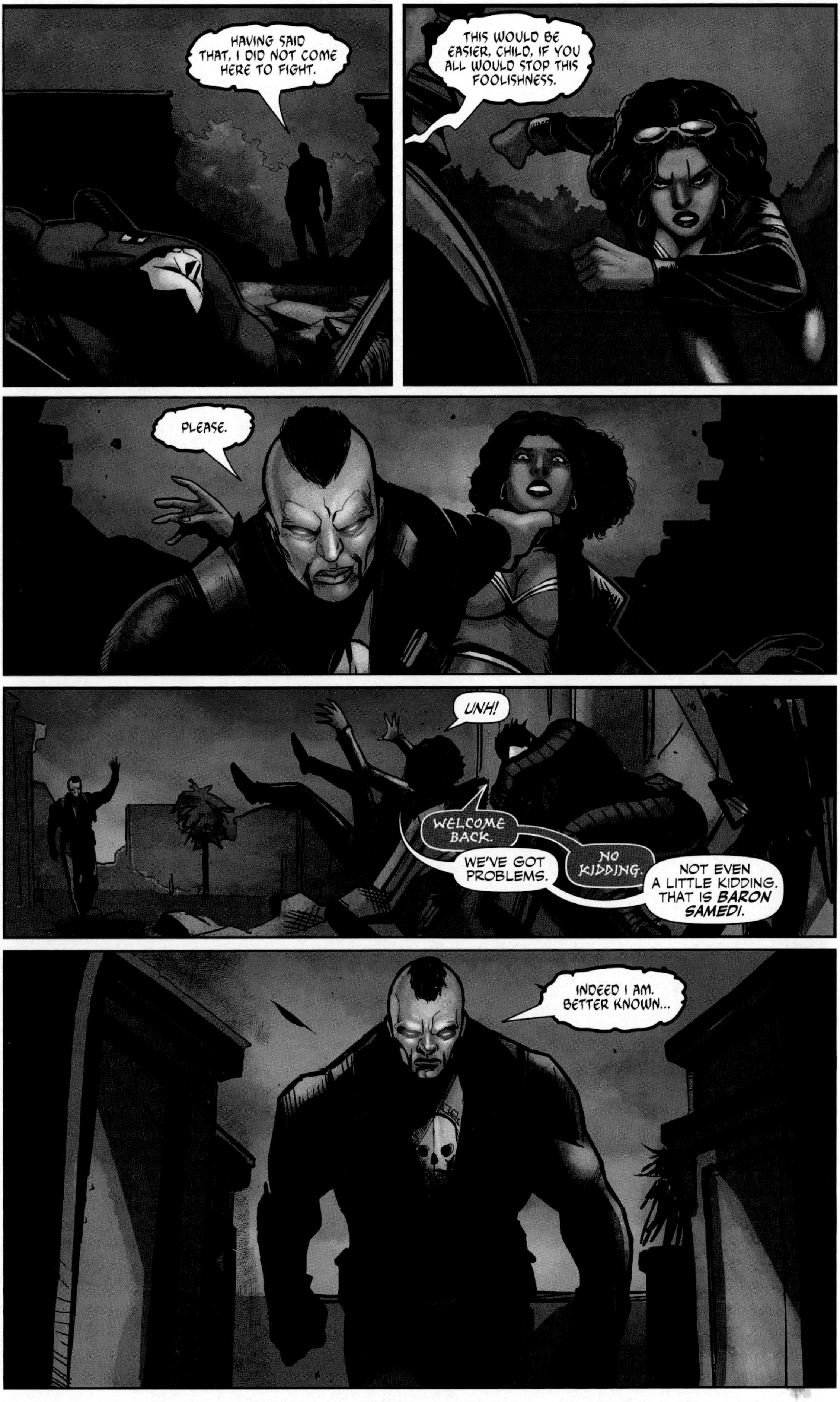
HAVING SAID THAT, I DID NOT COME HERE TO FIGHT.
THIS WOULD BE EASIER, CHILD, IF YOU ALL WOULD STOP THIS FOOLISHNESS.
PLEASE.
UNH!
WELCOME BACK.
NO KIDDING.
WE'VE GOT PROBLEMS.
NOT EVEN A LITTLE KIDDING. THAT IS *BARON SAMEDI*.
INDEED I AM. BETTER KNOWN...

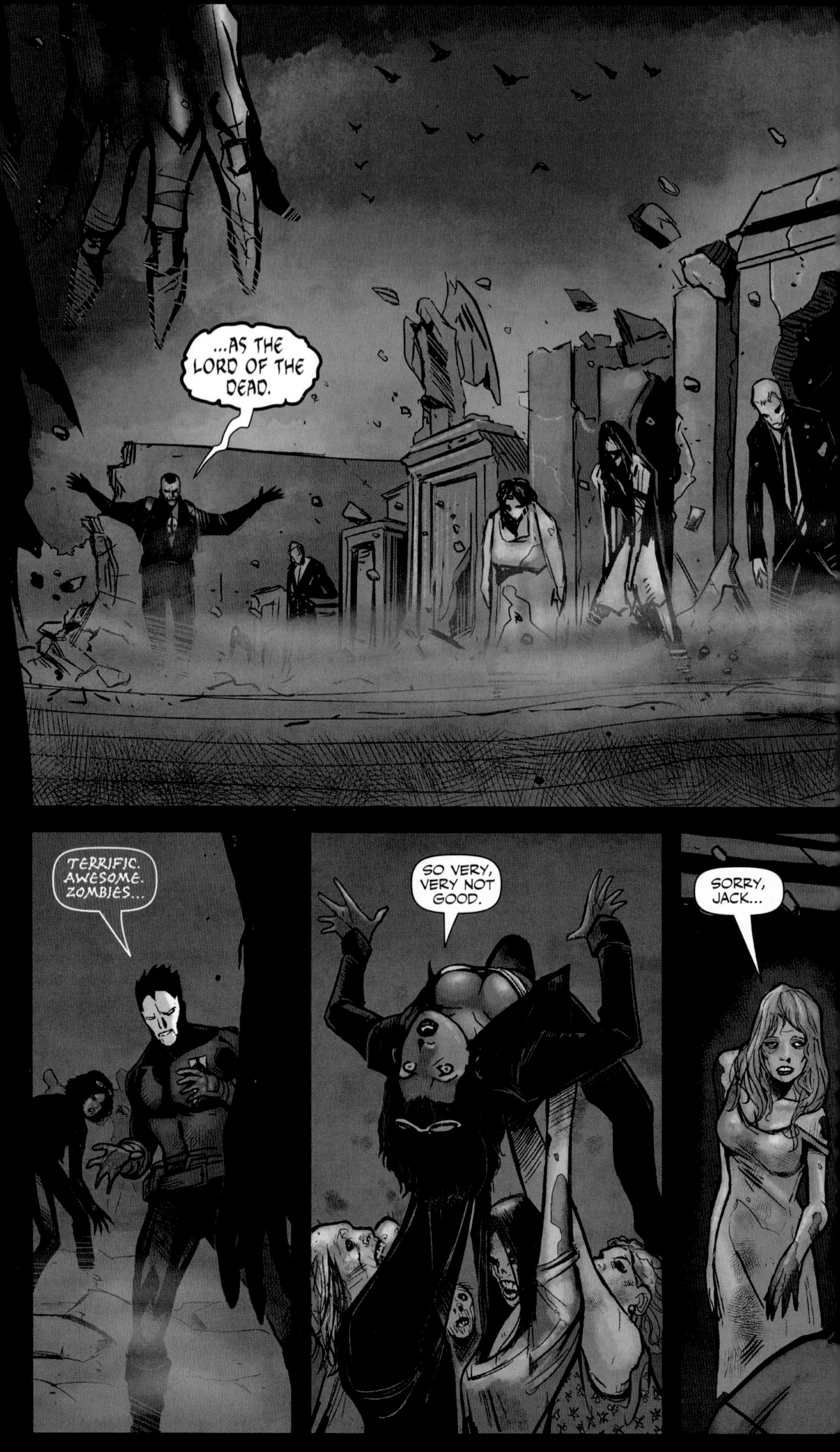
...AS THE LORD OF THE DEAD.
TERRIFIC. AWESOME. ZOMBIES...
SO VERY, VERY NOT GOOD.
SORRY, JACK...

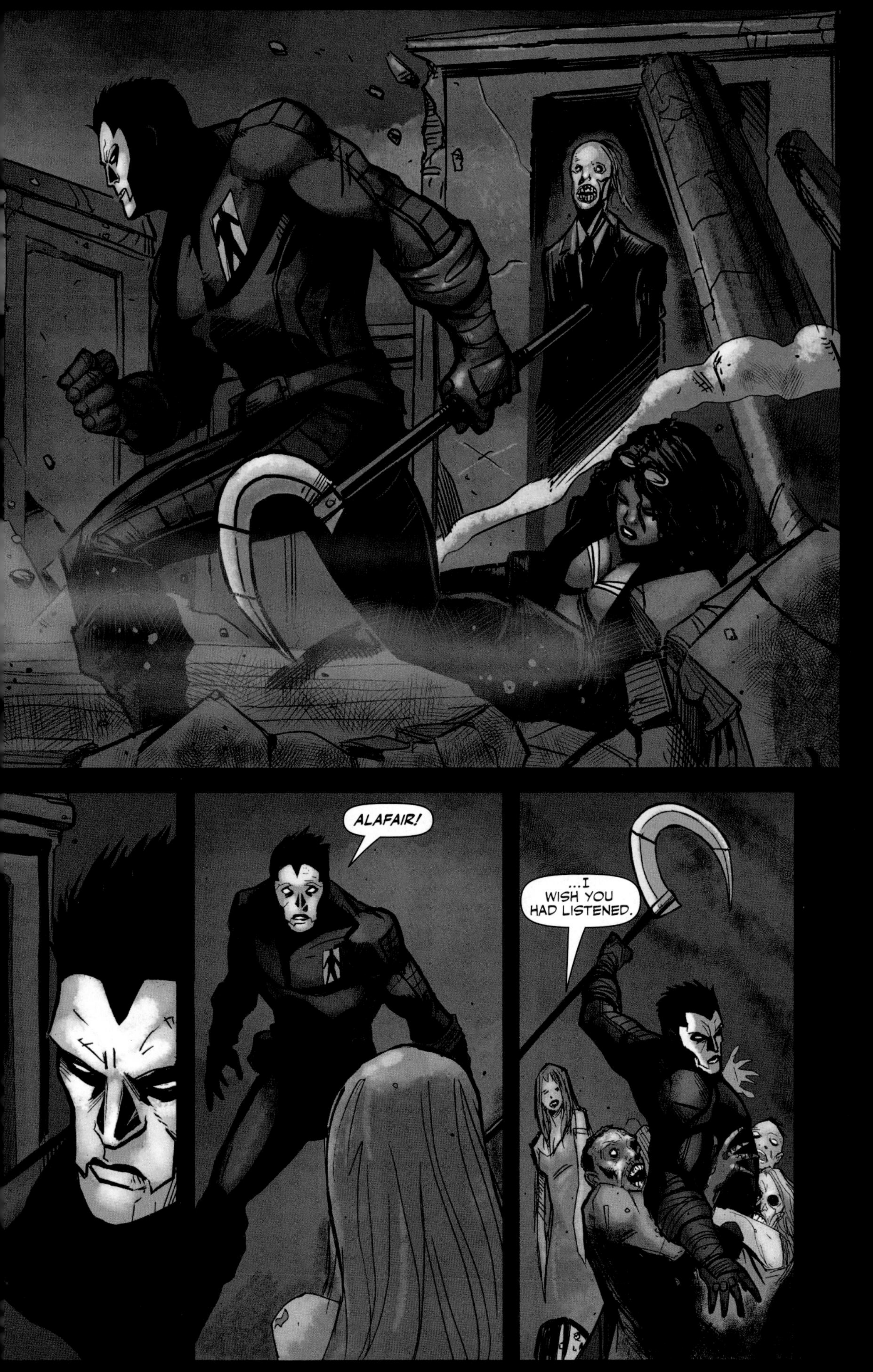
ALAFAIR!
...I WISH YOU HAD LISTENED.

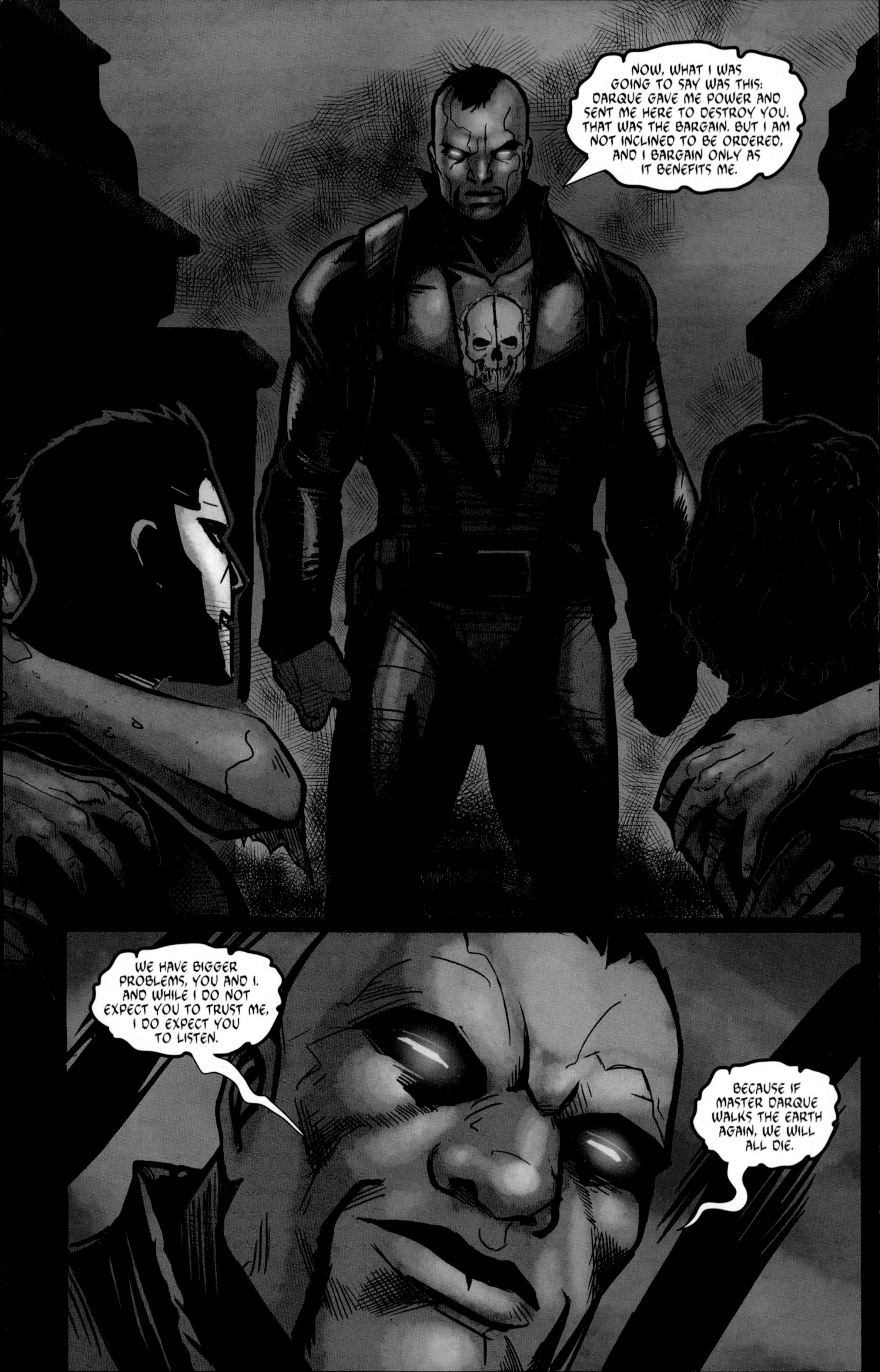
NOW, WHAT I WAS GOING TO SAY WAS THIS: DARQUE GAVE ME POWER AND SENT ME HERE TO DESTROY YOU. THAT WAS THE BARGAIN. BUT I AM NOT INCLINED TO BE ORDERED, AND I BARGAIN ONLY AS IT BENEFITS ME.
WE HAVE BIGGER PROBLEMS, YOU AND I. AND WHILE I DO NOT EXPECT YOU TO TRUST ME, I DO EXPECT YOU TO LISTEN.
BECAUSE IF MASTER DARQUE WALKS THE EARTH AGAIN, WE WILL ALL DIE.

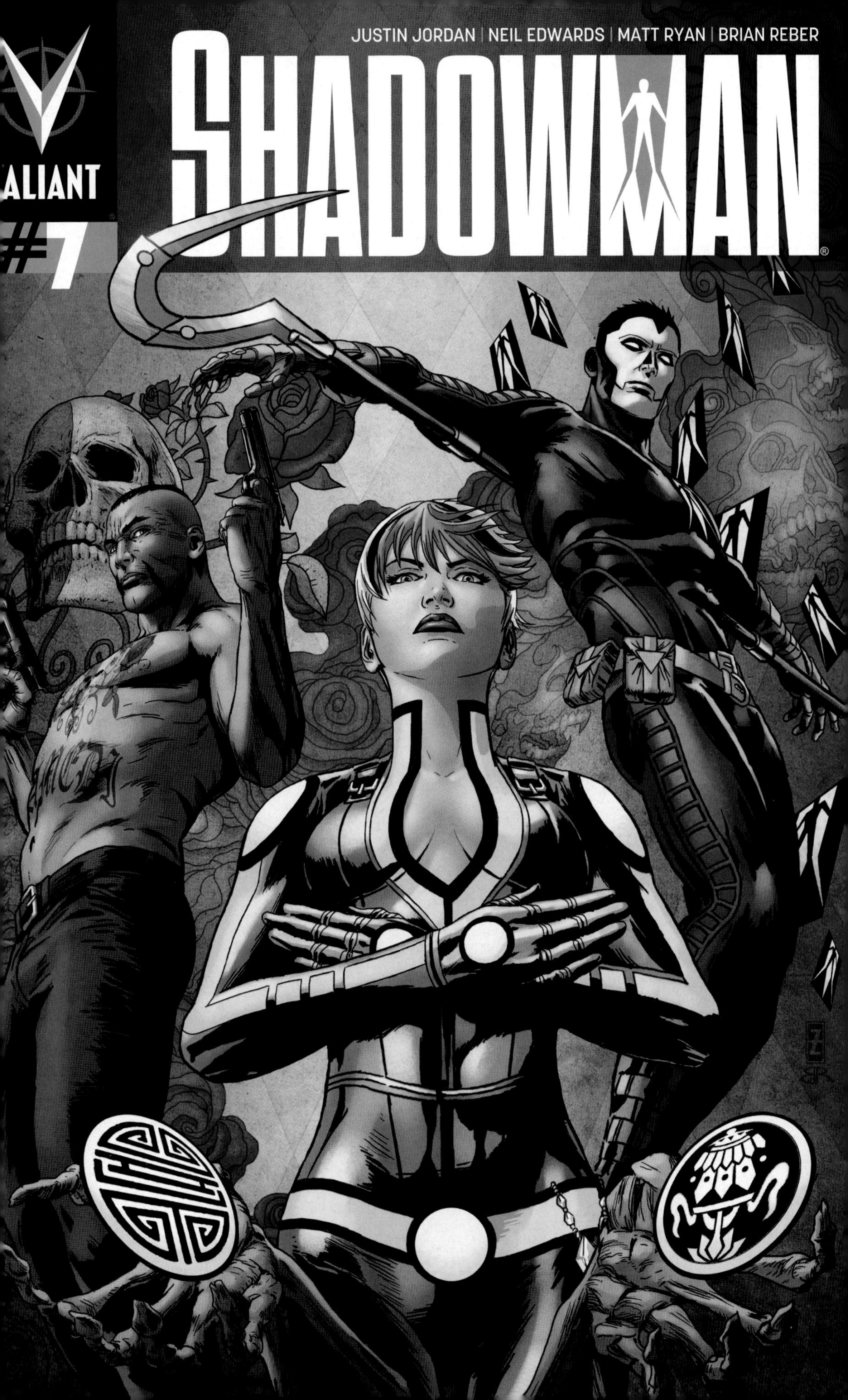
JUSTIN JORDAN | NEIL EDWARDS | MATT RYAN | BRIAN REBER
SHADOWMAN®
#7

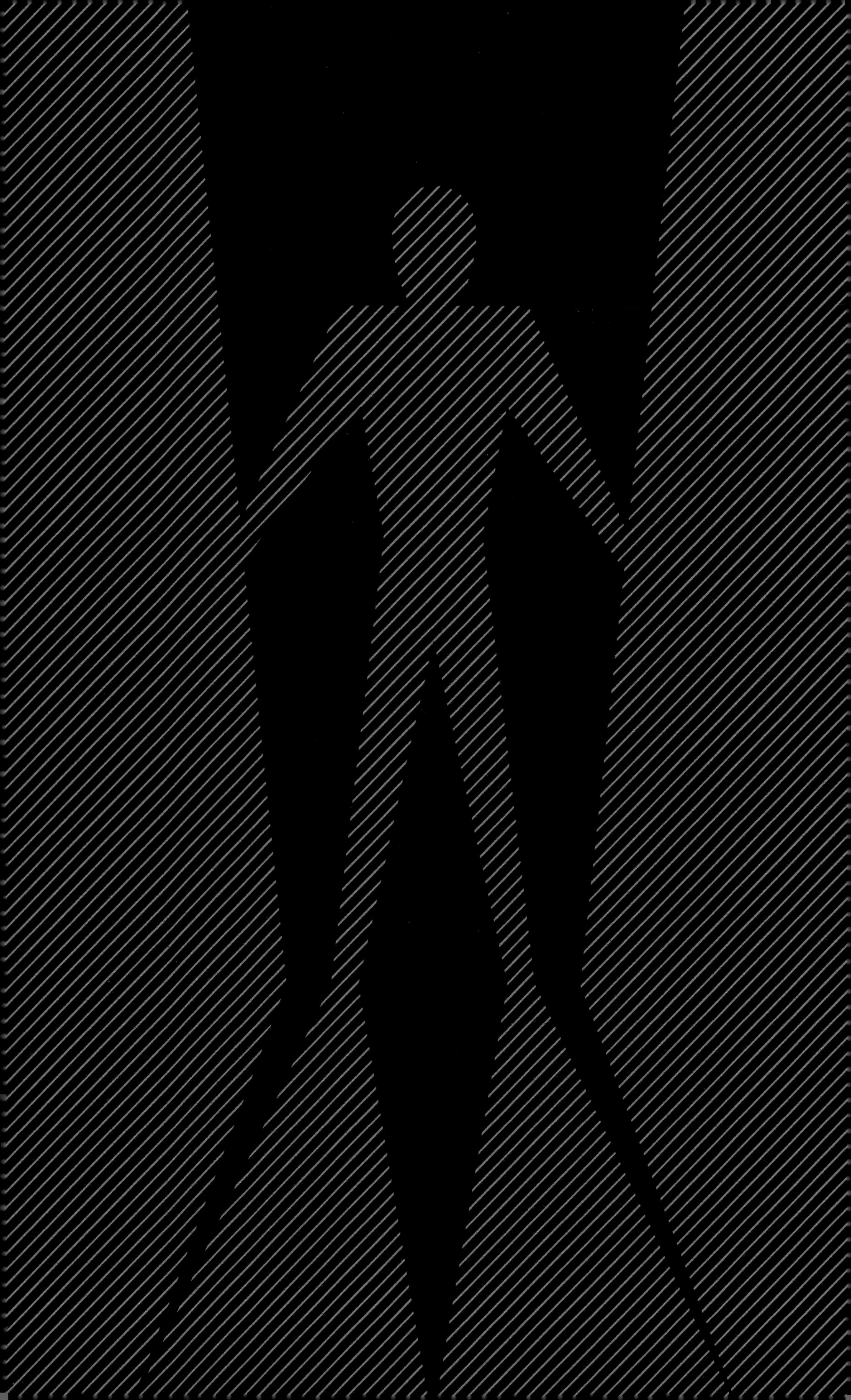

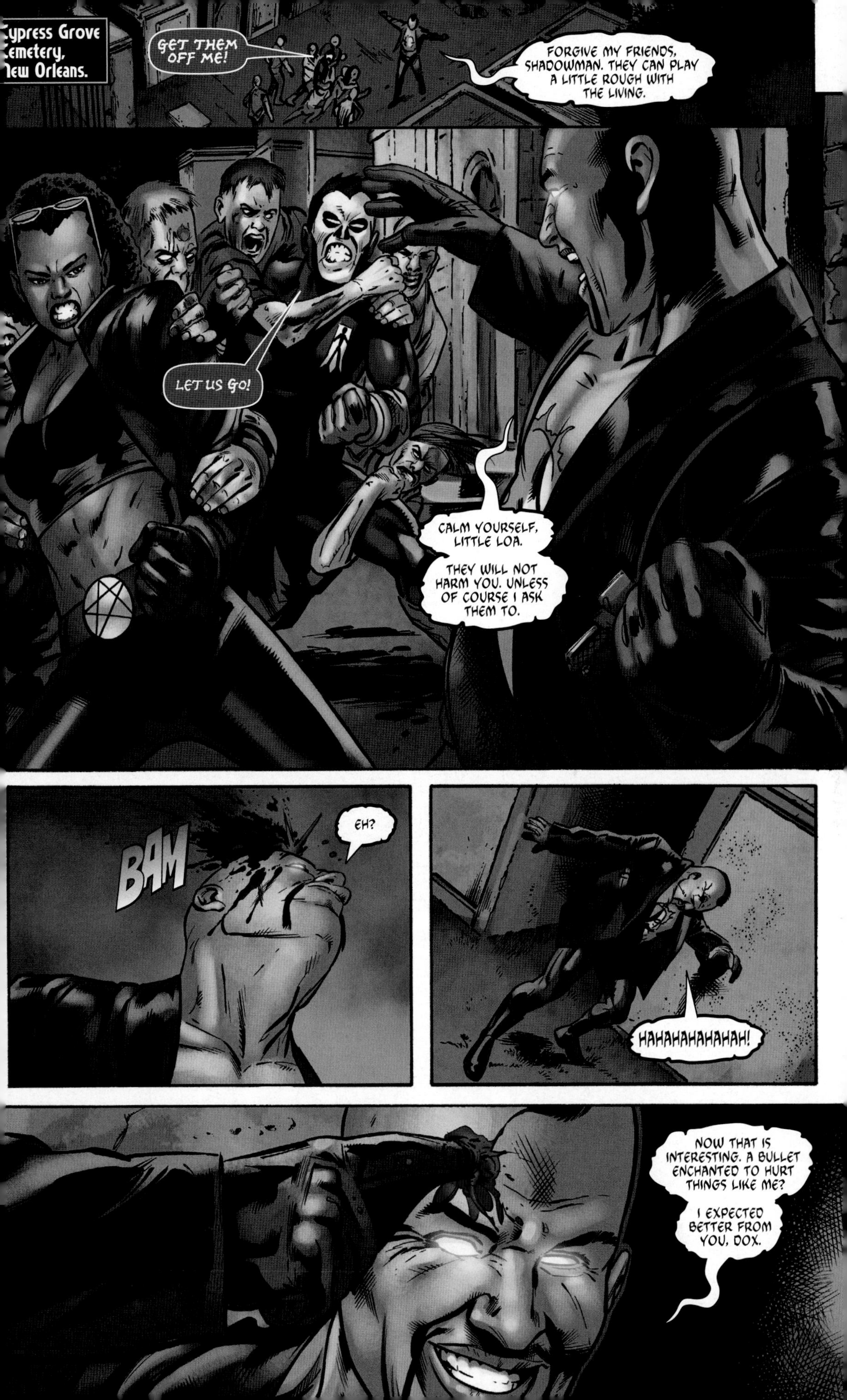
Cypress Grove Cemetery, New Orleans.
GET THEM OFF ME!
FORGIVE MY FRIENDS, SHADOWMAN. THEY CAN PLAY A LITTLE ROUGH WITH THE LIVING.
LET US GO!
CALM YOURSELF, LITTLE LOA.
THEY WILL NOT HARM YOU. UNLESS OF COURSE I ASK THEM TO.
BAM
EH?
HAHAHAHAHAHAH!
NOW THAT IS INTERESTING. A BULLET ENCHANTED TO HURT THINGS LIKE ME?
I EXPECTED BETTER FROM YOU, DOX.

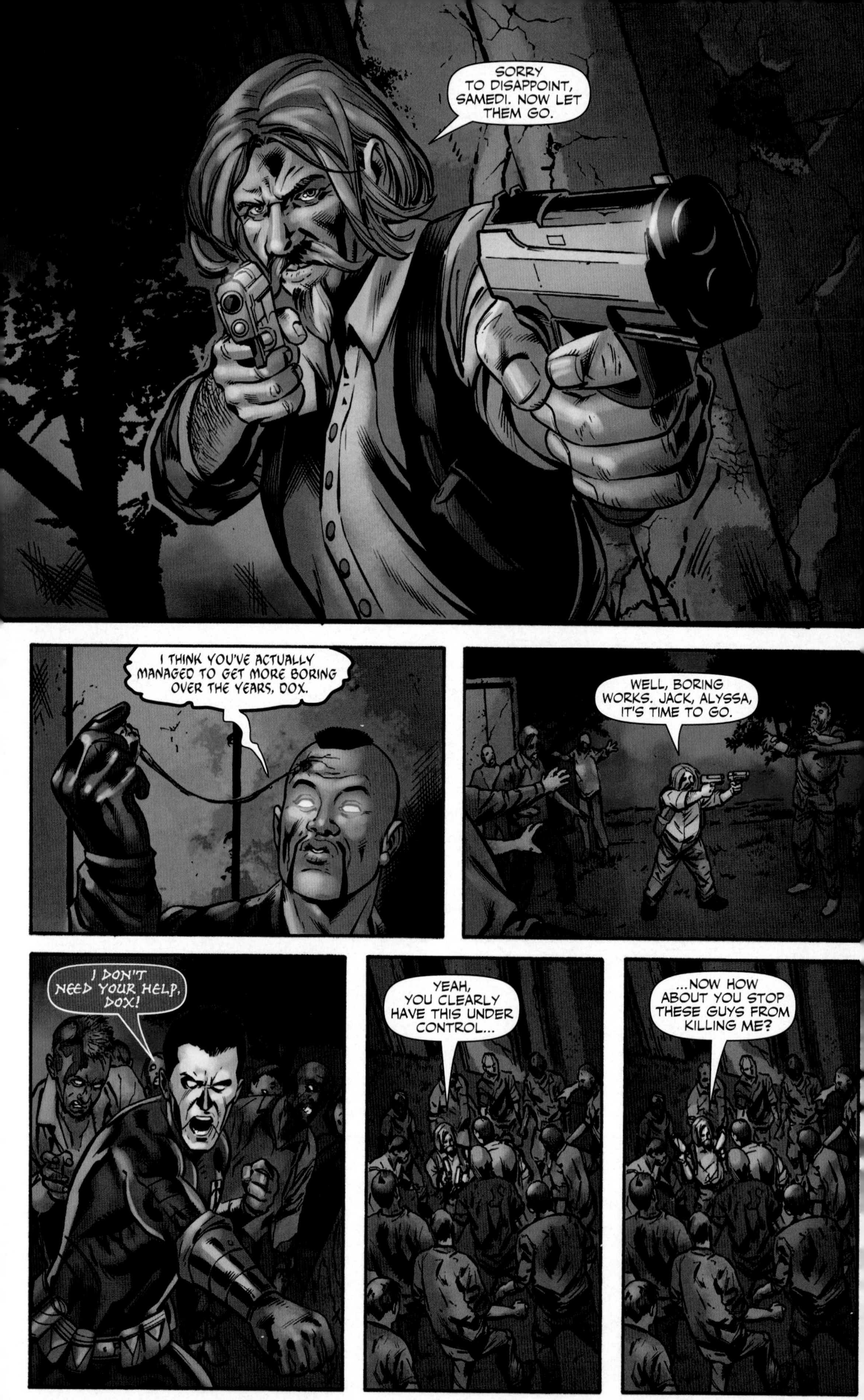
SORRY TO DISAPPOINT, SAMEDI. NOW LET THEM GO.
I THINK YOU'VE ACTUALLY MANAGED TO GET MORE BORING OVER THE YEARS, DOX.
WELL, BORING WORKS. JACK, ALYSSA, IT'S TIME TO GO.
I DON'T NEED YOUR HELP, DOX!
YEAH, YOU CLEARLY HAVE THIS UNDER CONTROL...
...NOW HOW ABOUT YOU STOP THESE GUYS FROM KILLING ME?

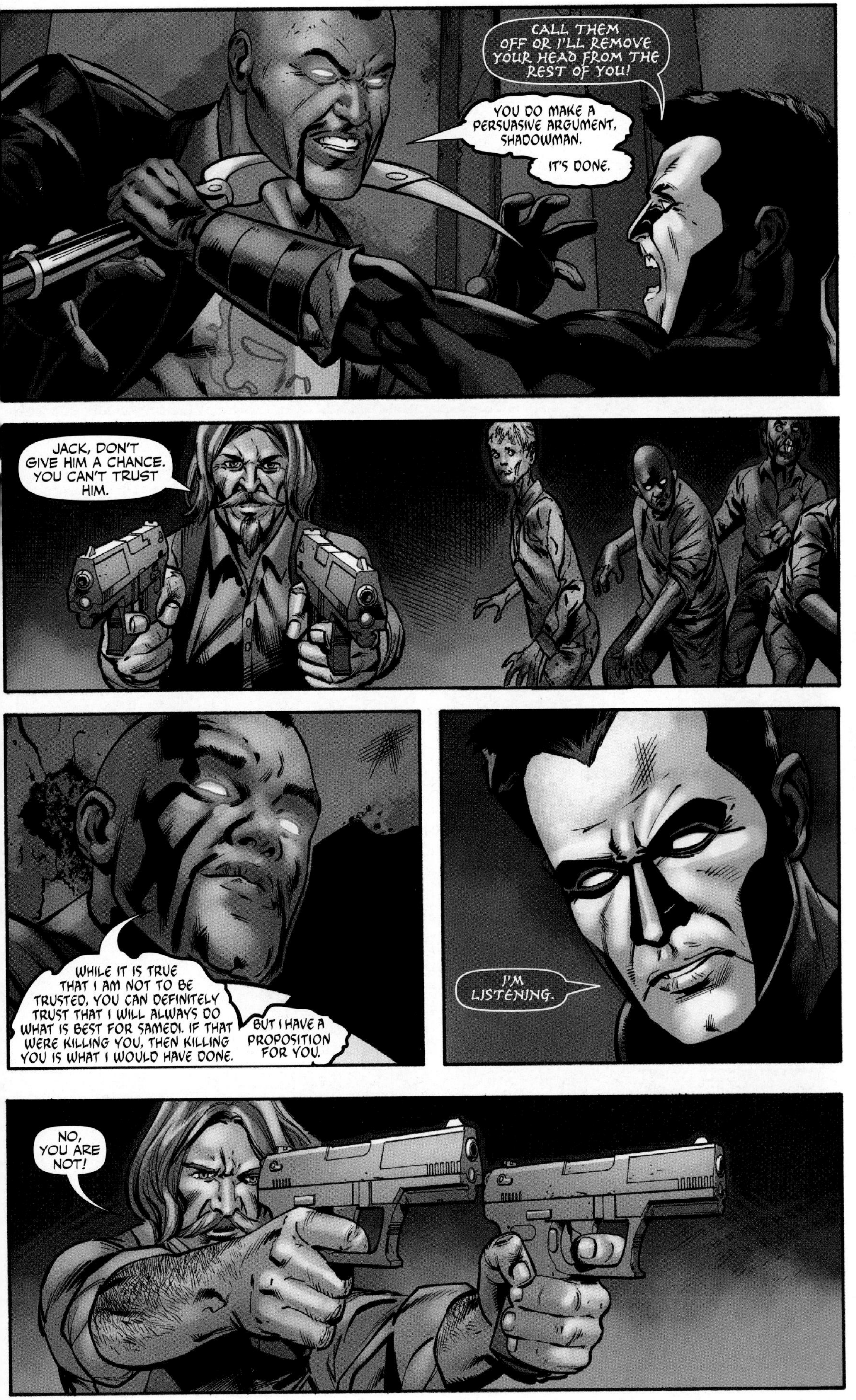
CALL THEM OFF OR I'LL REMOVE YOUR HEAD FROM THE REST OF YOU!
YOU DO MAKE A PERSUASIVE ARGUMENT, SHADOWMAN.
IT'S DONE.
JACK, DON'T GIVE HIM A CHANCE. YOU CAN'T TRUST HIM.
WHILE IT IS TRUE THAT I AM NOT TO BE TRUSTED, YOU CAN DEFINITELY TRUST THAT I WILL ALWAYS DO WHAT IS BEST FOR SAMEDI. IF THAT WERE KILLING YOU, THEN KILLING YOU IS WHAT I WOULD HAVE DONE.
BUT I HAVE A PROPOSITION FOR YOU.
I'M LISTENING.
NO, YOU ARE NOT!

YOU HEARD HIM--*LET GO OF ME!*

JACK, LISTEN TO DOX. THIS IS *BARON SAMEDI.*

I KNOW. AND HE'S GOING TO SAY WHAT HE CAME HERE TO SAY.

MASTER DARQUE IS TRAPPED IN THE DEADSIDE. BUT HE WILL NOT STAY THERE LONG. EVEN NOW THE BRETHREN ARE WORKING TO BRING THEIR MASTER TO EARTH UNDER THE LEADERSHIP OF THE MAN CALLED DEVEREAUX.

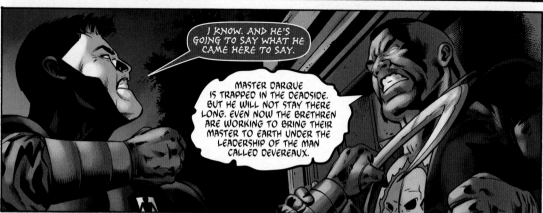

JACK, SAMEDI IS EXACTLY THE SORT OF THING THE ABETTORS ARE SUPPOSED TO STOP. THAT *YOU* ARE SUPPOSED TO STOP.

THINGS THAT THINK PEOPLE ARE TOYS, PETS, OR FOOD. OR ALL THREE.

JACK, PLEASE.

THE HUMAN I AM *RIDING* AMASSED A MAP OF THE BRETHREN OPERATIONS IN HIS HEAD. I KNOW WHAT HE KNEW.

AND I KNOW WHERE DEVEREAUX IS.

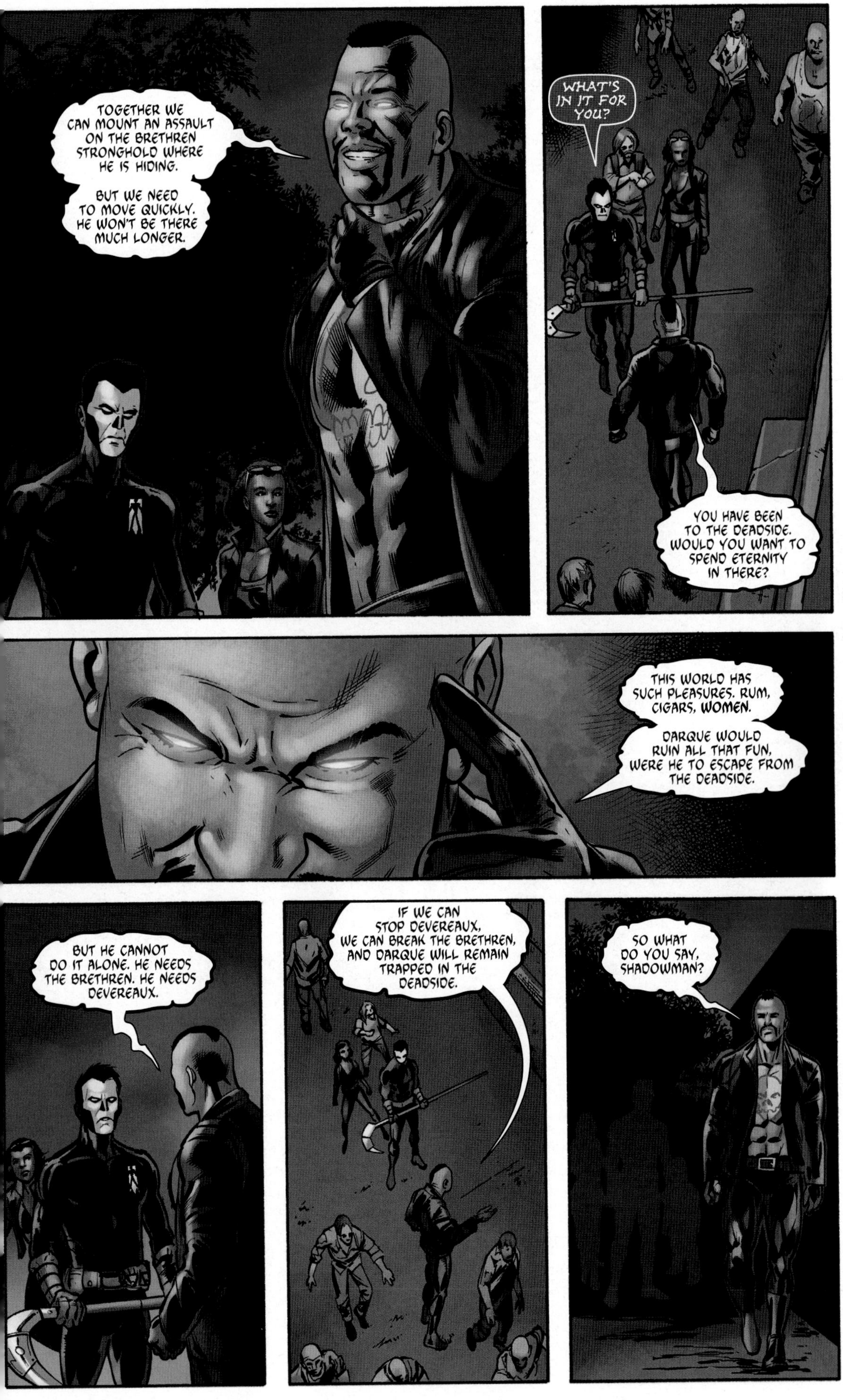

TOGETHER WE CAN MOUNT AN ASSAULT ON THE BRETHREN STRONGHOLD WHERE HE IS HIDING.
BUT WE NEED TO MOVE QUICKLY. HE WON'T BE THERE MUCH LONGER.
WHAT'S IN IT FOR YOU?
YOU HAVE BEEN TO THE DEADSIDE. WOULD YOU WANT TO SPEND ETERNITY IN THERE?
THIS WORLD HAS SUCH PLEASURES. RUM, CIGARS, WOMEN.
DARQUE WOULD RUIN ALL THAT FUN, WERE HE TO ESCAPE FROM THE DEADSIDE.
BUT HE CANNOT DO IT ALONE. HE NEEDS THE BRETHREN. HE NEEDS DEVEREAUX.
IF WE CAN STOP DEVEREAUX, WE CAN BREAK THE BRETHREN, AND DARQUE WILL REMAIN TRAPPED IN THE DEADSIDE.
SO WHAT DO YOU SAY, SHADOWMAN?

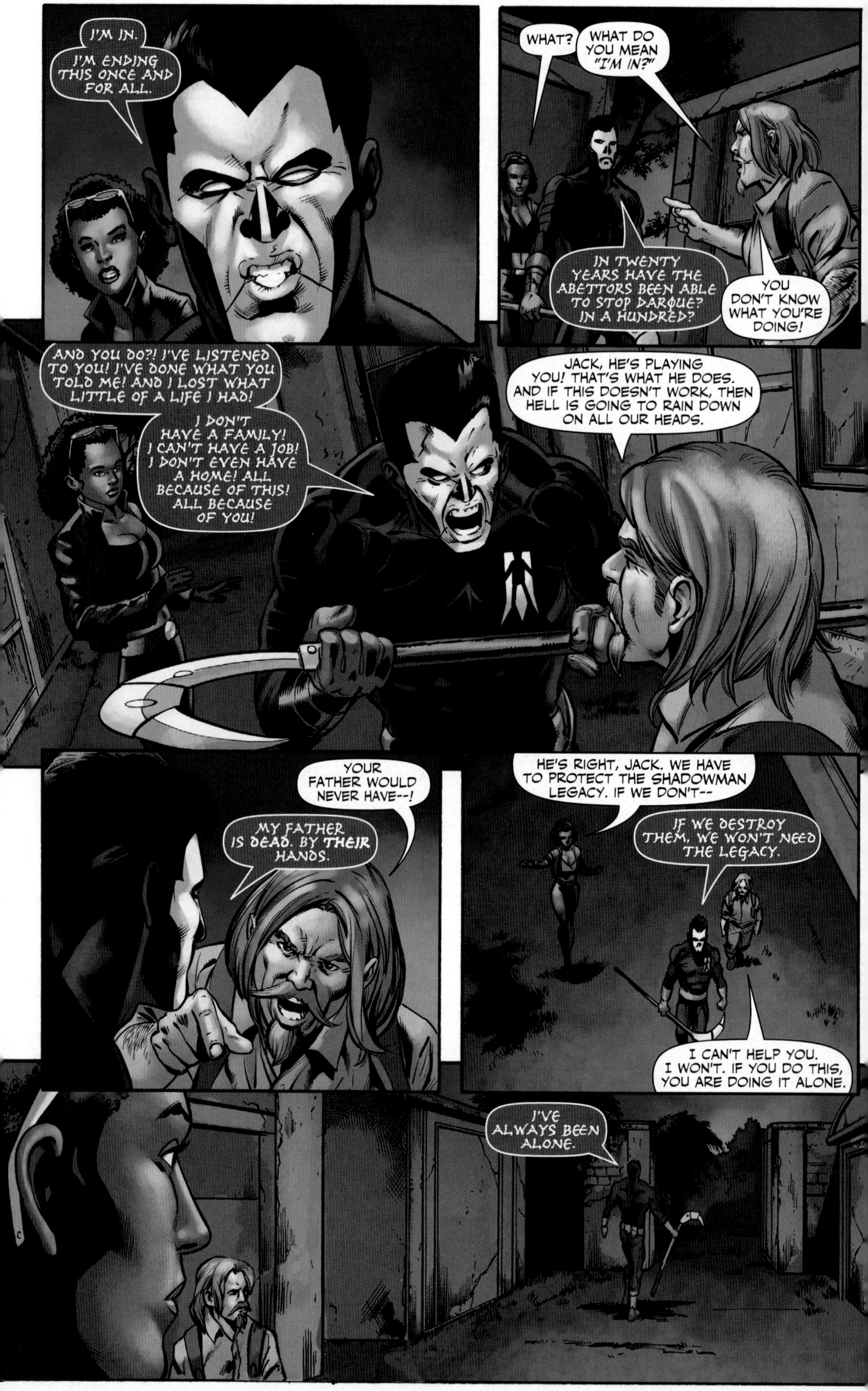

I'M IN.
I'M ENDING THIS ONCE AND FOR ALL.
WHAT?
WHAT DO YOU MEAN "I'M IN?"
IN TWENTY YEARS HAVE THE ABETTORS BEEN ABLE TO STOP DARQUE? IN A HUNDRED?
YOU DON'T KNOW WHAT YOU'RE DOING!
AND YOU DO?! I'VE LISTENED TO YOU! I'VE DONE WHAT YOU TOLD ME! AND I LOST WHAT LITTLE OF A LIFE I HAD!
I DON'T HAVE A FAMILY! I CAN'T HAVE A JOB! I DON'T EVEN HAVE A HOME! ALL BECAUSE OF THIS! ALL BECAUSE OF YOU!
JACK, HE'S PLAYING YOU! THAT'S WHAT HE DOES. AND IF THIS DOESN'T WORK, THEN HELL IS GOING TO RAIN DOWN ON ALL OUR HEADS.
YOUR FATHER WOULD NEVER HAVE--!
MY FATHER IS DEAD. BY THEIR HANDS.
HE'S RIGHT, JACK. WE HAVE TO PROTECT THE SHADOWMAN LEGACY. IF WE DON'T--
IF WE DESTROY THEM, WE WON'T NEED THE LEGACY.
I CAN'T HELP YOU. I WON'T. IF YOU DO THIS, YOU ARE DOING IT ALONE.
I'VE ALWAYS BEEN ALONE.

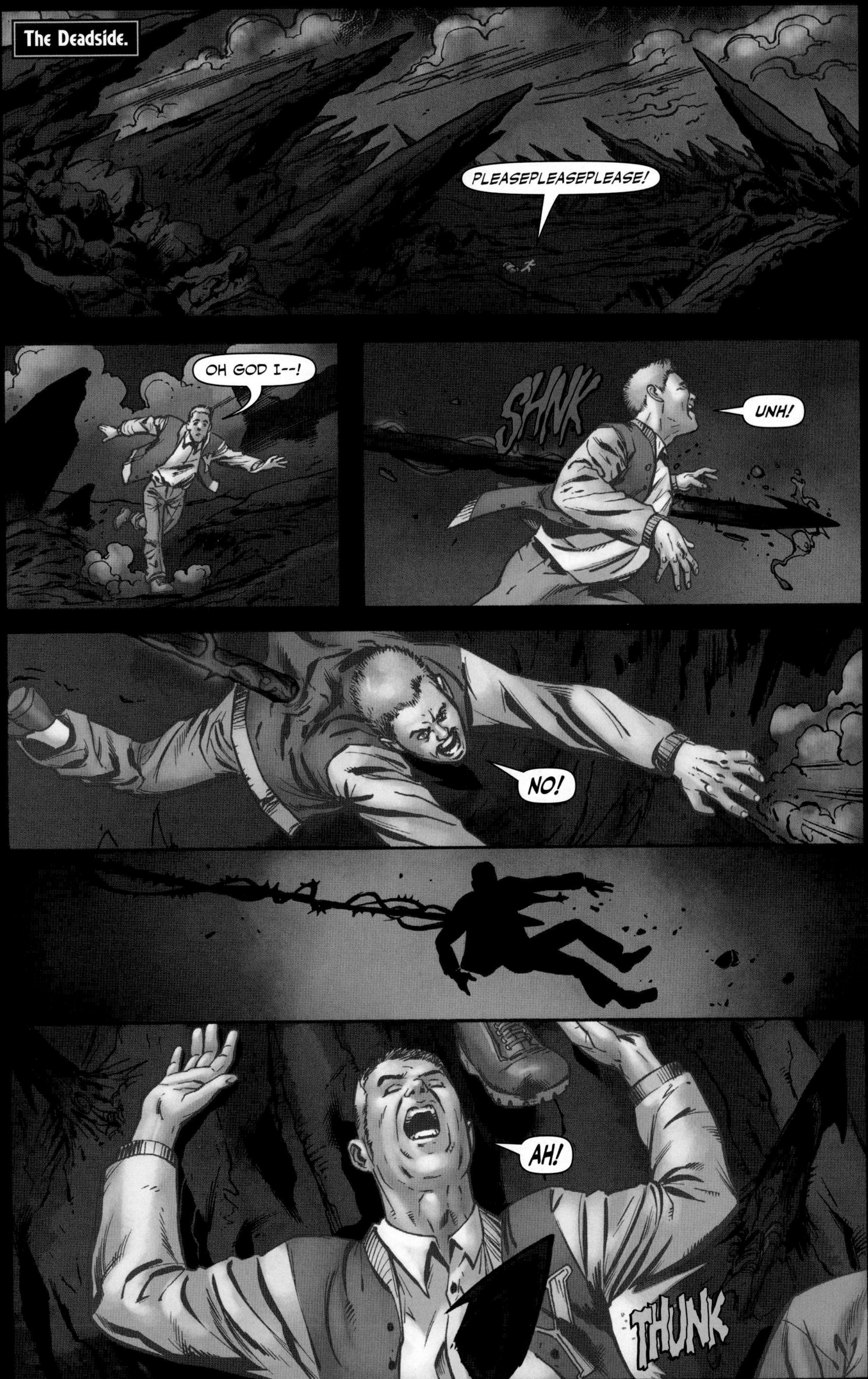
The Deadside.
PLEASEPLEASEPLEASE!
OH GOD I--!
SHNK
UNH!
NO!
AH!
THUNK

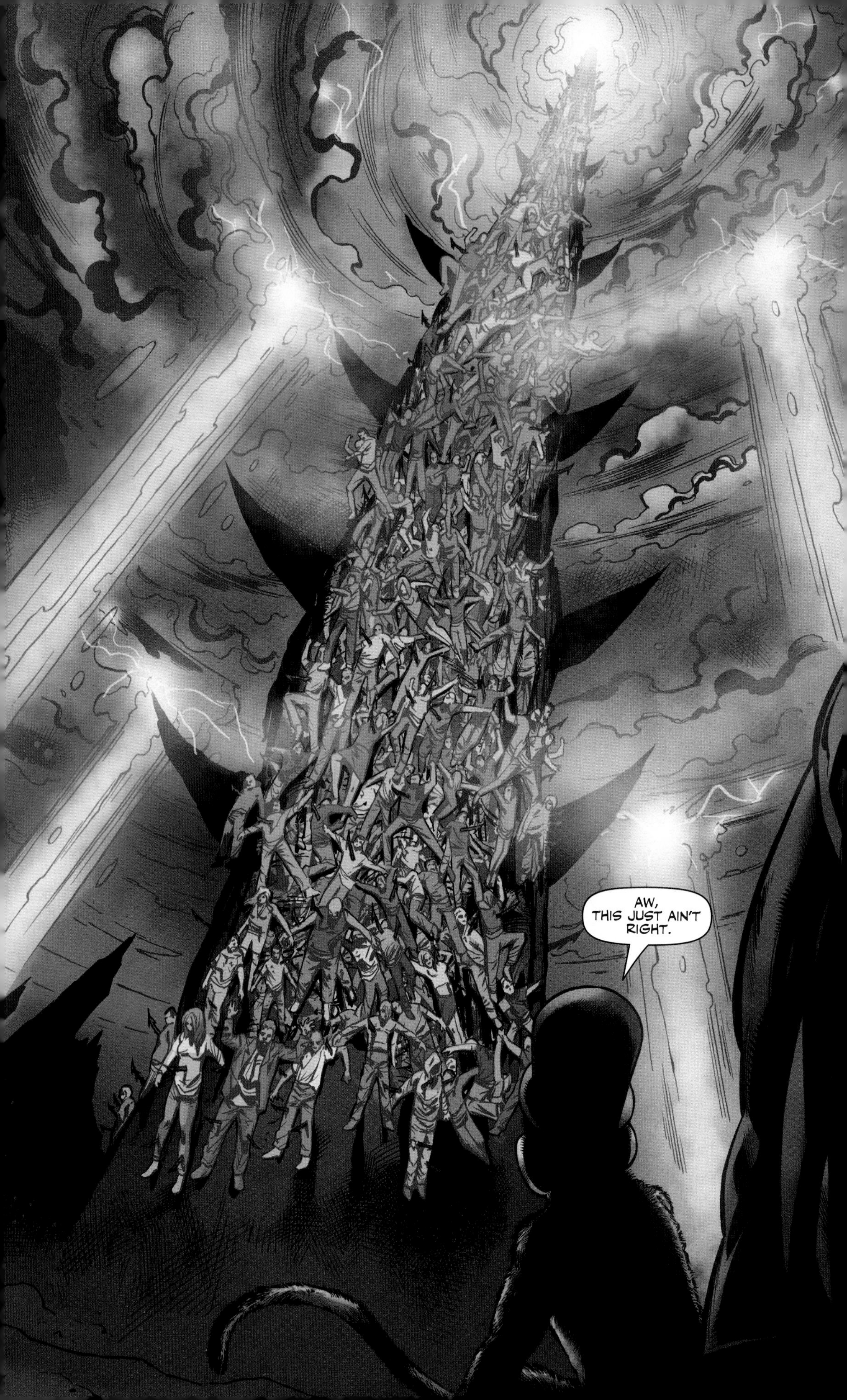
AW, THIS JUST AIN'T RIGHT.

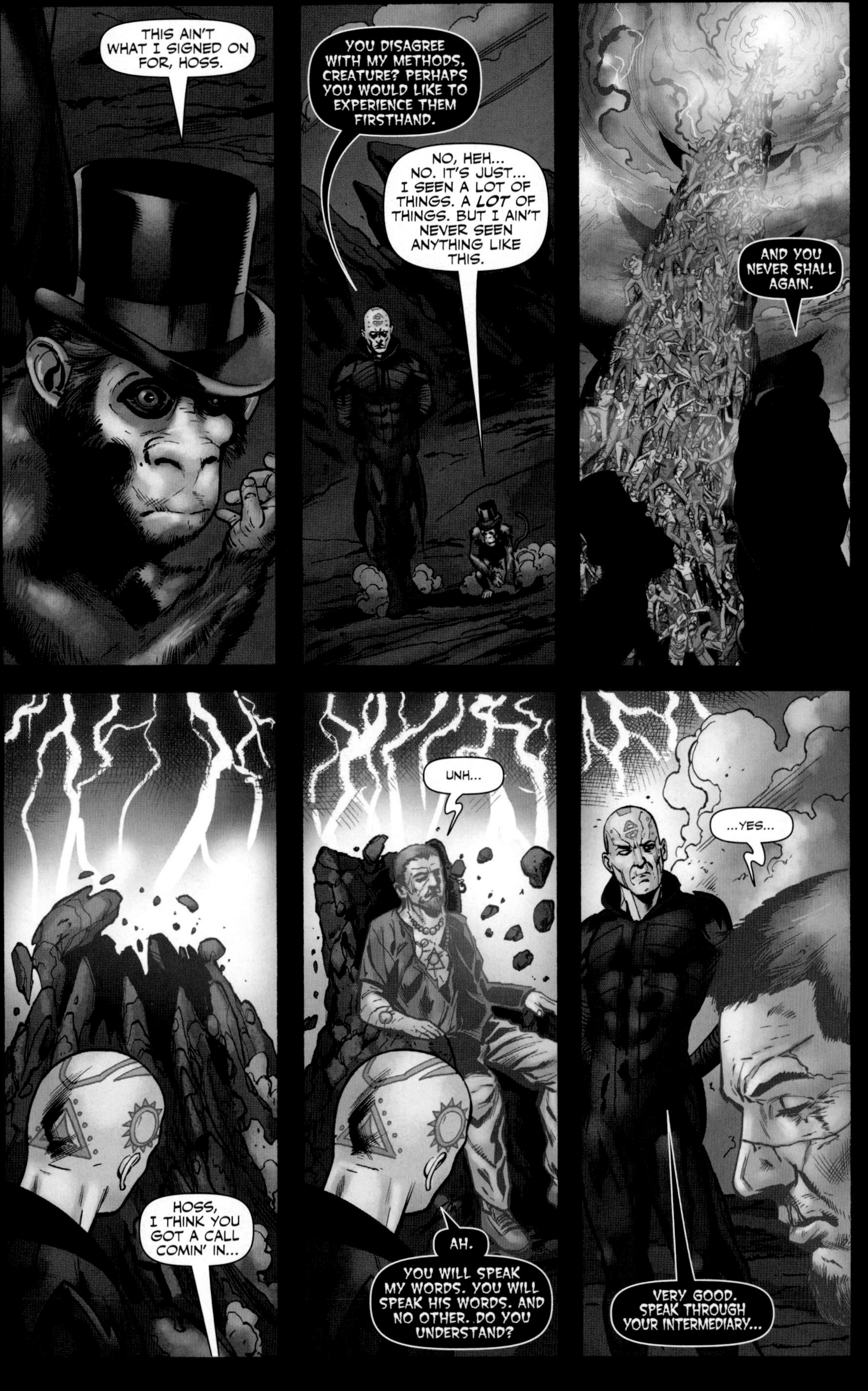
THIS AIN'T WHAT I SIGNED ON FOR, HOSS.
YOU DISAGREE WITH MY METHODS, CREATURE? PERHAPS YOU WOULD LIKE TO EXPERIENCE THEM FIRSTHAND.
NO, HEH... NO. IT'S JUST... I SEEN A LOT OF THINGS. A LOT OF THINGS. BUT I AIN'T NEVER SEEN ANYTHING LIKE THIS.
AND YOU NEVER SHALL AGAIN.
HOSS, I THINK YOU GOT A CALL COMIN' IN...
UNH...
AH.
YOU WILL SPEAK MY WORDS. YOU WILL SPEAK HIS WORDS. AND NO OTHER. DO YOU UNDERSTAND?
...YES...
VERY GOOD. SPEAK THROUGH YOUR INTERMEDIARY...

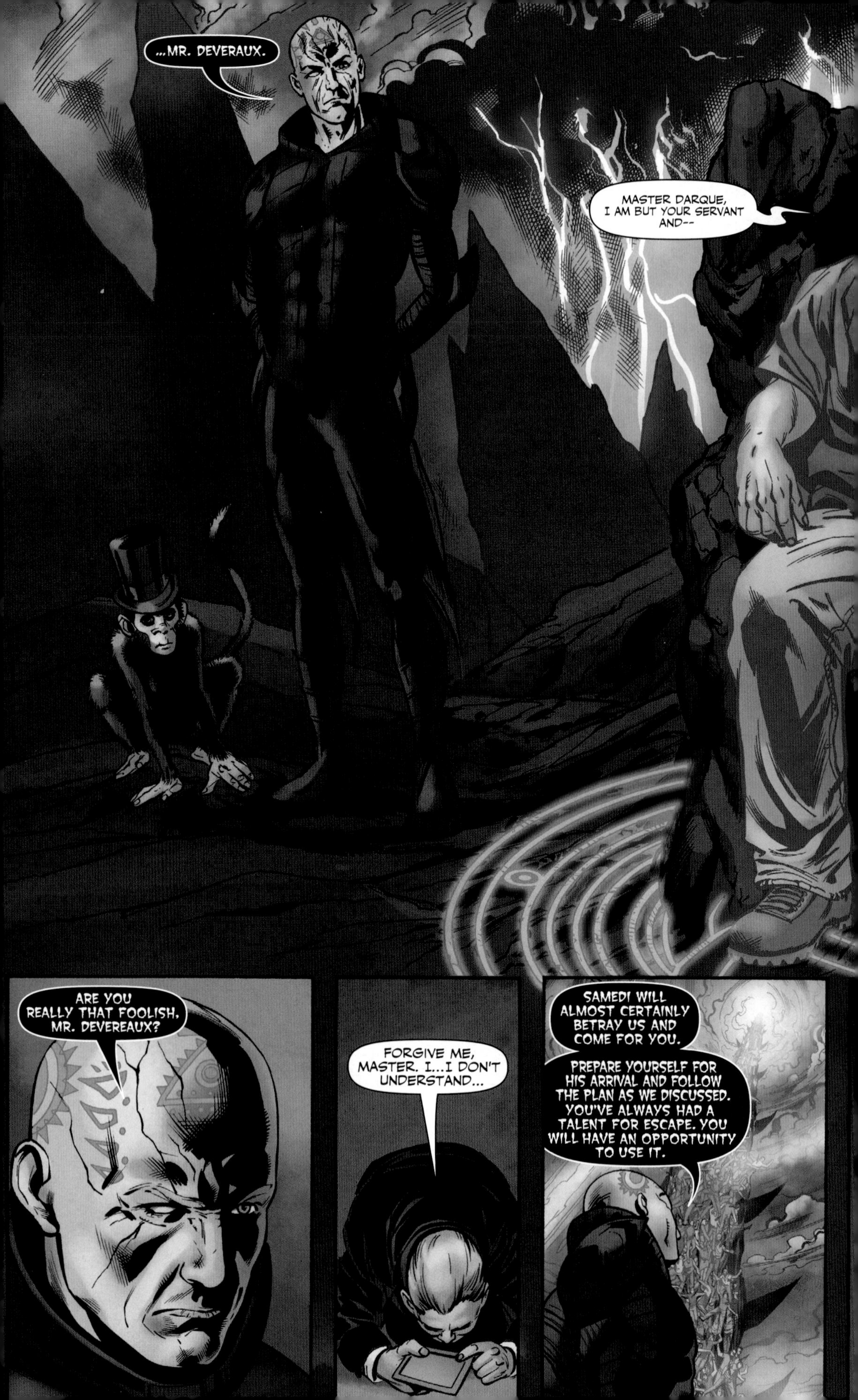
...MR. DEVERAUX.
MASTER DARQUE, I AM BUT YOUR SERVANT AND--
ARE YOU REALLY THAT FOOLISH, MR. DEVEREAUX?
FORGIVE ME, MASTER. I...I DON'T UNDERSTAND...
SAMEDI WILL ALMOST CERTAINLY BETRAY US AND COME FOR YOU.
PREPARE YOURSELF FOR HIS ARRIVAL AND FOLLOW THE PLAN AS WE DISCUSSED. YOU'VE ALWAYS HAD A TALENT FOR ESCAPE. YOU WILL HAVE AN OPPORTUNITY TO USE IT.

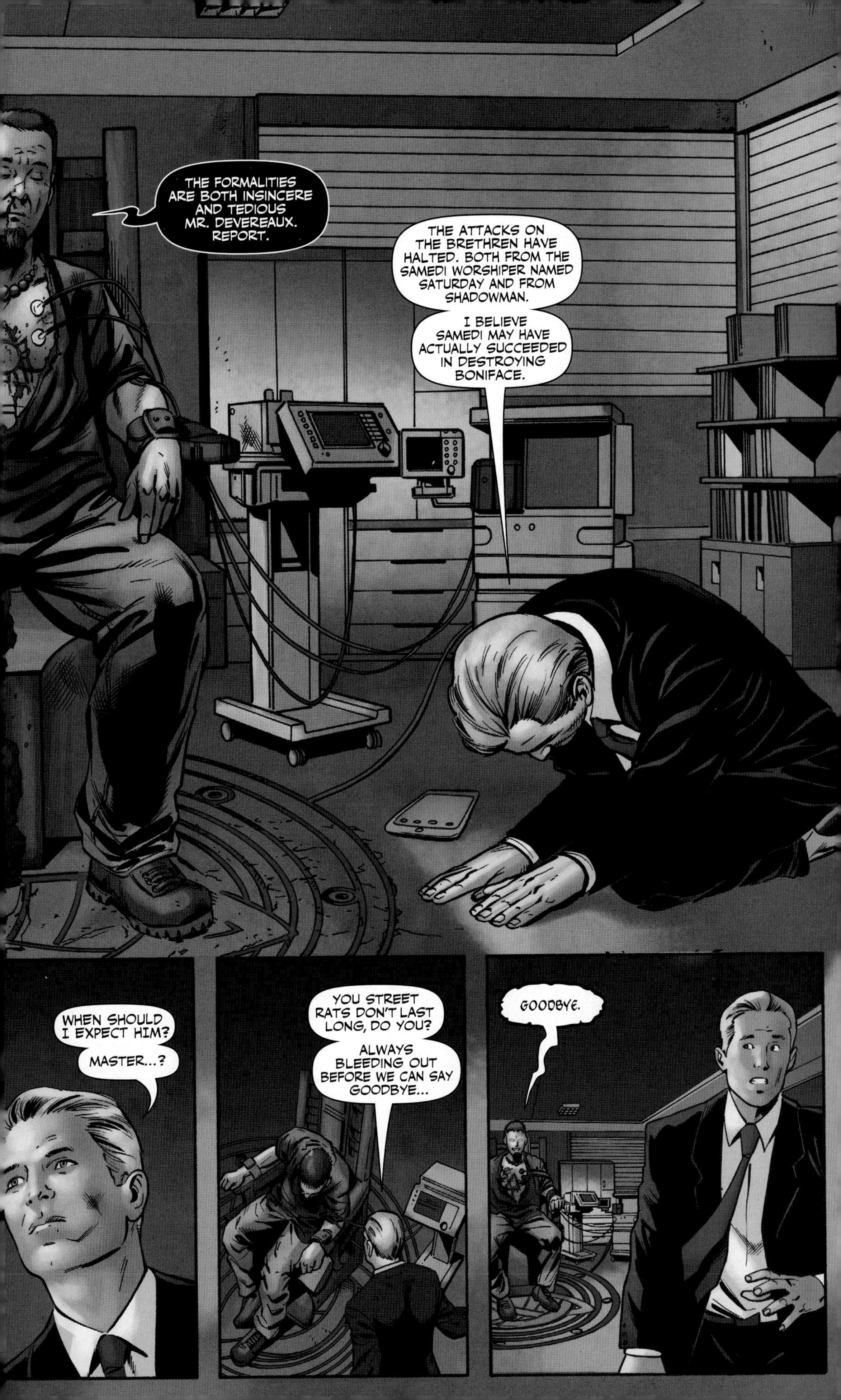
THE FORMALITIES ARE BOTH INSINCERE AND TEDIOUS MR. DEVEREAUX. REPORT.
THE ATTACKS ON THE BRETHREN HAVE HALTED. BOTH FROM THE SAMEDI WORSHIPER NAMED SATURDAY AND FROM SHADOWMAN.
I BELIEVE SAMEDI MAY HAVE ACTUALLY SUCCEEDED IN DESTROYING BONIFACE.
WHEN SHOULD I EXPECT HIM?
MASTER...?
YOU STREET RATS DON'T LAST LONG, DO YOU?
ALWAYS BLEEDING OUT BEFORE WE CAN SAY GOODBYE...
GOODBYE.

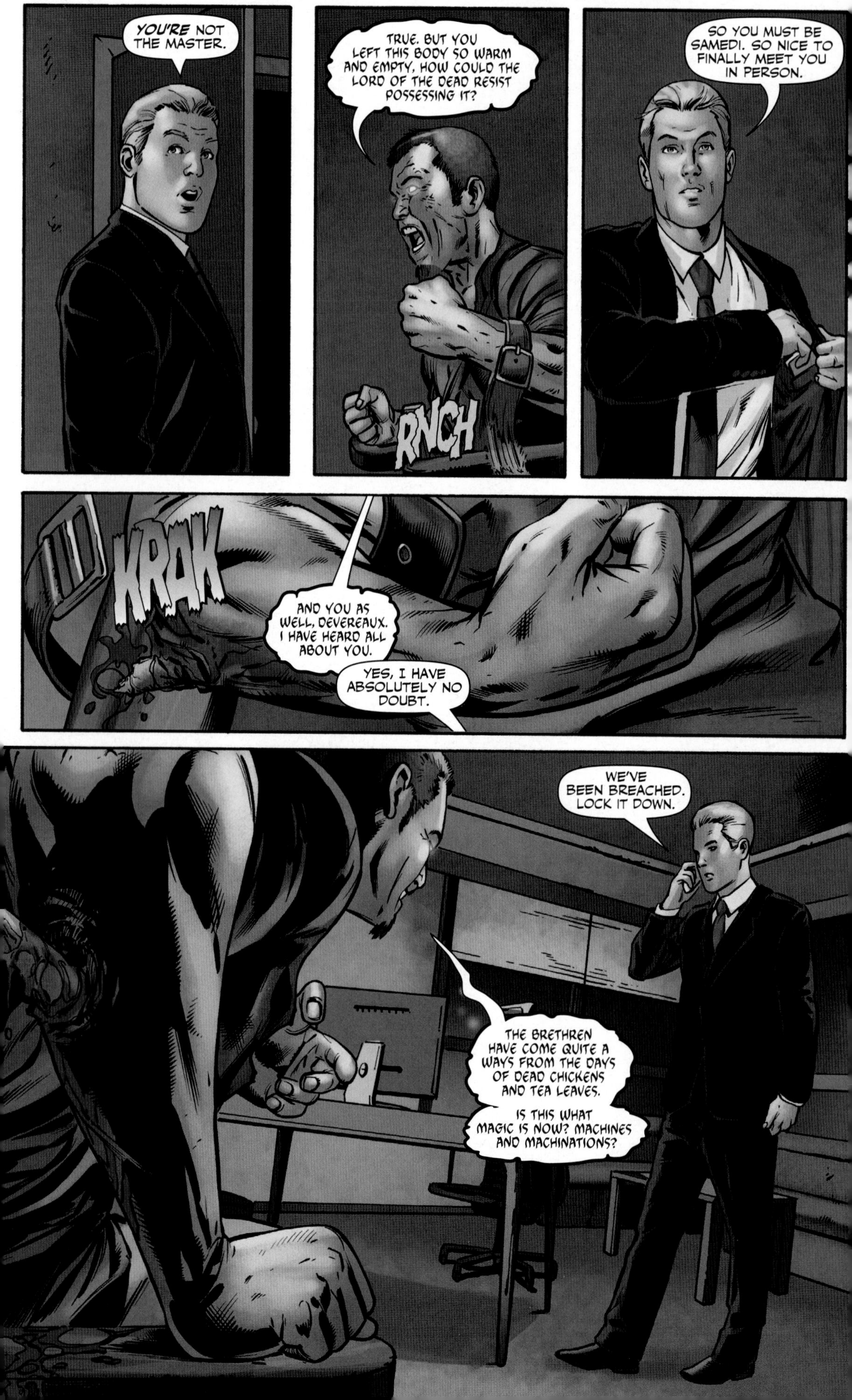
YOU'RE NOT THE MASTER.
TRUE. BUT YOU LEFT THIS BODY SO WARM AND EMPTY, HOW COULD THE LORD OF THE DEAD RESIST POSSESSING IT?
RNCH
SO YOU MUST BE SAMEDI. SO NICE TO FINALLY MEET YOU IN PERSON.
KRAK
AND YOU AS WELL, DEVEREAUX. I HAVE HEARD ALL ABOUT YOU.
YES, I HAVE ABSOLUTELY NO DOUBT.
WE'VE BEEN BREACHED. LOCK IT DOWN.
THE BRETHREN HAVE COME QUITE A WAYS FROM THE DAYS OF DEAD CHICKENS AND TEA LEAVES.
IS THIS WHAT MAGIC IS NOW? MACHINES AND MACHINATIONS?

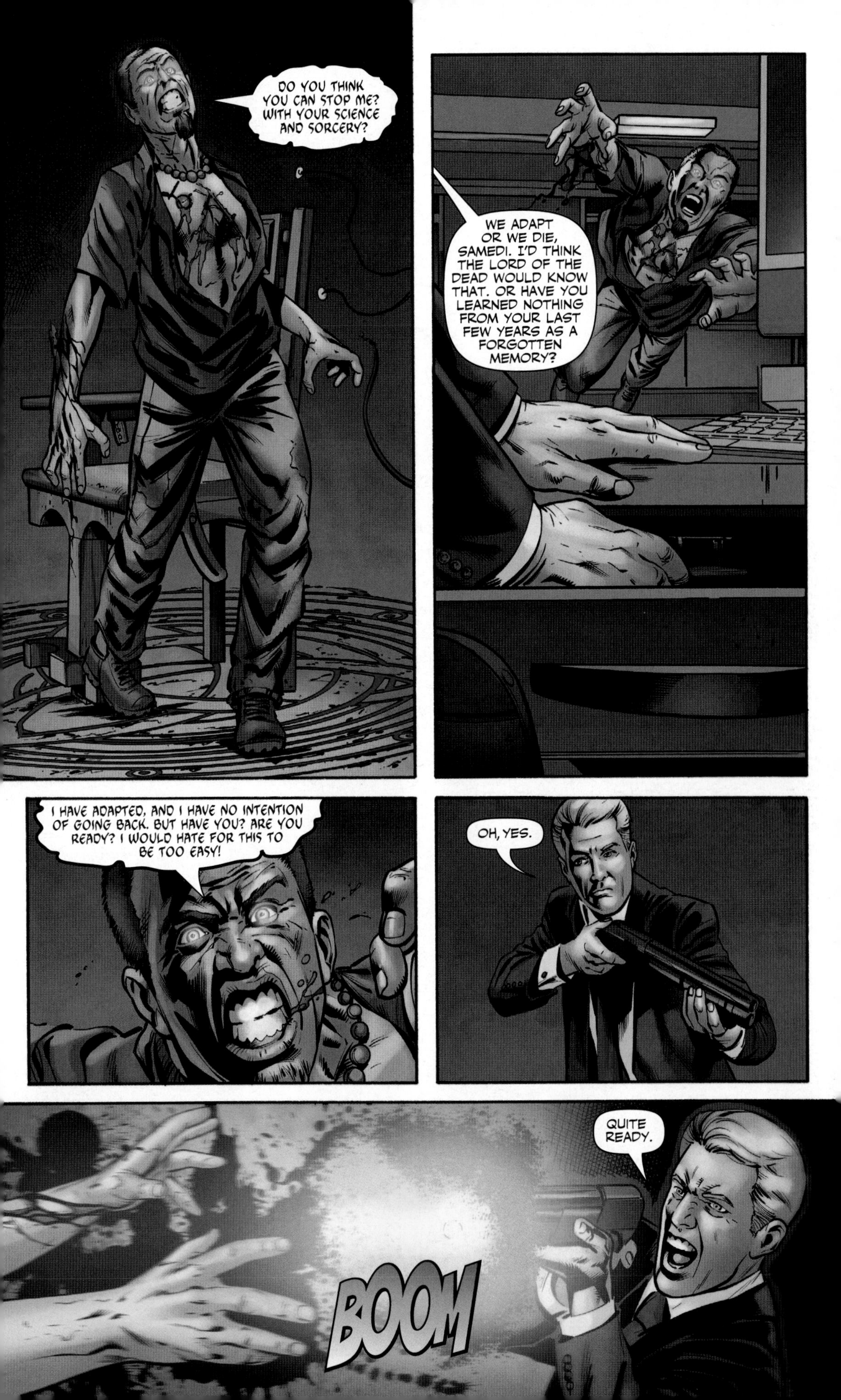
DO YOU THINK YOU CAN STOP ME? WITH YOUR SCIENCE AND SORCERY?
WE ADAPT OR WE DIE, SAMEDI. I'D THINK THE LORD OF THE DEAD WOULD KNOW THAT. OR HAVE YOU LEARNED NOTHING FROM YOUR LAST FEW YEARS AS A FORGOTTEN MEMORY?
I HAVE ADAPTED, AND I HAVE NO INTENTION OF GOING BACK. BUT HAVE YOU? ARE YOU READY? I WOULD HATE FOR THIS TO BE TOO EASY!
OH, YES.
QUITE READY.
BOOM

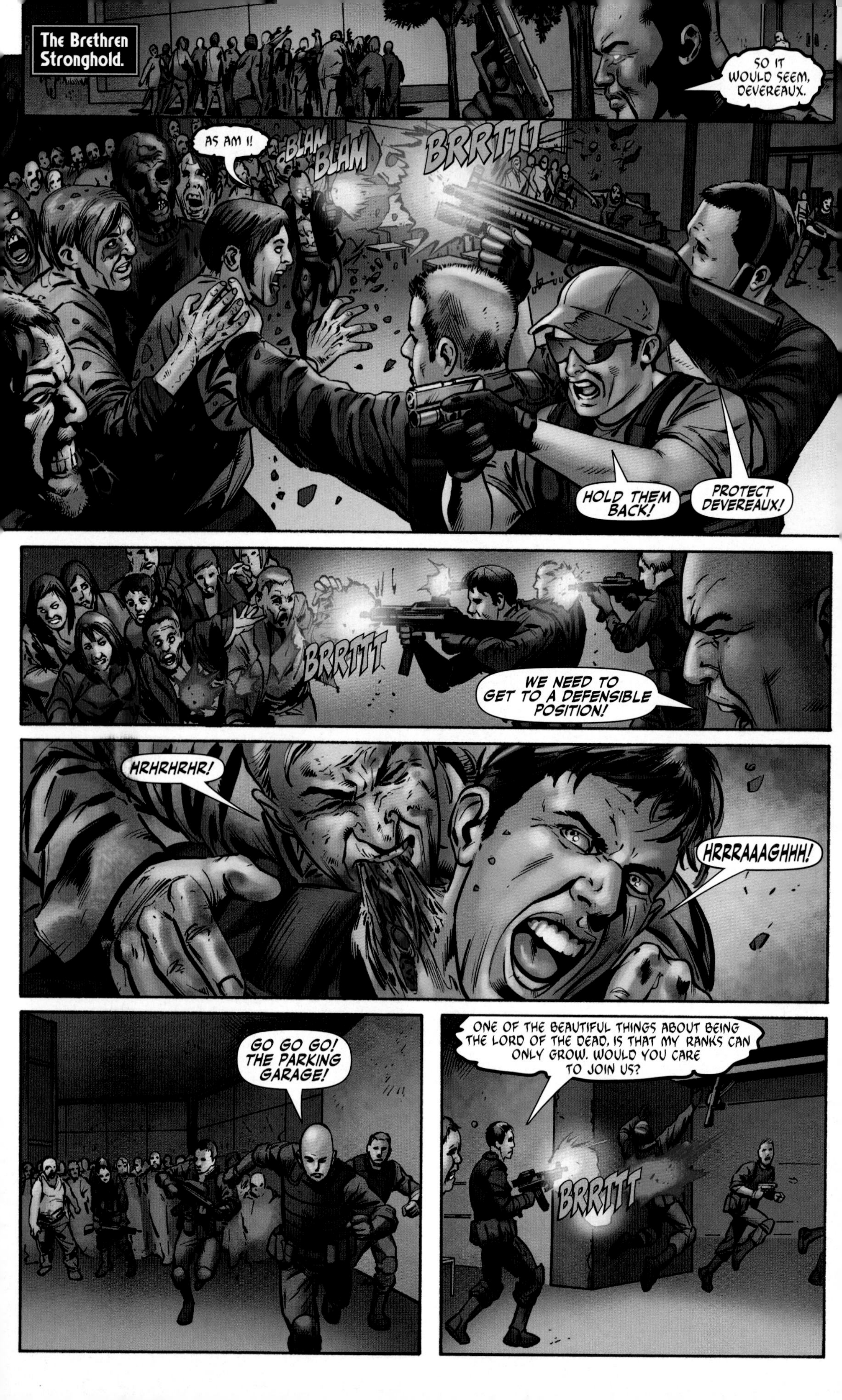

The Brethren Stronghold.
SO IT WOULD SEEM, DEVEREAUX.
AS AM I!
BLAM BLAM
BRRTTT
HOLD THEM BACK!
PROTECT DEVEREAUX!
BRRTTT
WE NEED TO GET TO A DEFENSIBLE POSITION!
HRHRHRHR!
HRRRAAAGHHH!
GO GO GO! THE PARKING GARAGE!
ONE OF THE BEAUTIFUL THINGS ABOUT BEING THE LORD OF THE DEAD, IS THAT MY RANKS CAN ONLY GROW. WOULD YOU CARE TO JOIN US?
BRRTTT

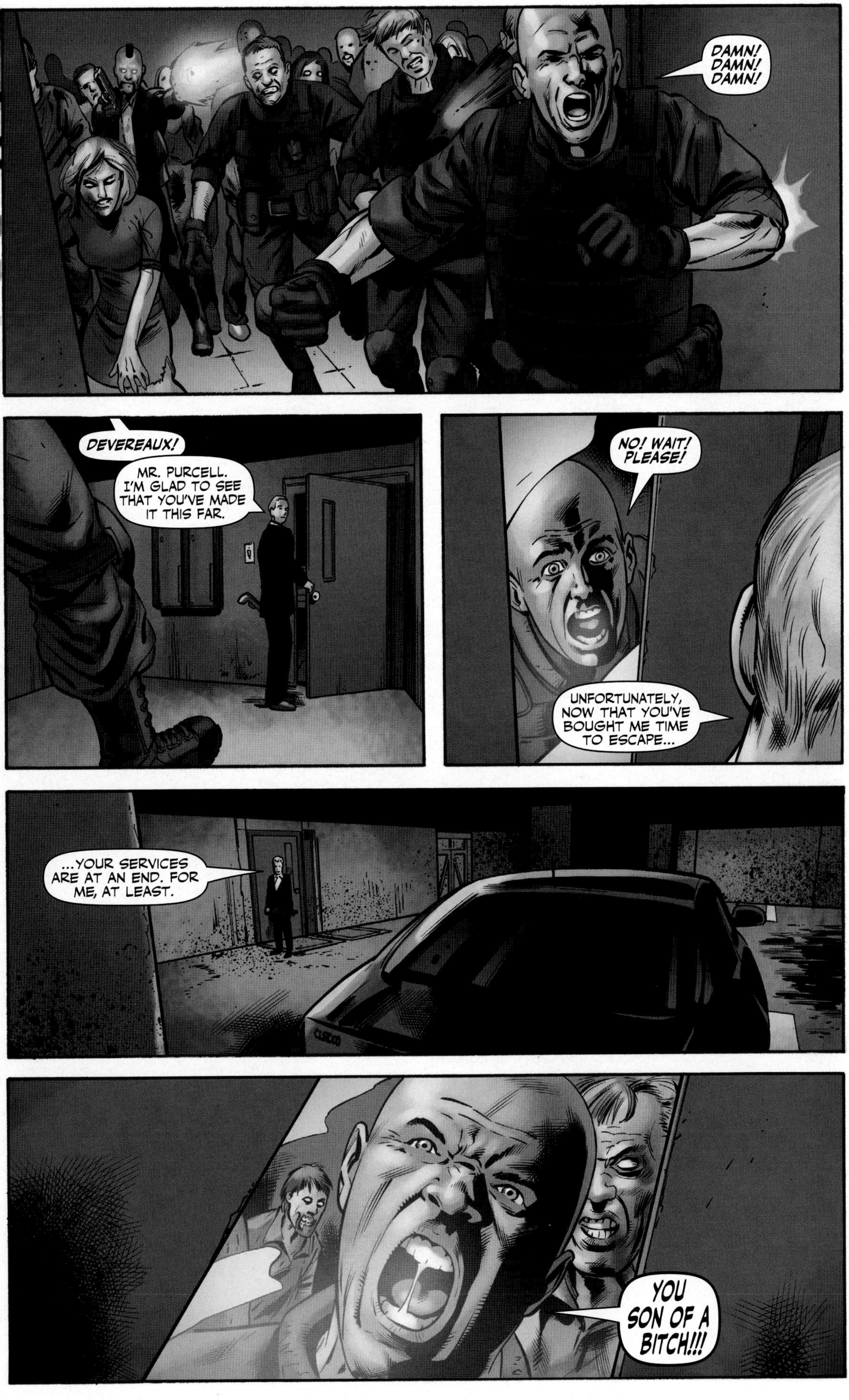
DAMN! DAMN! DAMN!
DEVEREAUX!
MR. PURCELL. I'M GLAD TO SEE THAT YOU'VE MADE IT THIS FAR.
NO! WAIT! PLEASE!
UNFORTUNATELY, NOW THAT YOU'VE BOUGHT ME TIME TO ESCAPE...
...YOUR SERVICES ARE AT AN END. FOR ME, AT LEAST.
YOU SON OF A BITCH!!!

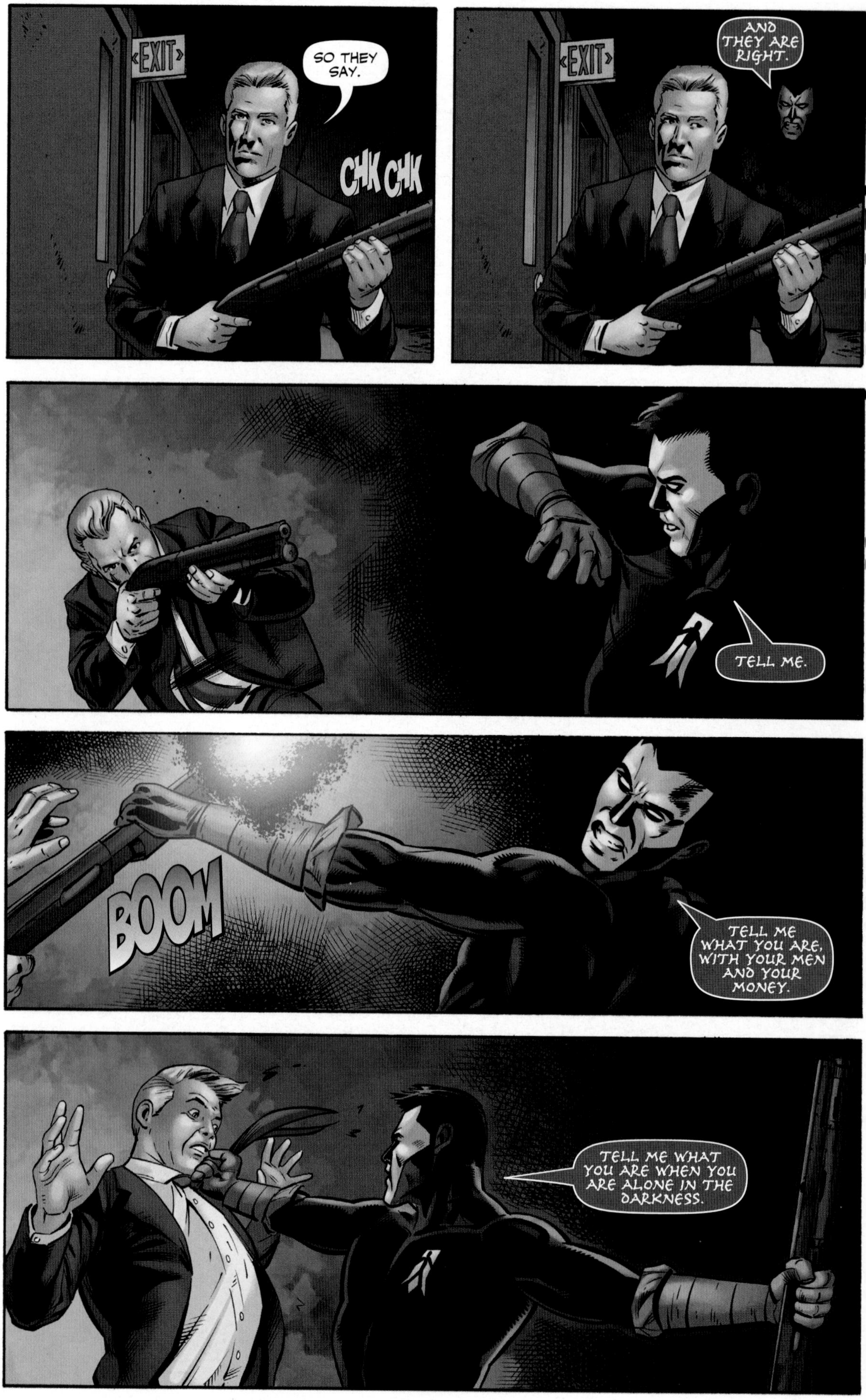
EXIT
SO THEY SAY.
CHK CHK
EXIT
AND THEY ARE RIGHT.
TELL ME.
BOOM
TELL ME WHAT YOU ARE, WITH YOUR MEN AND YOUR MONEY.
TELL ME WHAT YOU ARE WHEN YOU ARE ALONE IN THE DARKNESS.

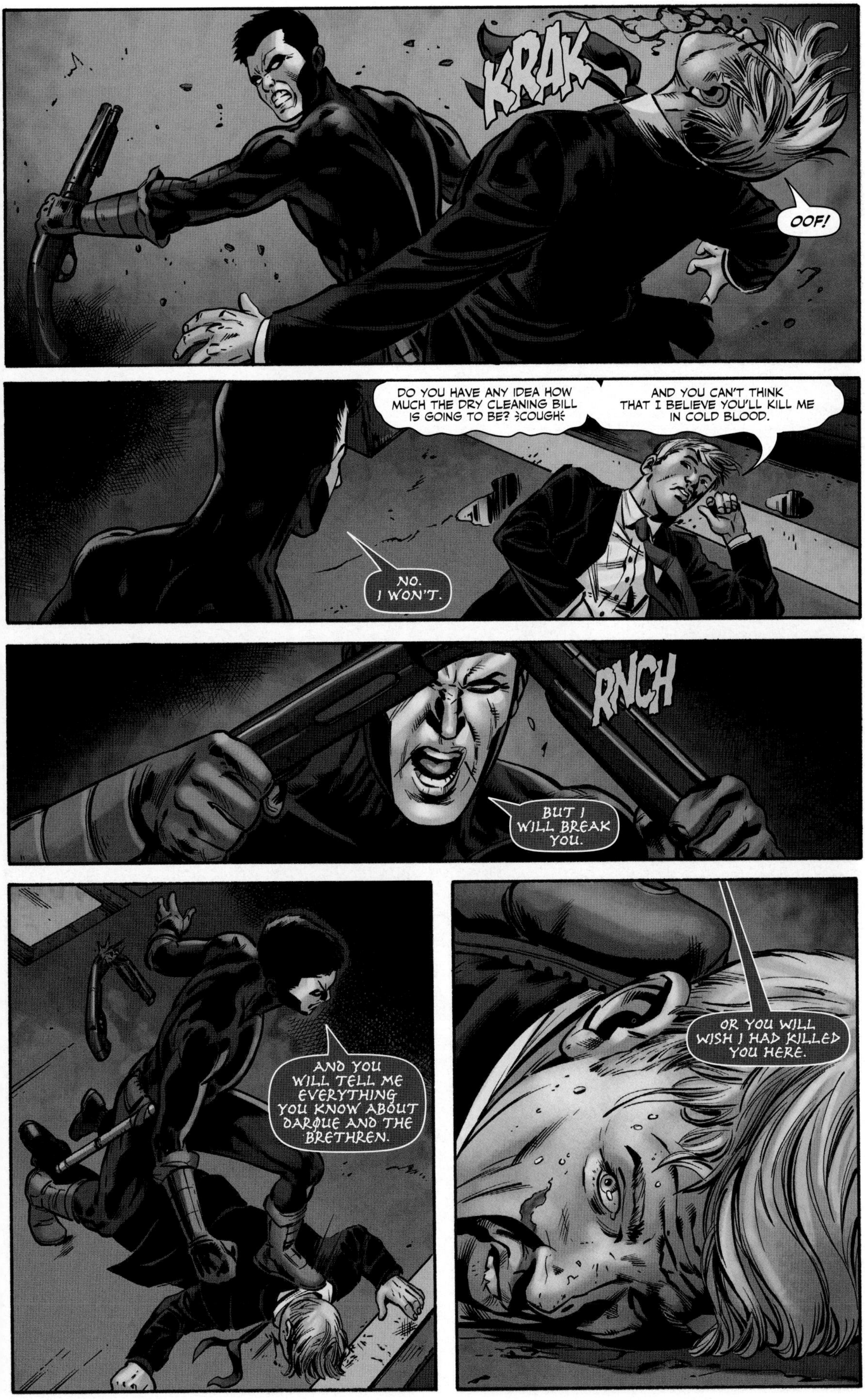
KRAK
OOF!
DO YOU HAVE ANY IDEA HOW MUCH THE DRY CLEANING BILL IS GOING TO BE? ;COUGH;
AND YOU CAN'T THINK THAT I BELIEVE YOU'LL KILL ME IN COLD BLOOD.
NO. I WON'T.
RNCH
BUT I WILL BREAK YOU.
AND YOU WILL TELL ME EVERYTHING YOU KNOW ABOUT DARQUE AND THE BRETHREN.
OR YOU WILL WISH I HAD KILLED YOU HERE.

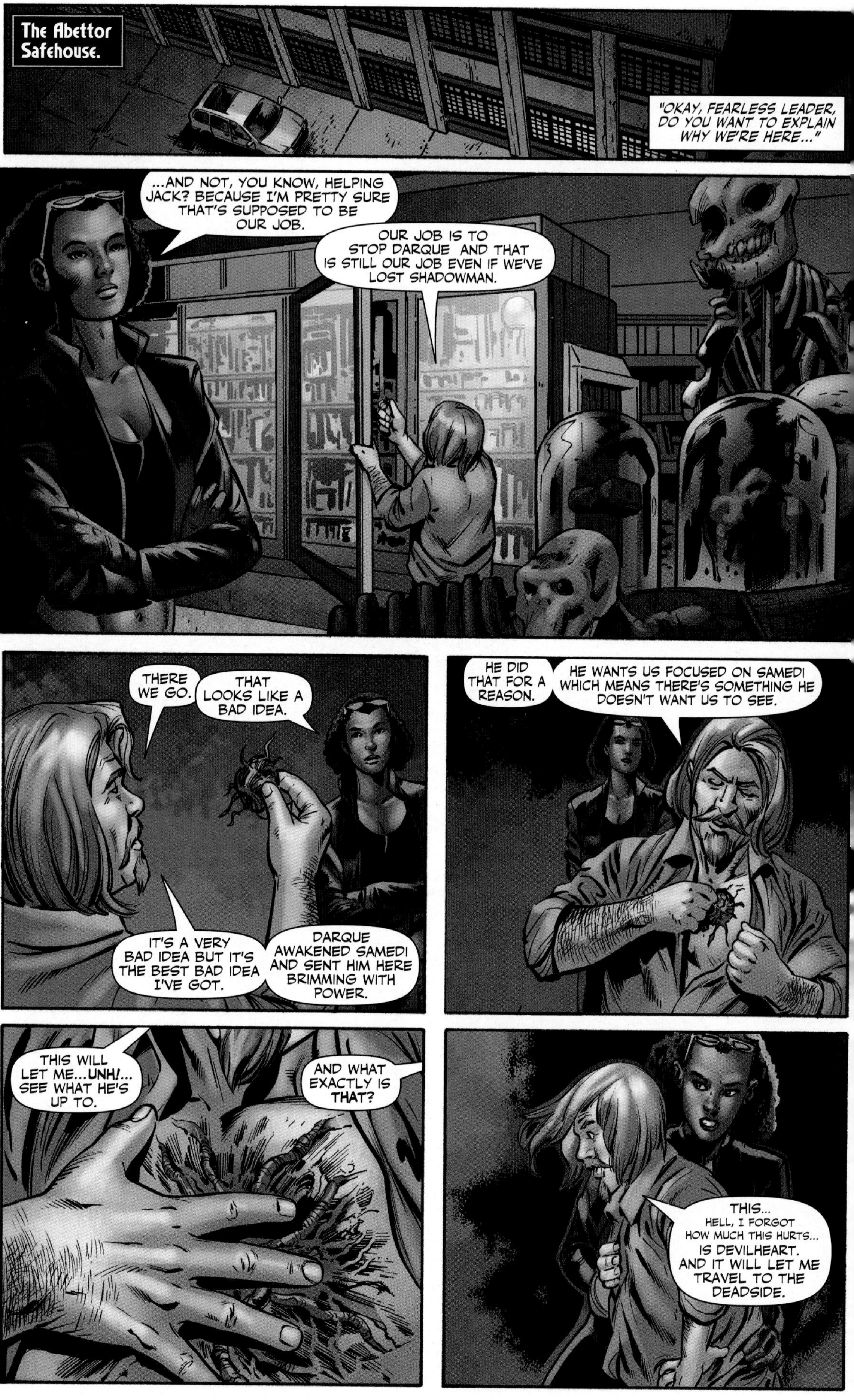
The Abettor Safehouse.
"OKAY, FEARLESS LEADER, DO YOU WANT TO EXPLAIN WHY WE'RE HERE..."
...AND NOT, YOU KNOW, HELPING JACK? BECAUSE I'M PRETTY SURE THAT'S SUPPOSED TO BE OUR JOB.
OUR JOB IS TO STOP DARQUE AND THAT IS STILL OUR JOB EVEN IF WE'VE LOST SHADOWMAN.
THERE WE GO.
THAT LOOKS LIKE A BAD IDEA.
IT'S A VERY BAD IDEA BUT IT'S THE BEST BAD IDEA I'VE GOT.
DARQUE AWAKENED SAMEDI AND SENT HIM HERE BRIMMING WITH POWER.
HE DID THAT FOR A REASON.
HE WANTS US FOCUSED ON SAMEDI WHICH MEANS THERE'S SOMETHING HE DOESN'T WANT US TO SEE.
THIS WILL LET ME...UNH!... SEE WHAT HE'S UP TO.
AND WHAT EXACTLY IS THAT?
THIS... HELL, I FORGOT HOW MUCH THIS HURTS... IS DEVILHEART. AND IT WILL LET ME TRAVEL TO THE DEADSIDE.

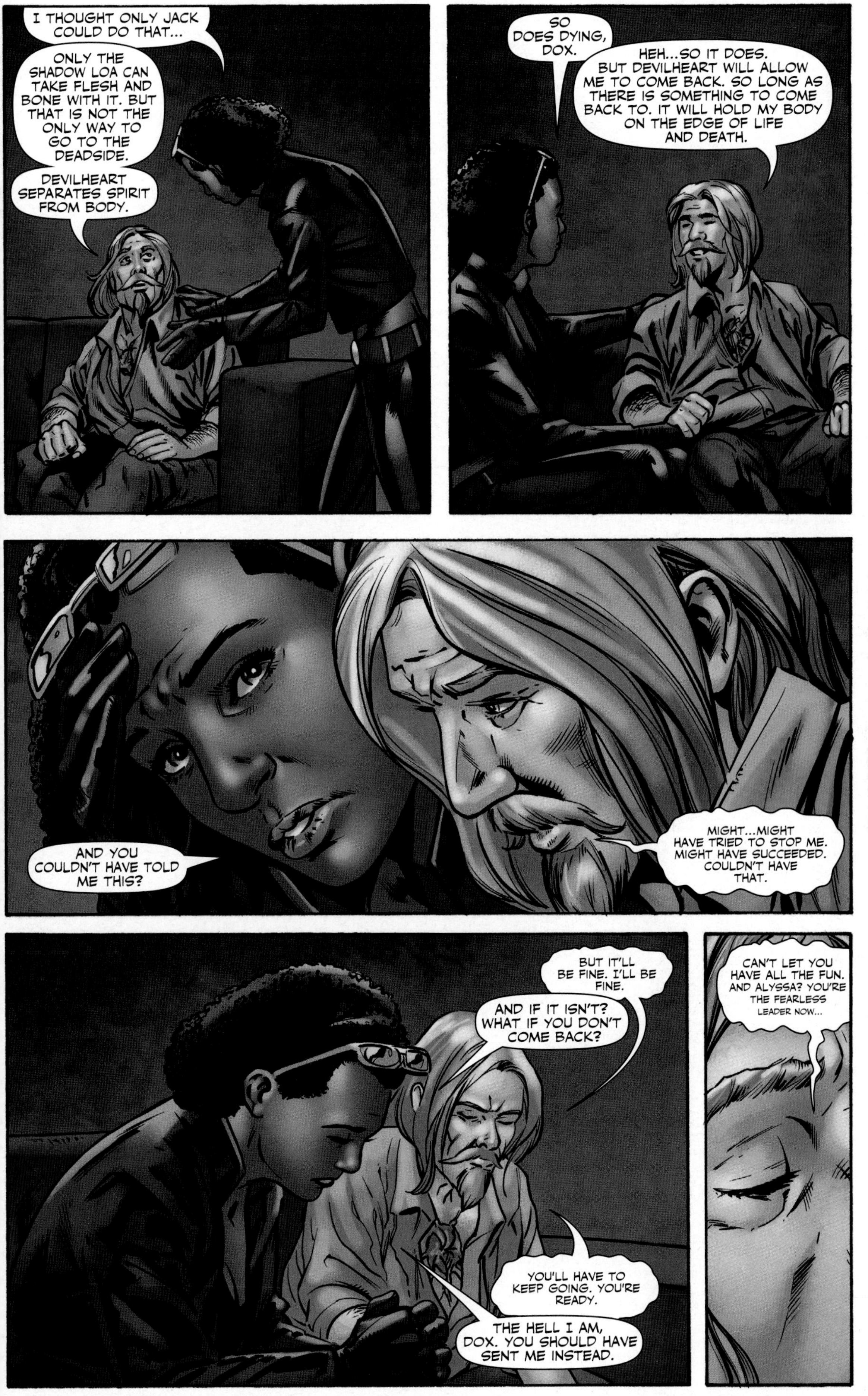
I THOUGHT ONLY JACK COULD DO THAT...
ONLY THE SHADOW LOA CAN TAKE FLESH AND BONE WITH IT. BUT THAT IS NOT THE ONLY WAY TO GO TO THE DEADSIDE.
DEVILHEART SEPARATES SPIRIT FROM BODY.
SO DOES DYING, DOX.
HEH...SO IT DOES. BUT DEVILHEART WILL ALLOW ME TO COME BACK. SO LONG AS THERE IS SOMETHING TO COME BACK TO. IT WILL HOLD MY BODY ON THE EDGE OF LIFE AND DEATH.
AND YOU COULDN'T HAVE TOLD ME THIS?
MIGHT...MIGHT HAVE TRIED TO STOP ME. MIGHT HAVE SUCCEEDED. COULDN'T HAVE THAT.
BUT IT'LL BE FINE. I'LL BE FINE.
AND IF IT ISN'T? WHAT IF YOU DON'T COME BACK?
YOU'LL HAVE TO KEEP GOING. YOU'RE READY.
THE HELL I AM, DOX. YOU SHOULD HAVE SENT ME INSTEAD.
CAN'T LET YOU HAVE ALL THE FUN. AND ALYSSA? YOU'RE THE FEARLESS LEADER NOW...

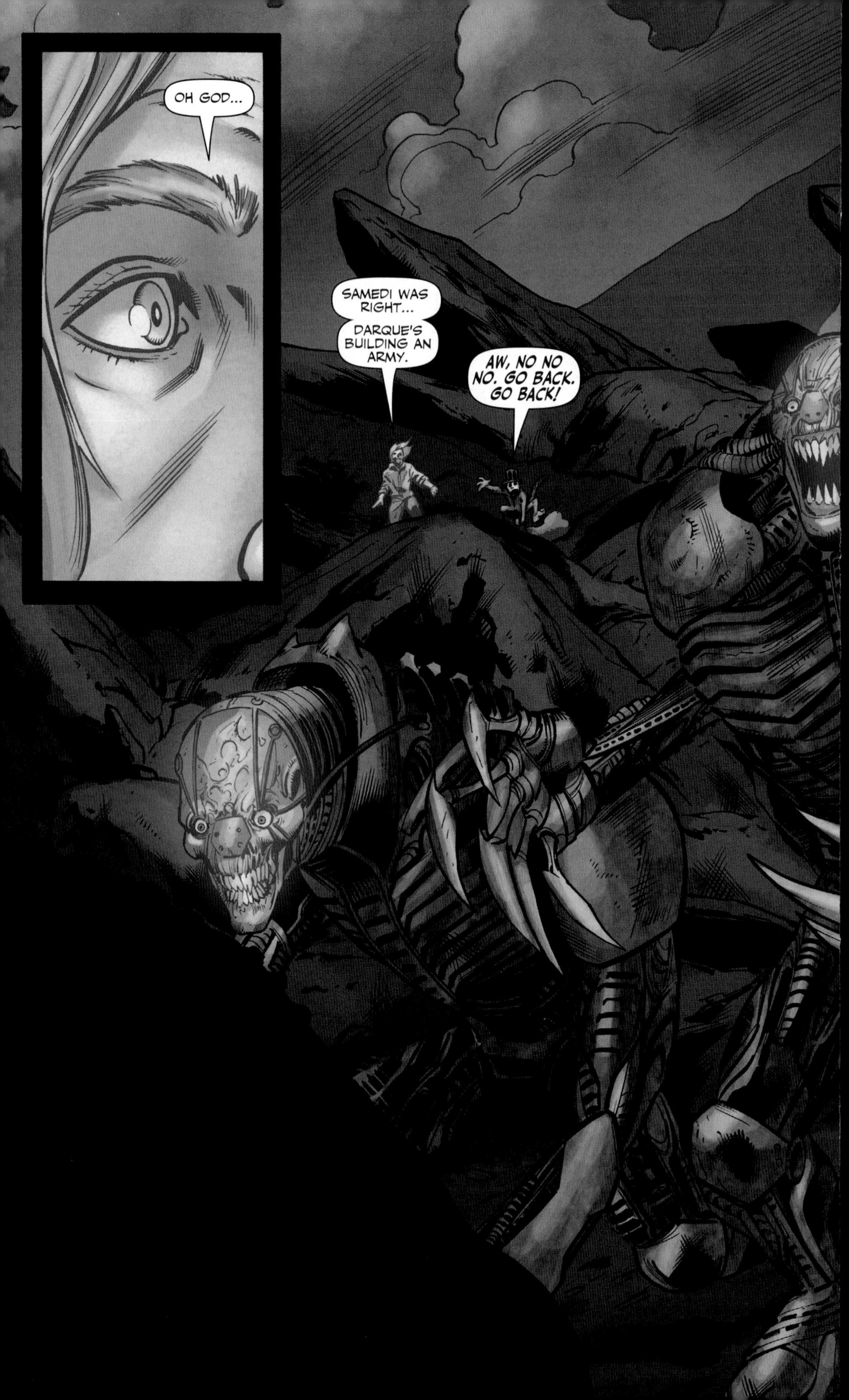
OH GOD...
SAMEDI WAS RIGHT...
DARQUE'S BUILDING AN ARMY.
AW, NO NO NO. GO BACK. GO BACK!

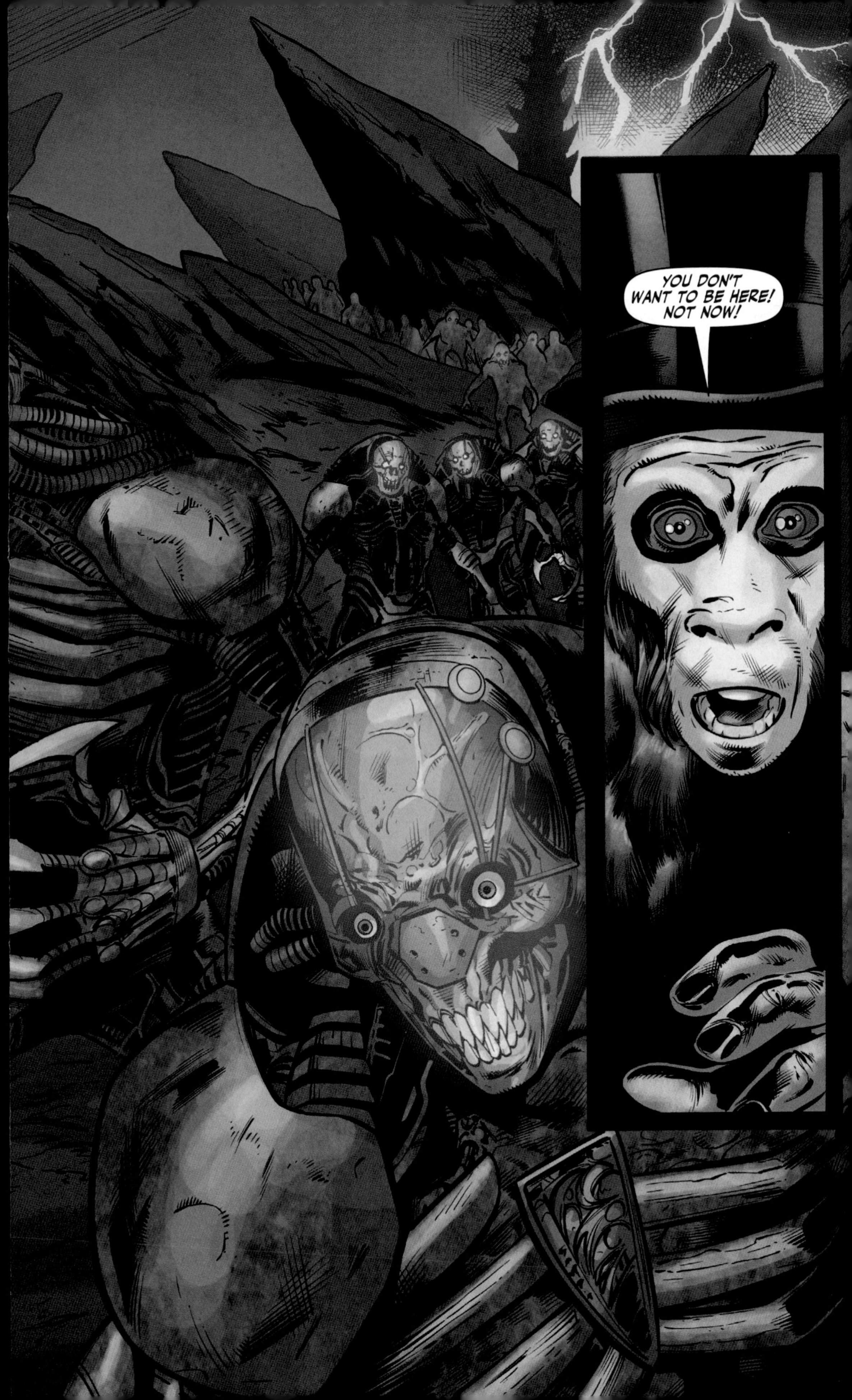
YOU DON'T
WANT TO BE HERE!
NOT NOW!

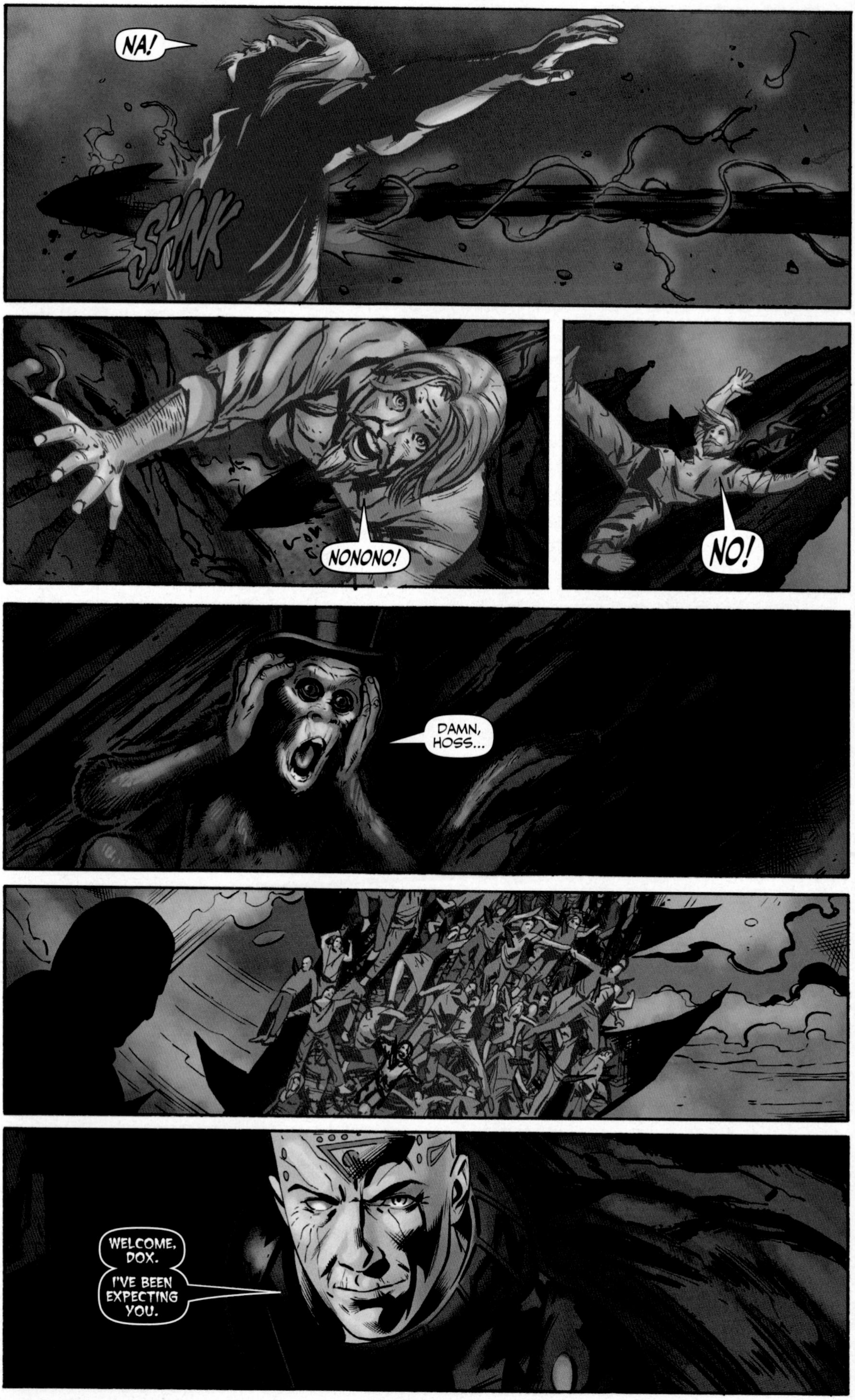
NA!
SHNK
NONONO!
NO!
DAMN, HOSS...
WELCOME, DOX.
I'VE BEEN EXPECTING YOU.

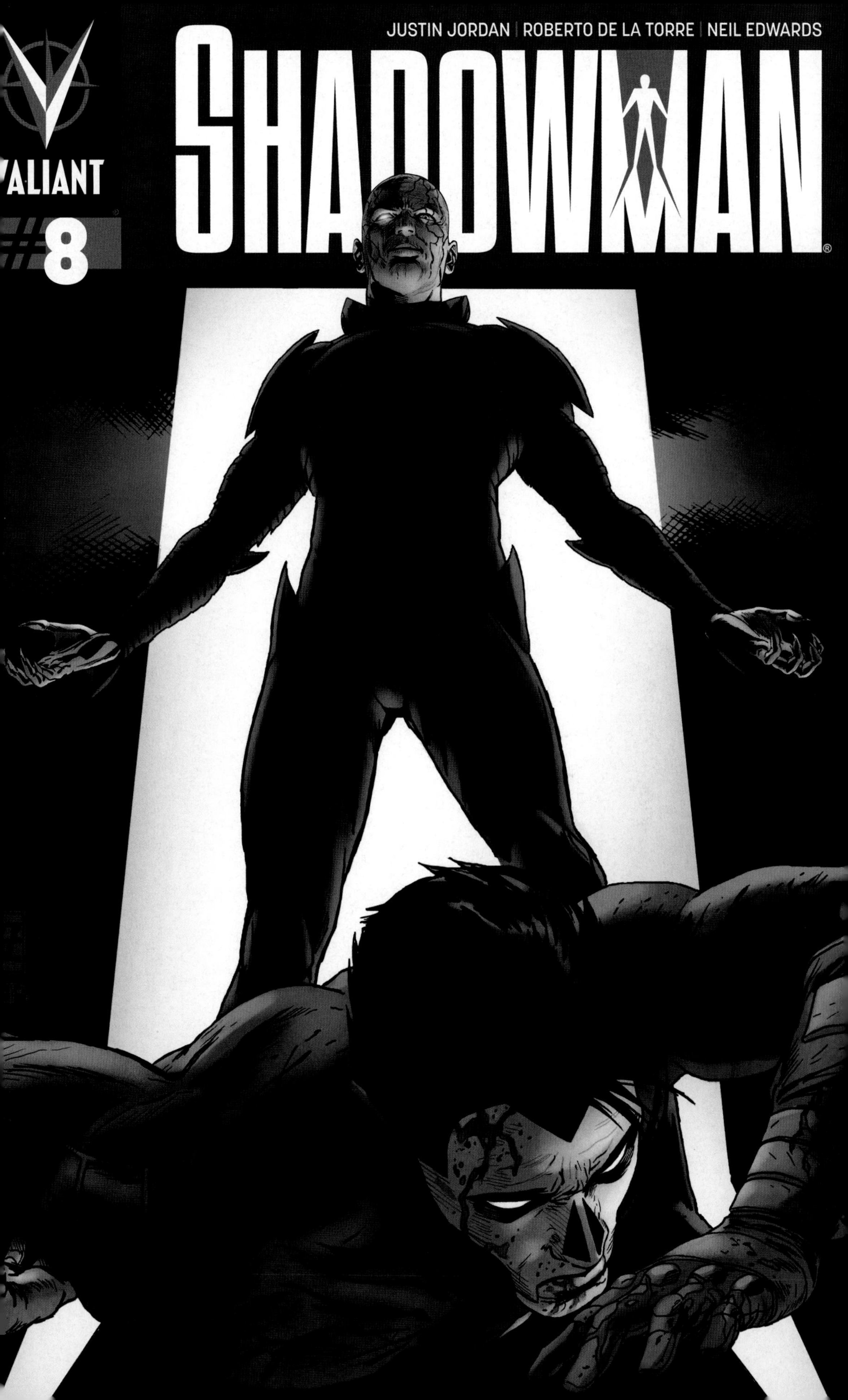

JUSTIN JORDAN | ROBERTO DE LA TORRE | NEIL EDWARDS
VALIANT
#8
SHADOWMAN

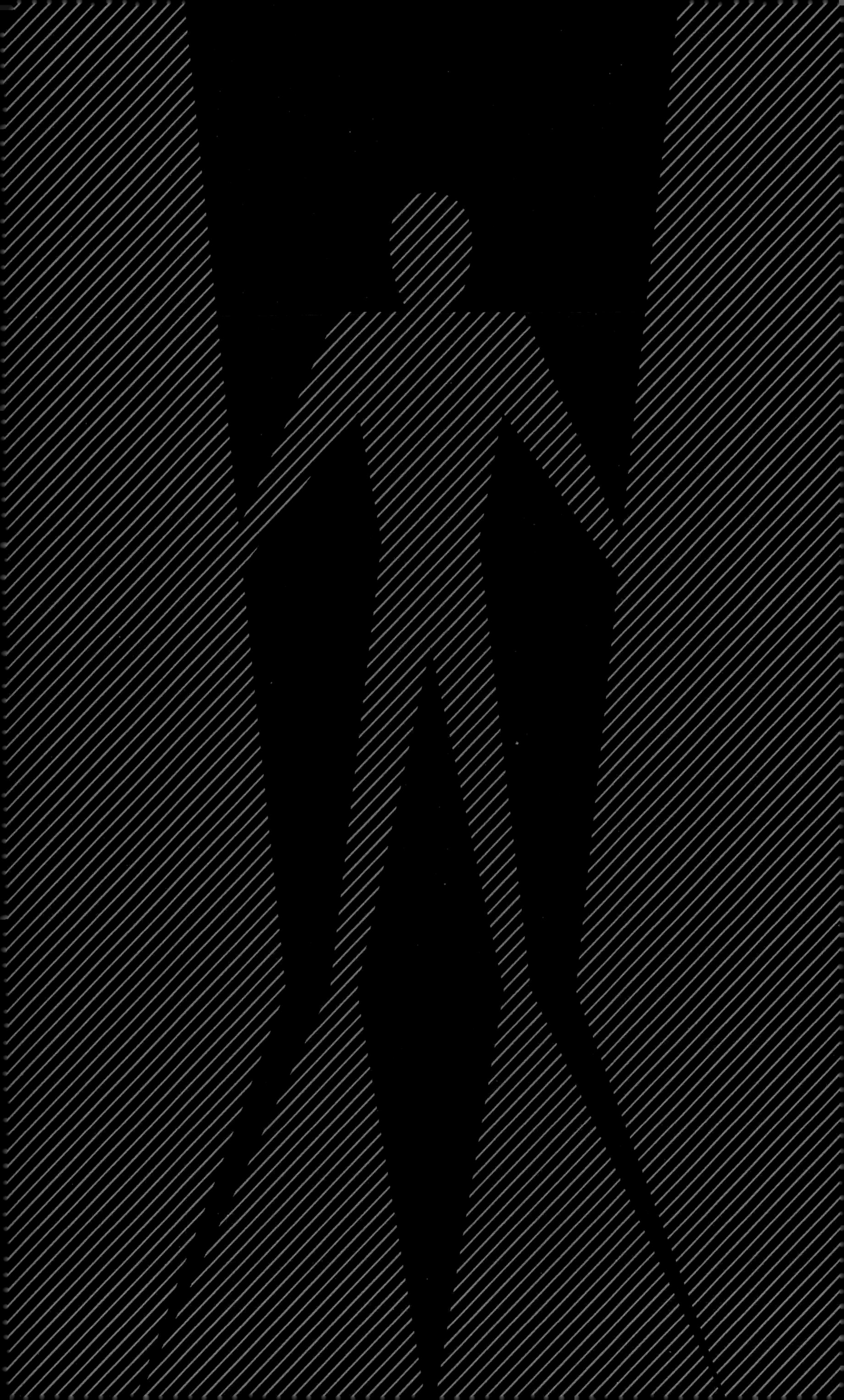

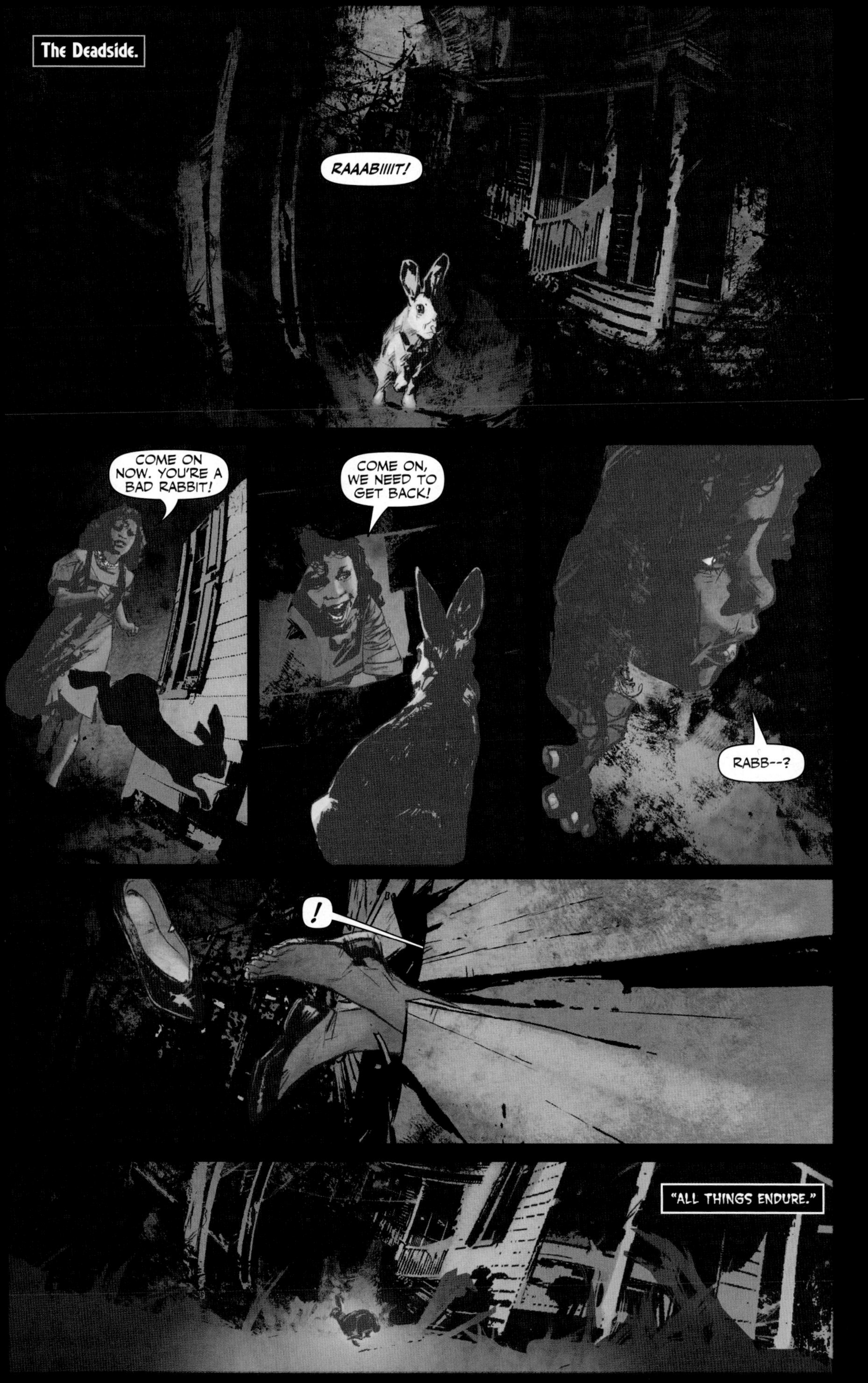
The Deadside.
RAAABIIIIT!
COME ON NOW. YOU'RE A BAD RABBIT!
COME ON, WE NEED TO GET BACK!
RABB--?
!
"ALL THINGS ENDURE."

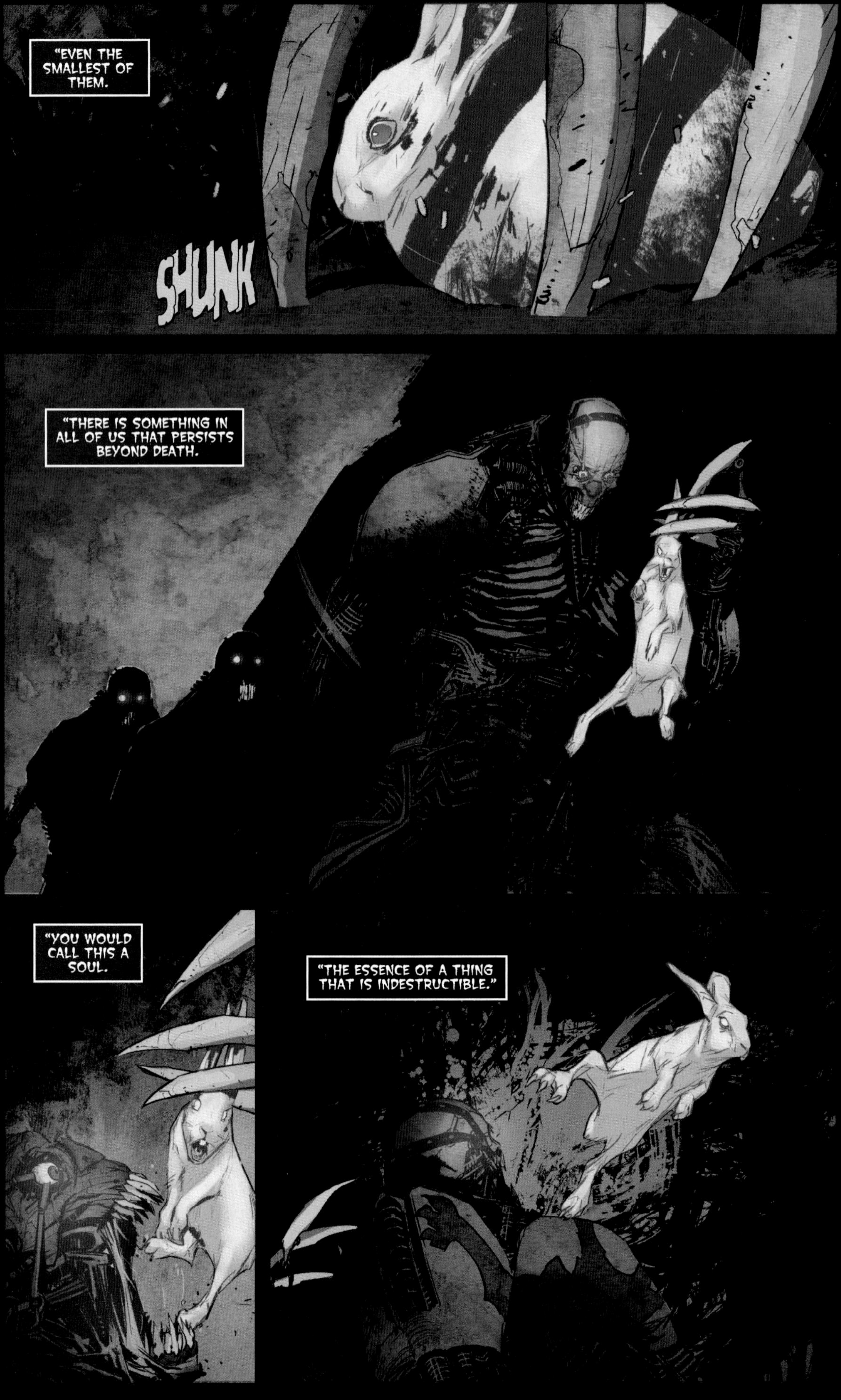
"EVEN THE SMALLEST OF THEM.
SHUNK
"THERE IS SOMETHING IN ALL OF US THAT PERSISTS BEYOND DEATH.
"YOU WOULD CALL THIS A SOUL.
"THE ESSENCE OF A THING THAT IS INDESTRUCTIBLE."

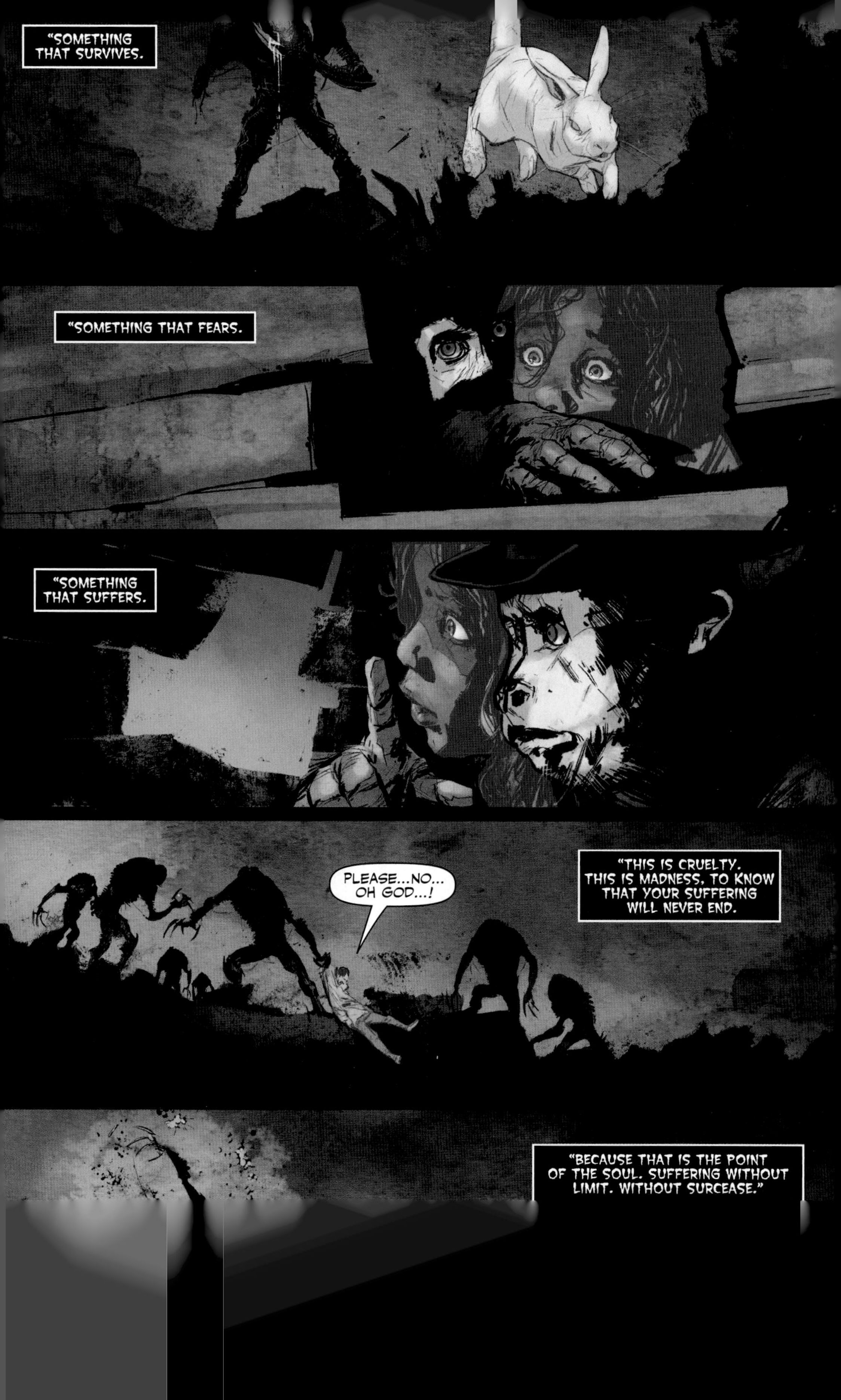
"SOMETHING THAT SURVIVES.
"SOMETHING THAT FEARS.
"SOMETHING THAT SUFFERS.
PLEASE...NO... OH GOD...!
"THIS IS CRUELTY. THIS IS MADNESS, TO KNOW THAT YOUR SUFFERING WILL NEVER END.
"BECAUSE THAT IS THE POINT OF THE SOUL. SUFFERING WITHOUT LIMIT. WITHOUT SURCEASE."

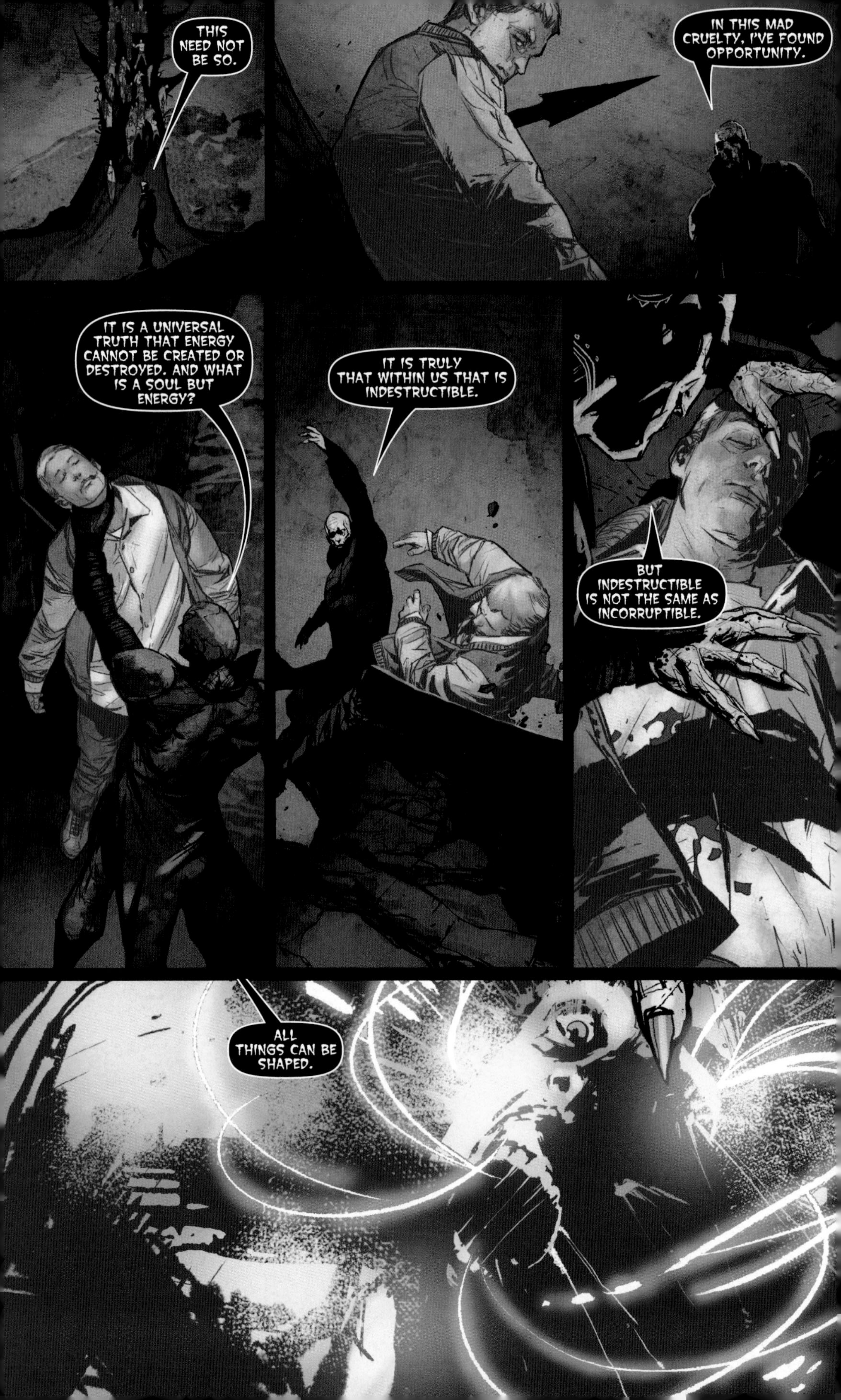
THIS NEED NOT BE SO.
IN THIS MAD CRUELTY, I'VE FOUND OPPORTUNITY.
IT IS A UNIVERSAL TRUTH THAT ENERGY CANNOT BE CREATED OR DESTROYED. AND WHAT IS A SOUL BUT ENERGY?
IT IS TRULY THAT WITHIN US THAT IS INDESTRUCTIBLE.
BUT INDESTRUCTIBLE IS NOT THE SAME AS INCORRUPTIBLE.
ALL THINGS CAN BE SHAPED.

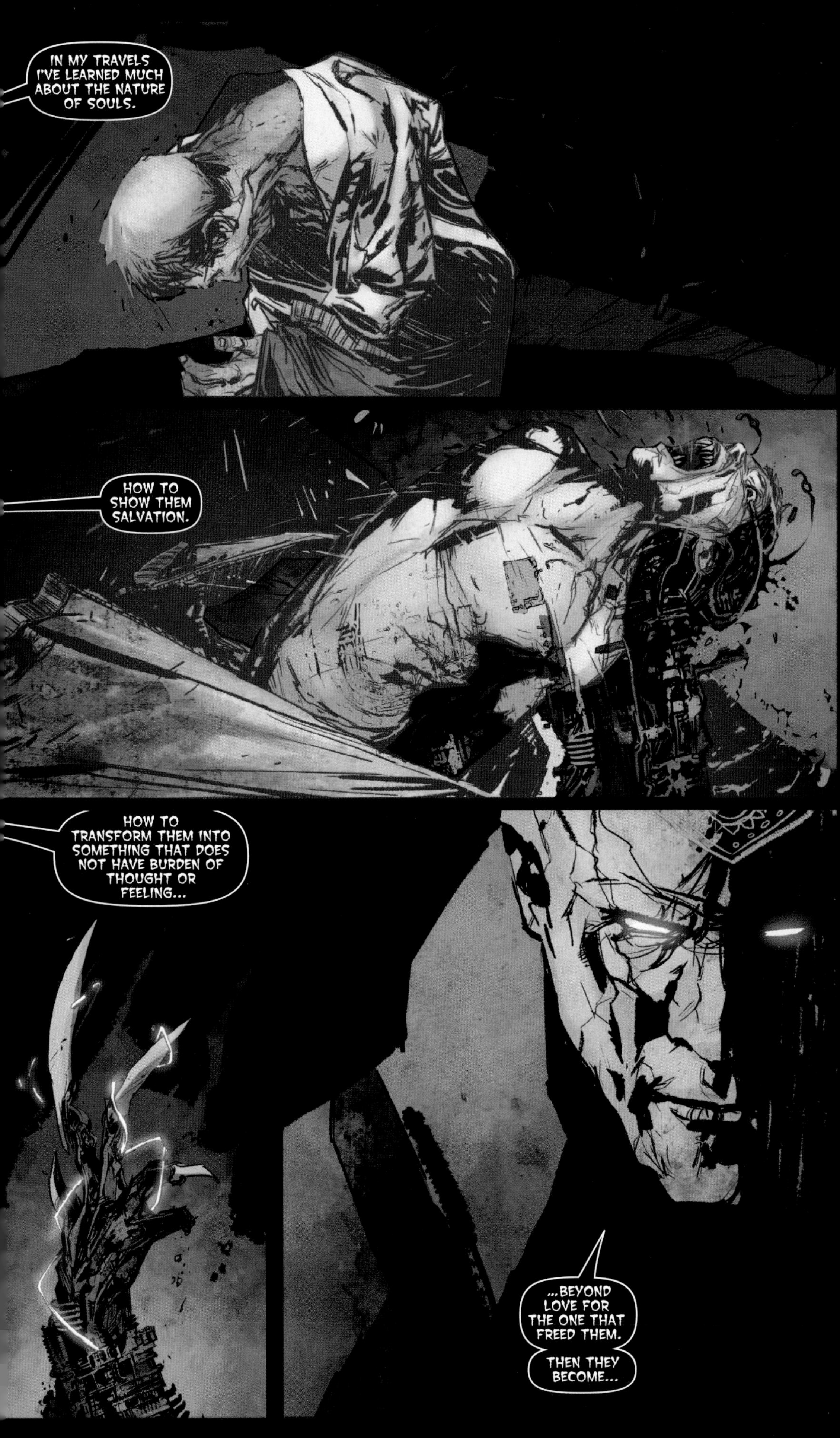
IN MY TRAVELS I'VE LEARNED MUCH ABOUT THE NATURE OF SOULS.
HOW TO SHOW THEM SALVATION.
HOW TO TRANSFORM THEM INTO SOMETHING THAT DOES NOT HAVE BURDEN OF THOUGHT OR FEELING...
...BEYOND LOVE FOR THE ONE THAT FREED THEM.
THEN THEY BECOME...

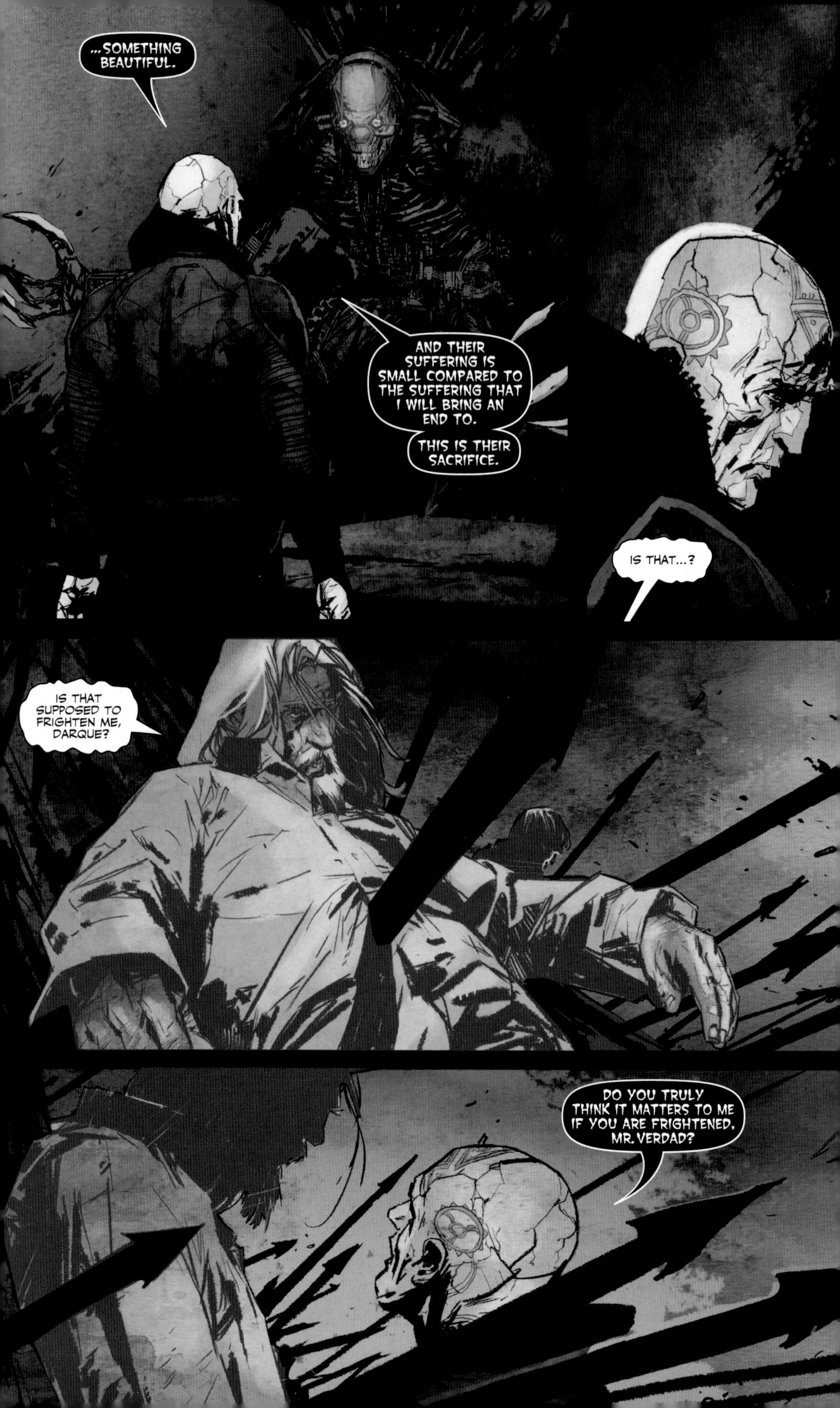
...SOMETHING BEAUTIFUL.
AND THEIR SUFFERING IS SMALL COMPARED TO THE SUFFERING THAT I WILL BRING AN END TO.
THIS IS THEIR SACRIFICE.
IS THAT...?
IS THAT SUPPOSED TO FRIGHTEN ME, DARQUE?
DO YOU TRULY THINK IT MATTERS TO ME IF YOU ARE FRIGHTENED, MR. VERDAD?

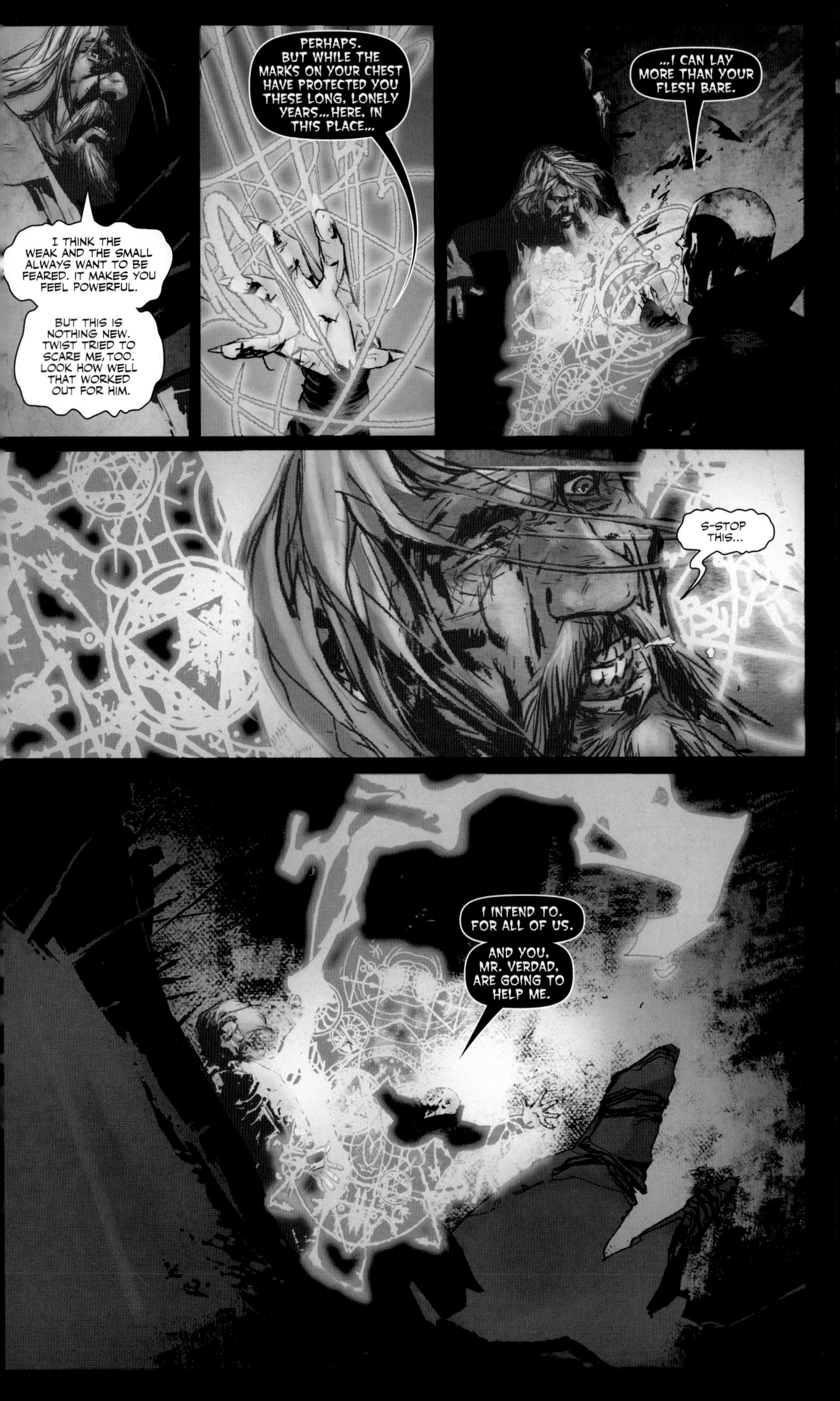
I THINK THE WEAK AND THE SMALL ALWAYS WANT TO BE FEARED. IT MAKES YOU FEEL POWERFUL.
BUT THIS IS NOTHING NEW. TWIST TRIED TO SCARE ME, TOO. LOOK HOW WELL THAT WORKED OUT FOR HIM.
PERHAPS. BUT WHILE THE MARKS ON YOUR CHEST HAVE PROTECTED YOU THESE LONG, LONELY YEARS...HERE, IN THIS PLACE...
...I CAN LAY MORE THAN YOUR FLESH BARE.
S-STOP THIS...
I INTEND TO. FOR ALL OF US.
AND YOU, MR. VERDAD, ARE GOING TO HELP ME.

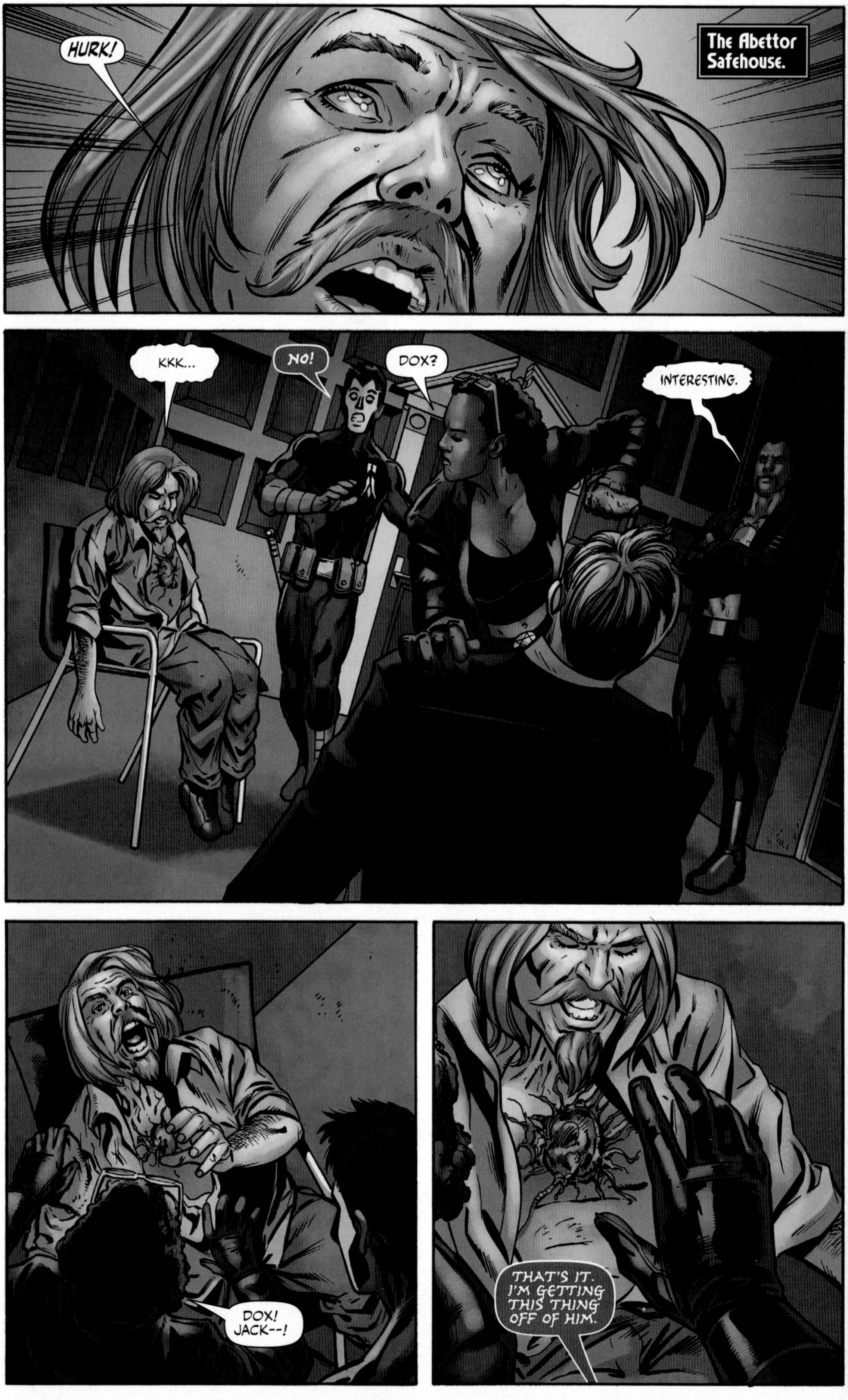
The Abettor Safehouse.
HURK!
KKK...
NO!
DOX?
INTERESTING.
DOX! JACK--!
THAT'S IT. I'M GETTING THIS THING OFF OF HIM.

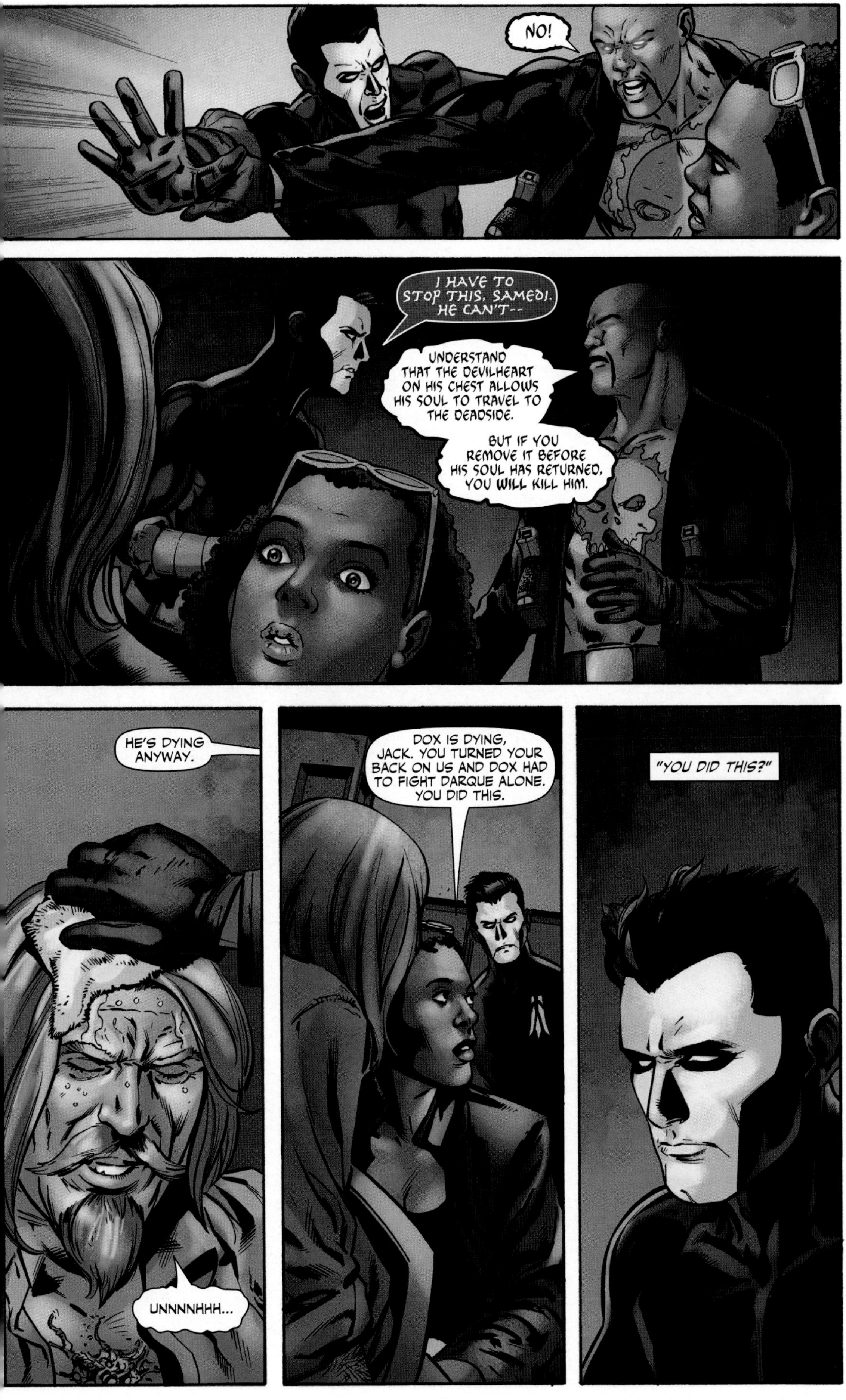
NO!
I HAVE TO STOP THIS, SAMEDI. HE CAN'T--
UNDERSTAND THAT THE DEVILHEART ON HIS CHEST ALLOWS HIS SOUL TO TRAVEL TO THE DEADSIDE.
BUT IF YOU REMOVE IT BEFORE HIS SOUL HAS RETURNED, YOU WILL KILL HIM.
HE'S DYING ANYWAY.
UNNNNHHH...
DOX IS DYING, JACK. YOU TURNED YOUR BACK ON US AND DOX HAD TO FIGHT DARQUE ALONE. YOU DID THIS.
"YOU DID THIS?"

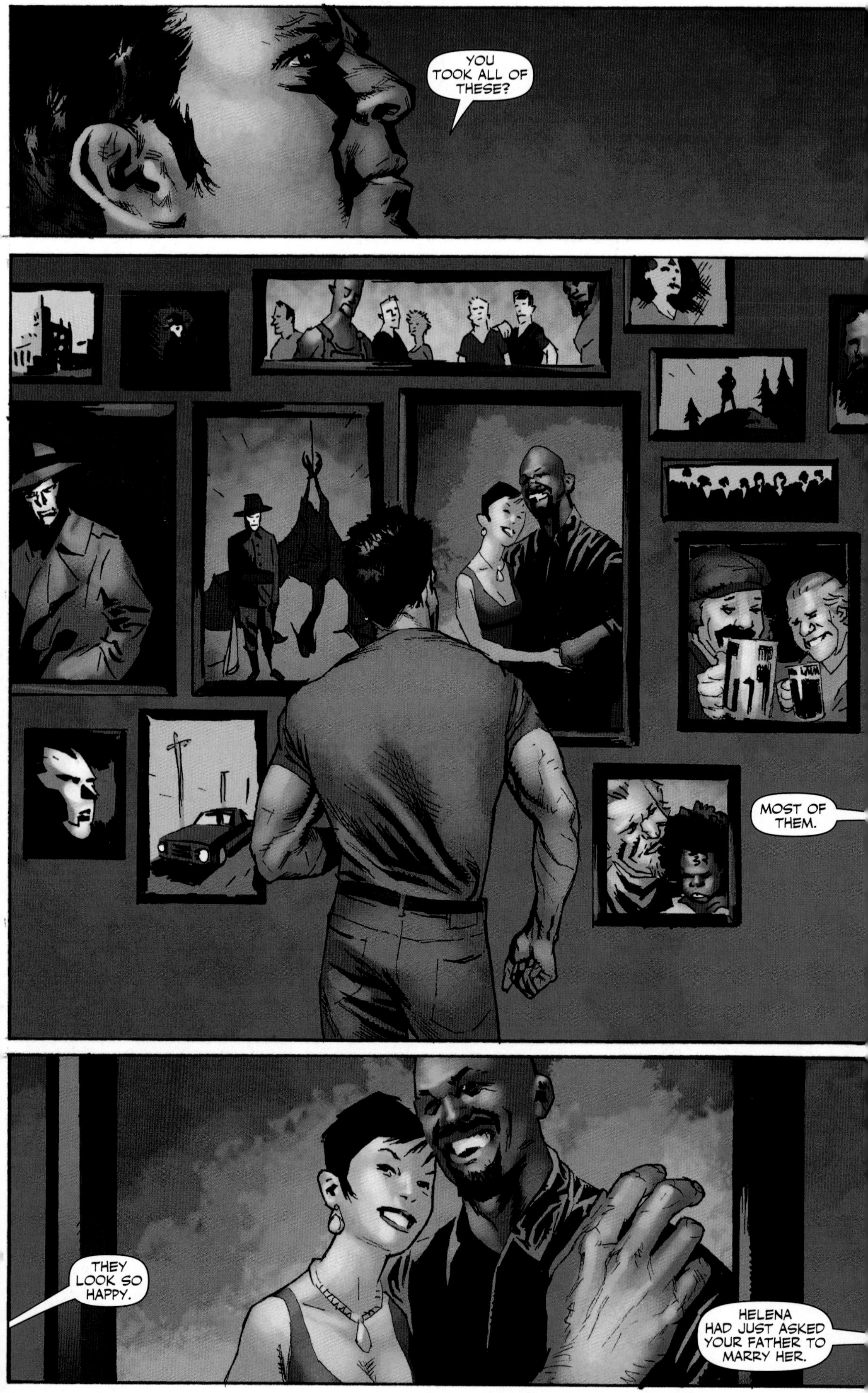
YOU TOOK ALL OF THESE?
MOST OF THEM.
THEY LOOK SO HAPPY.
HELENA HAD JUST ASKED YOUR FATHER TO MARRY HER.

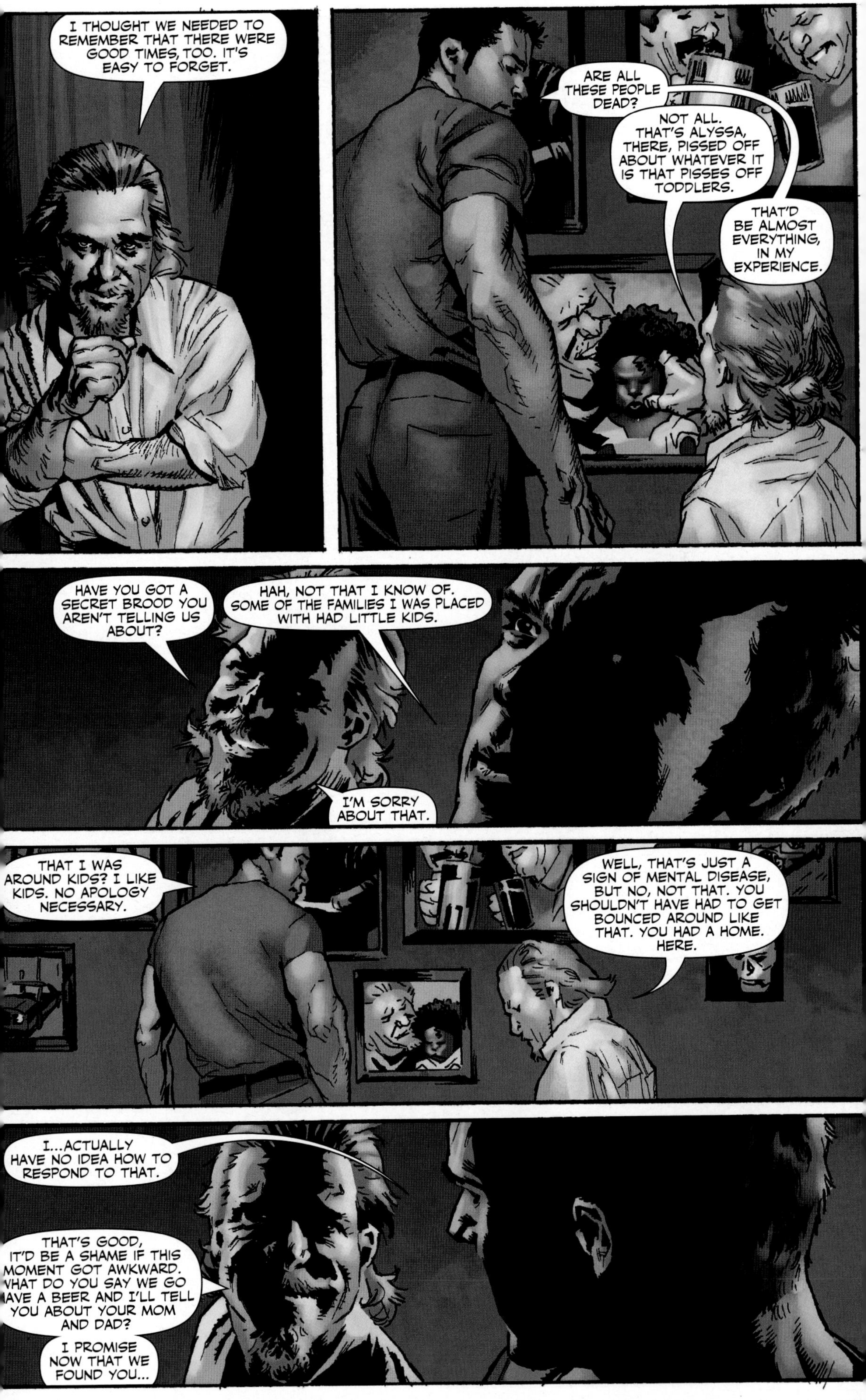
I THOUGHT WE NEEDED TO REMEMBER THAT THERE WERE GOOD TIMES, TOO. IT'S EASY TO FORGET.
ARE ALL THESE PEOPLE DEAD?
NOT ALL. THAT'S ALYSSA, THERE, PISSED OFF ABOUT WHATEVER IT IS THAT PISSES OFF TODDLERS.
THAT'D BE ALMOST EVERYTHING, IN MY EXPERIENCE.
HAVE YOU GOT A SECRET BROOD YOU AREN'T TELLING US ABOUT?
HAH, NOT THAT I KNOW OF. SOME OF THE FAMILIES I WAS PLACED WITH HAD LITTLE KIDS.
I'M SORRY ABOUT THAT.
THAT I WAS AROUND KIDS? I LIKE KIDS. NO APOLOGY NECESSARY.
WELL, THAT'S JUST A SIGN OF MENTAL DISEASE, BUT NO, NOT THAT. YOU SHOULDN'T HAVE HAD TO GET BOUNCED AROUND LIKE THAT. YOU HAD A HOME. HERE.
I...ACTUALLY HAVE NO IDEA HOW TO RESPOND TO THAT.
THAT'S GOOD, IT'D BE A SHAME IF THIS MOMENT GOT AWKWARD. WHAT DO YOU SAY WE GO HAVE A BEER AND I'LL TELL YOU ABOUT YOUR MOM AND DAD?
I PROMISE NOW THAT WE FOUND YOU...

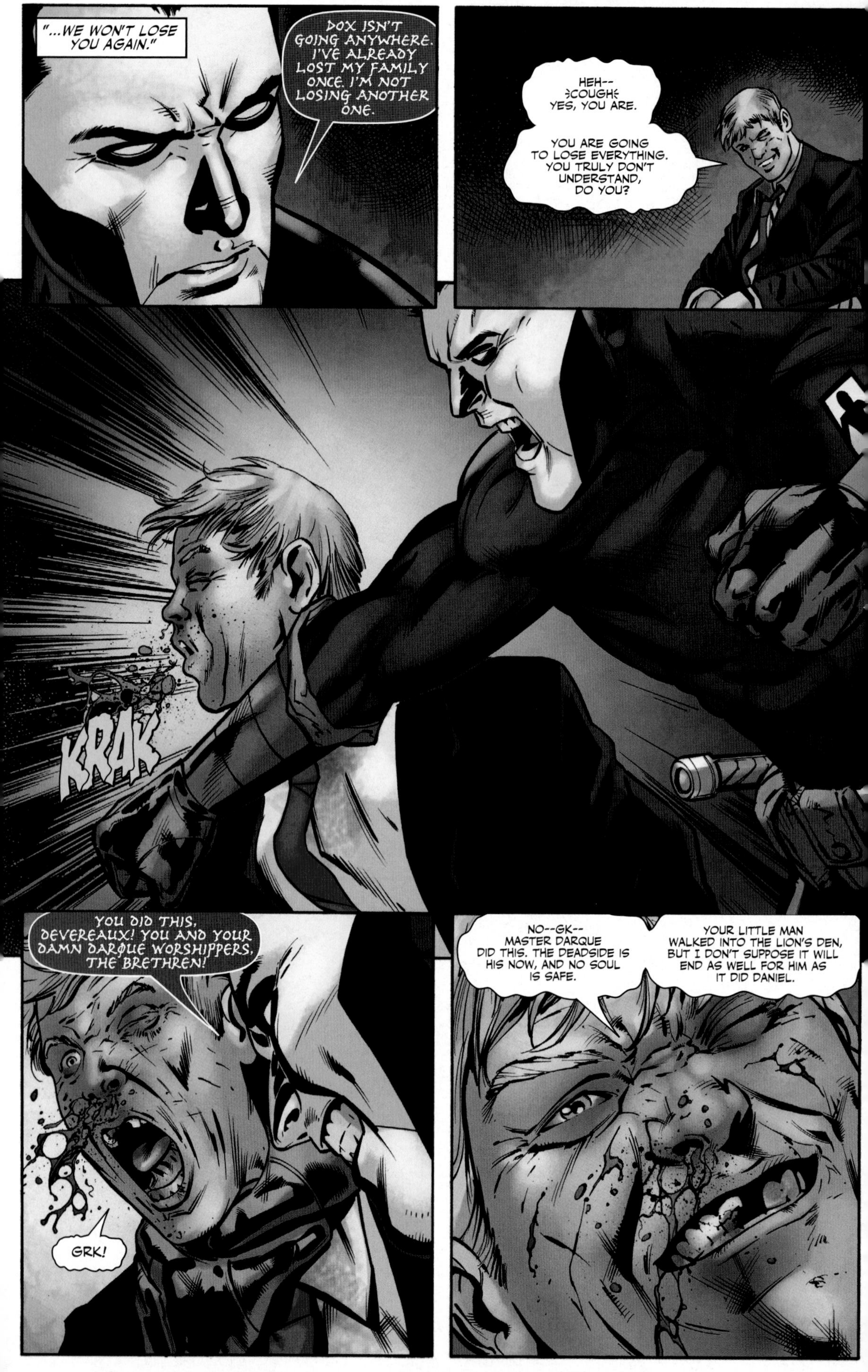
"...WE WON'T LOSE YOU AGAIN."
DOX ISN'T GOING ANYWHERE. I'VE ALREADY LOST MY FAMILY ONCE. I'M NOT LOSING ANOTHER ONE.
HEH-- *COUGH* YES, YOU ARE.
YOU ARE GOING TO LOSE EVERYTHING. YOU TRULY DON'T UNDERSTAND, DO YOU?
KRAK
YOU DID THIS, DEVEREAUX! YOU AND YOUR DAMN DARQUE WORSHIPPERS, THE BRETHREN!
GRK!
NO--GK-- MASTER DARQUE DID THIS. THE DEADSIDE IS HIS NOW, AND NO SOUL IS SAFE.
YOUR LITTLE MAN WALKED INTO THE LION'S DEN, BUT I DON'T SUPPOSE IT WILL END AS WELL FOR HIM AS IT DID DANIEL.

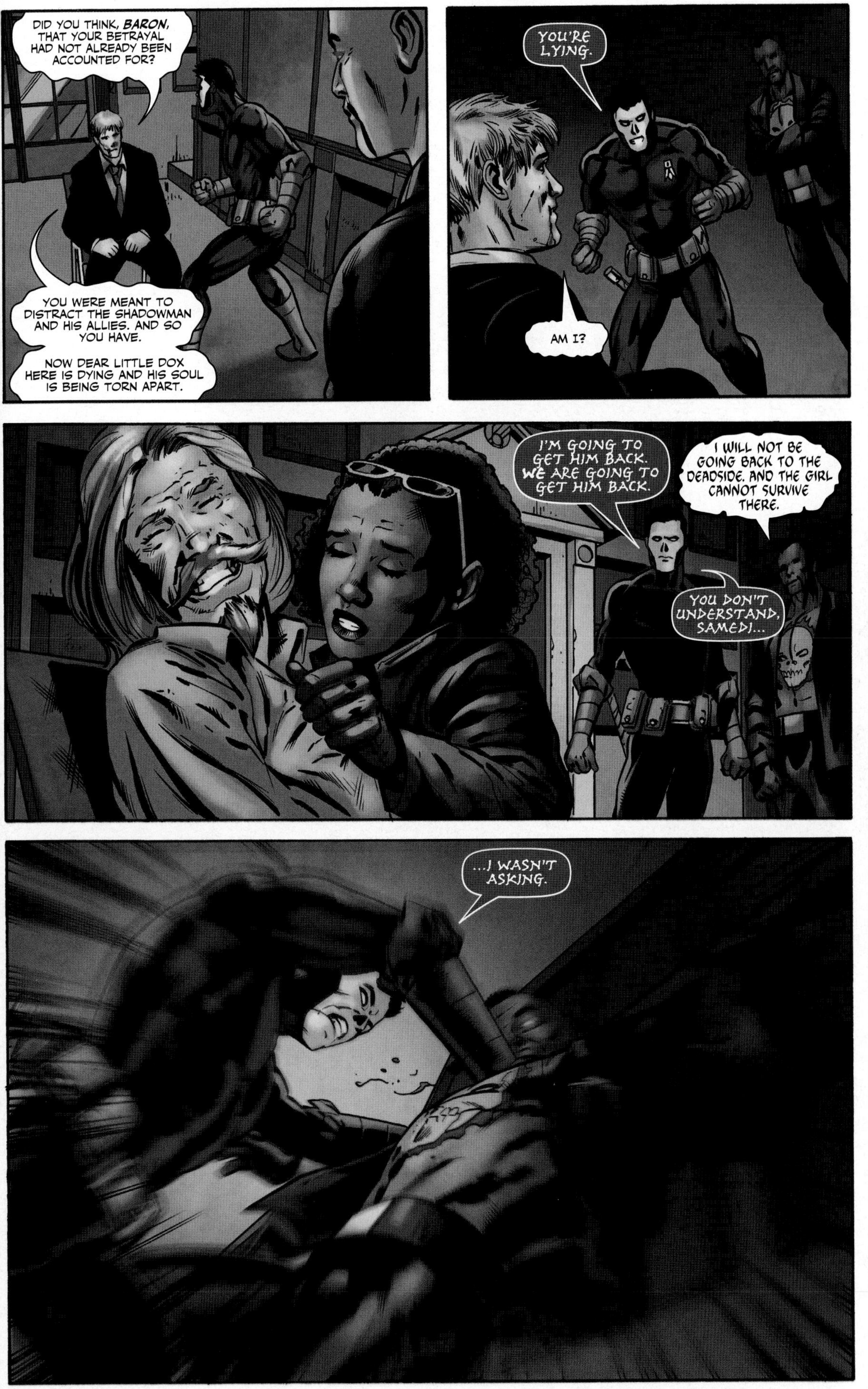
DID YOU THINK, BARON, THAT YOUR BETRAYAL HAD NOT ALREADY BEEN ACCOUNTED FOR?
YOU WERE MEANT TO DISTRACT THE SHADOWMAN AND HIS ALLIES. AND SO YOU HAVE.
NOW DEAR LITTLE DOX HERE IS DYING AND HIS SOUL IS BEING TORN APART.
YOU'RE LYING.
AM I?
I'M GOING TO GET HIM BACK. WE ARE GOING TO GET HIM BACK.
I WILL NOT BE GOING BACK TO THE DEADSIDE. AND THE GIRL CANNOT SURVIVE THERE.
YOU DON'T UNDERSTAND, SAMEDI...
...I WASN'T ASKING.

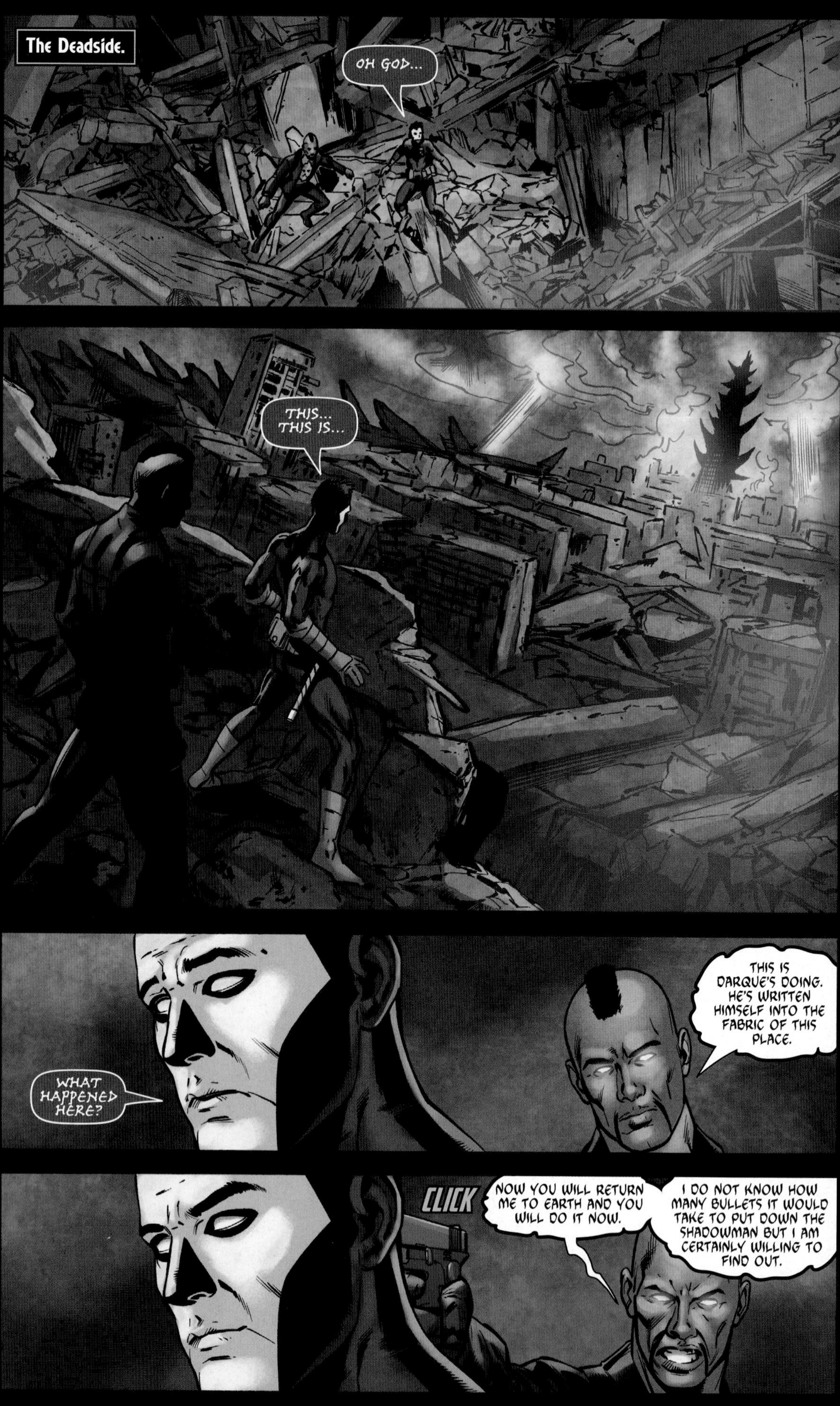
The Deadside.
OH GOD...
THIS... THIS IS...
WHAT HAPPENED HERE?
THIS IS DARQUE'S DOING. HE'S WRITTEN HIMSELF INTO THE FABRIC OF THIS PLACE.
CLICK
NOW YOU WILL RETURN ME TO EARTH AND YOU WILL DO IT NOW.
I DO NOT KNOW HOW MANY BULLETS IT WOULD TAKE TO PUT DOWN THE SHADOWMAN BUT I AM CERTAINLY WILLING TO FIND OUT.

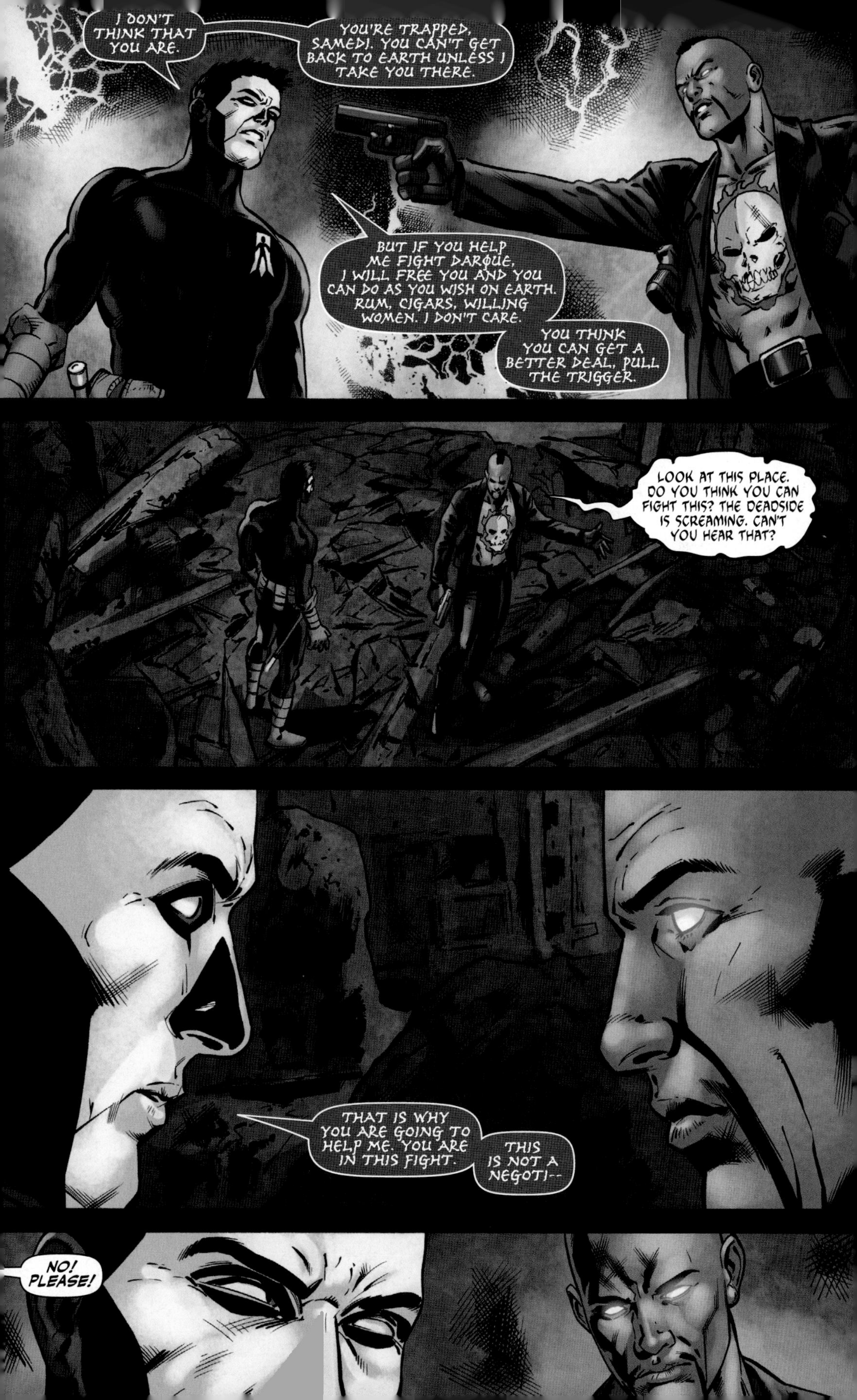
YOU'RE TRAPPED, SAMEDI. YOU CAN'T GET BACK TO EARTH UNLESS I TAKE YOU THERE.
I DON'T THINK THAT YOU ARE.
BUT IF YOU HELP ME FIGHT DARQUE, I WILL FREE YOU AND YOU CAN DO AS YOU WISH ON EARTH. RUM, CIGARS, WILLING WOMEN. I DON'T CARE.
YOU THINK YOU CAN GET A BETTER DEAL, PULL THE TRIGGER.
LOOK AT THIS PLACE. DO YOU THINK YOU CAN FIGHT THIS? THE DEADSIDE IS SCREAMING. CAN'T YOU HEAR THAT?
THAT IS WHY YOU ARE GOING TO HELP ME. YOU ARE IN THIS FIGHT.
THIS IS NOT A NEGOTI--
NO! PLEASE!

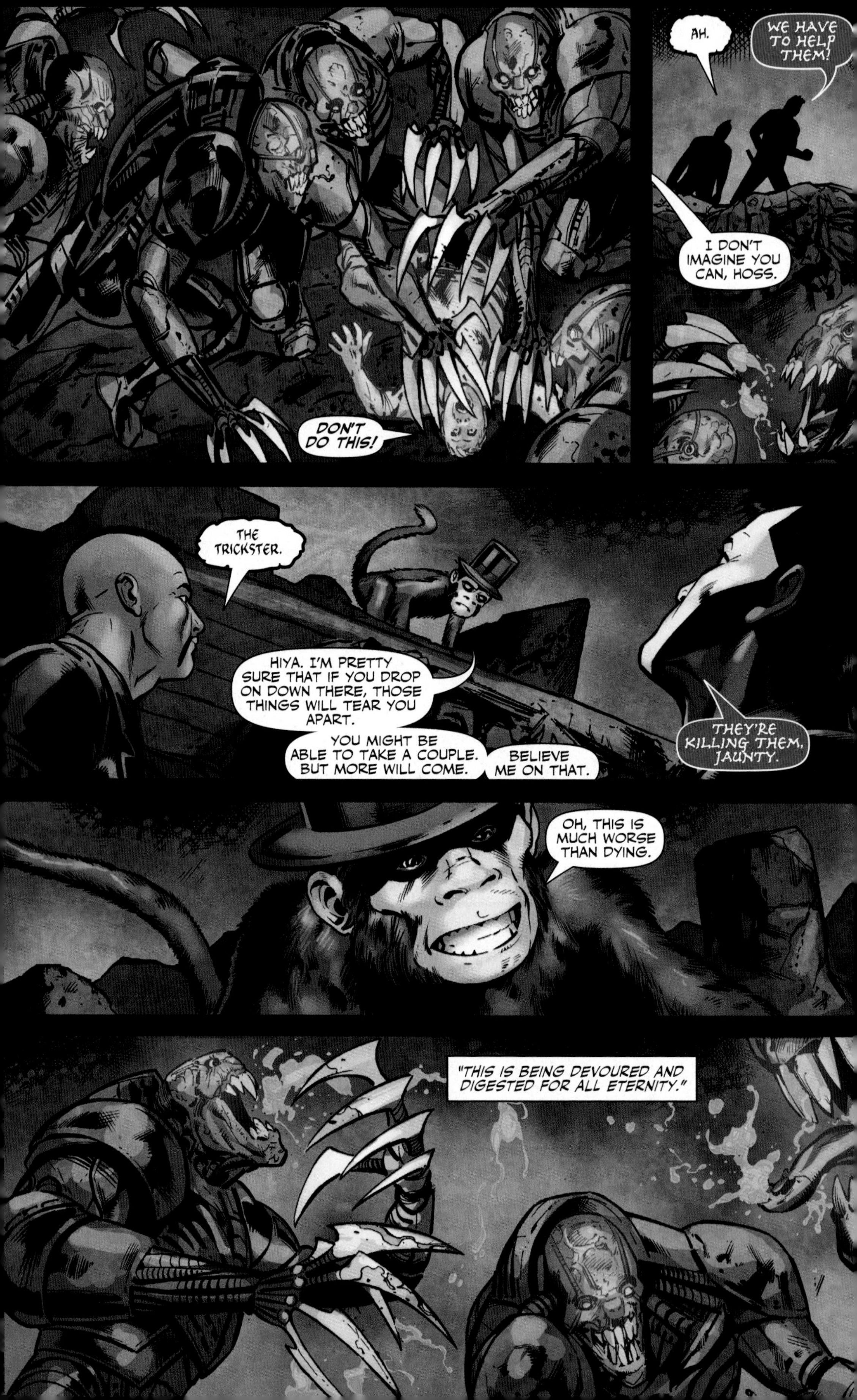
DON'T DO THIS!
AH.
WE HAVE TO HELP THEM!
I DON'T IMAGINE YOU CAN, HOSS.
THE TRICKSTER.
HIYA. I'M PRETTY SURE THAT IF YOU DROP ON DOWN THERE, THOSE THINGS WILL TEAR YOU APART.
YOU MIGHT BE ABLE TO TAKE A COUPLE. BUT MORE WILL COME.
BELIEVE ME ON THAT.
THEY'RE KILLING THEM, JAUNTY.
OH, THIS IS MUCH WORSE THAN DYING.
"THIS IS BEING DEVOURED AND DIGESTED FOR ALL ETERNITY."

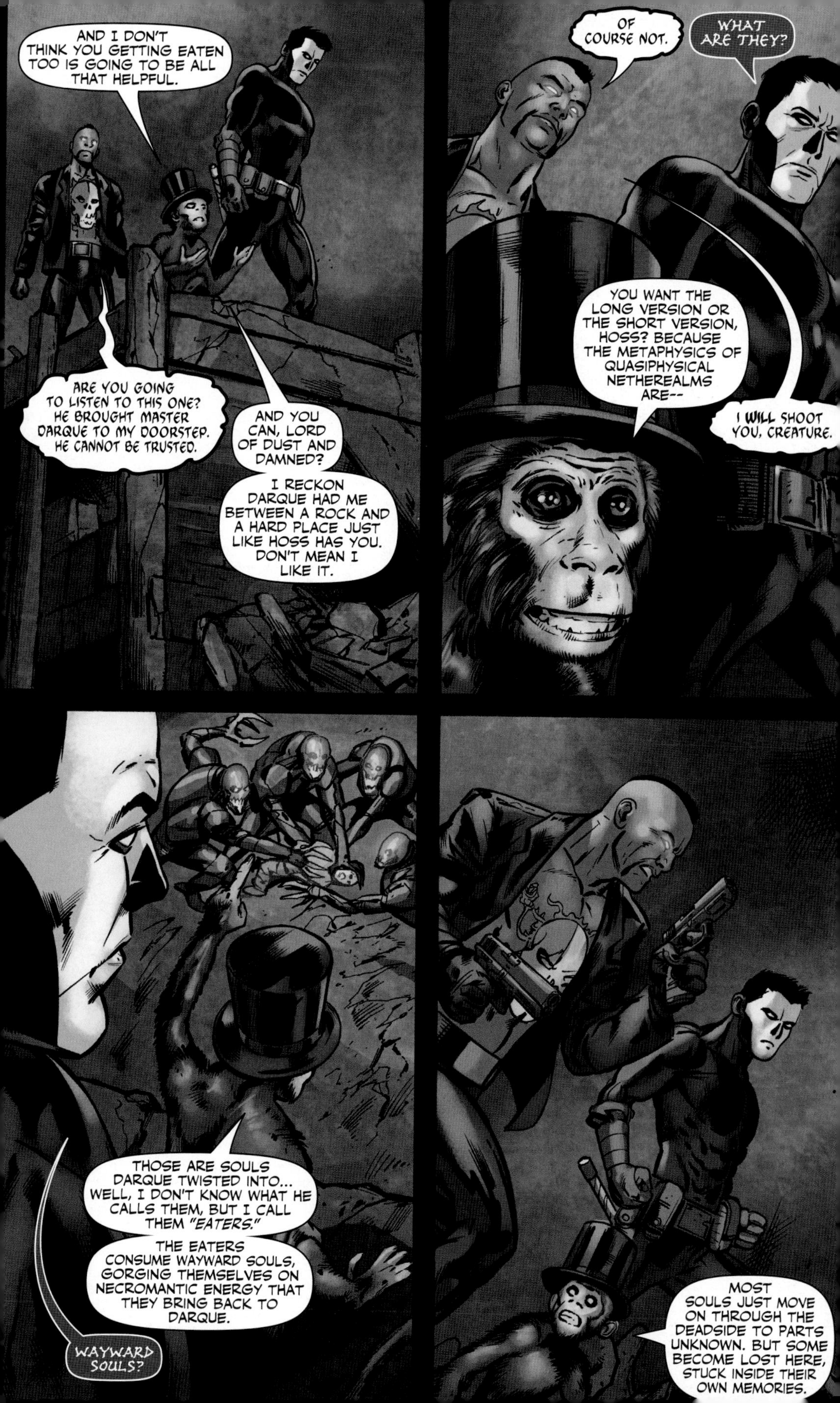

AND I DON'T THINK YOU GETTING EATEN TOO IS GOING TO BE ALL THAT HELPFUL.
ARE YOU GOING TO LISTEN TO THIS ONE? HE BROUGHT MASTER DARQUE TO MY DOORSTEP. HE CANNOT BE TRUSTED.
AND YOU CAN, LORD OF DUST AND DAMNED?
I RECKON DARQUE HAD ME BETWEEN A ROCK AND A HARD PLACE JUST LIKE HOSS HAS YOU. DON'T MEAN I LIKE IT.
OF COURSE NOT.
WHAT ARE THEY?
YOU WANT THE LONG VERSION OR THE SHORT VERSION, HOSS? BECAUSE THE METAPHYSICS OF QUASIPHYSICAL NETHEREALMS ARE--
I **WILL** SHOOT YOU, CREATURE.
THOSE ARE SOULS DARQUE TWISTED INTO... WELL, I DON'T KNOW WHAT HE CALLS THEM, BUT I CALL THEM *"EATERS."*
THE EATERS CONSUME WAYWARD SOULS, GORGING THEMSELVES ON NECROMANTIC ENERGY THAT THEY BRING BACK TO DARQUE.
WAYWARD SOULS?
MOST SOULS JUST MOVE ON THROUGH THE DEADSIDE TO PARTS UNKNOWN. BUT SOME BECOME LOST HERE, STUCK INSIDE THEIR OWN MEMORIES.

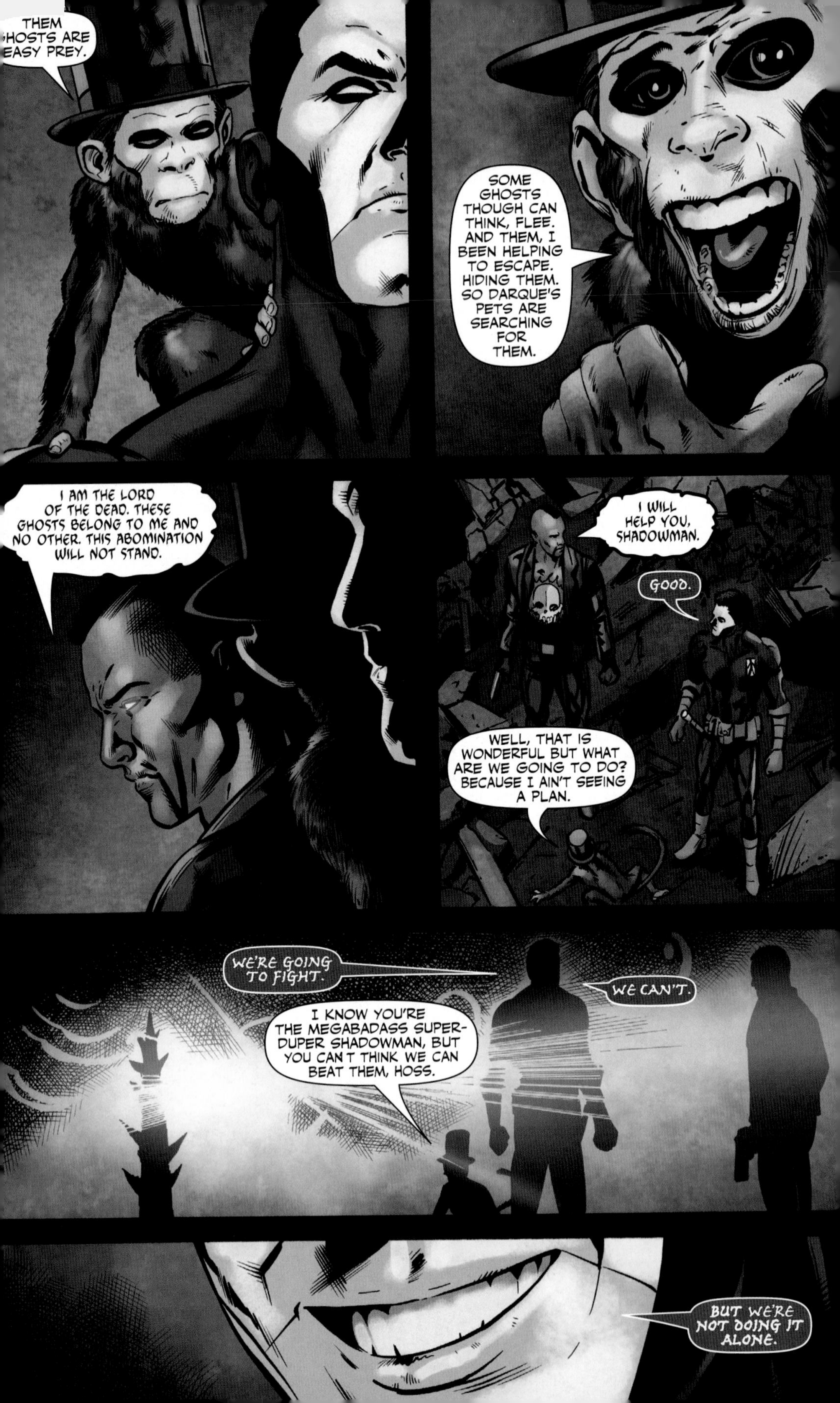
THEM GHOSTS ARE EASY PREY.
SOME GHOSTS THOUGH CAN THINK, FLEE. AND THEM, I BEEN HELPING TO ESCAPE. HIDING THEM. SO DARQUE'S PETS ARE SEARCHING FOR THEM.
I AM THE LORD OF THE DEAD. THESE GHOSTS BELONG TO ME AND NO OTHER. THIS ABOMINATION WILL NOT STAND.
I WILL HELP YOU, SHADOWMAN.
GOOD.
WELL, THAT IS WONDERFUL BUT WHAT ARE WE GOING TO DO? BECAUSE I AIN'T SEEING A PLAN.
WE'RE GOING TO FIGHT.
WE CAN'T.
I KNOW YOU'RE THE MEGABADASS SUPER-DUPER SHADOWMAN, BUT YOU CAN'T THINK WE CAN BEAT THEM, HOSS.
BUT WE'RE NOT DOING IT ALONE.

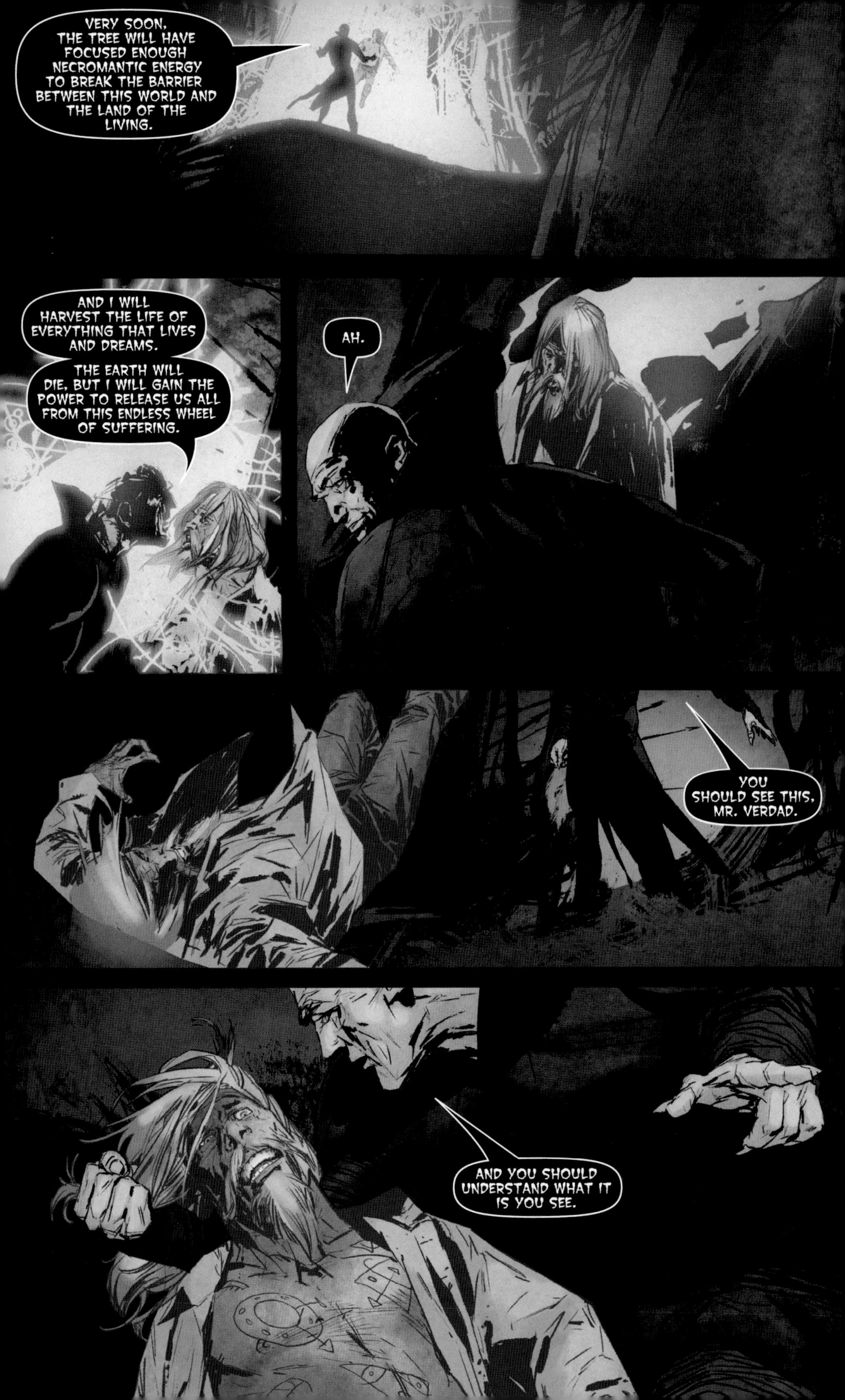
VERY SOON, THE TREE WILL HAVE FOCUSED ENOUGH NECROMANTIC ENERGY TO BREAK THE BARRIER BETWEEN THIS WORLD AND THE LAND OF THE LIVING.
AND I WILL HARVEST THE LIFE OF EVERYTHING THAT LIVES AND DREAMS.
THE EARTH WILL DIE, BUT I WILL GAIN THE POWER TO RELEASE US ALL FROM THIS ENDLESS WHEEL OF SUFFERING.
AH.
YOU SHOULD SEE THIS, MR. VERDAD.
AND YOU SHOULD UNDERSTAND WHAT IT IS YOU SEE.

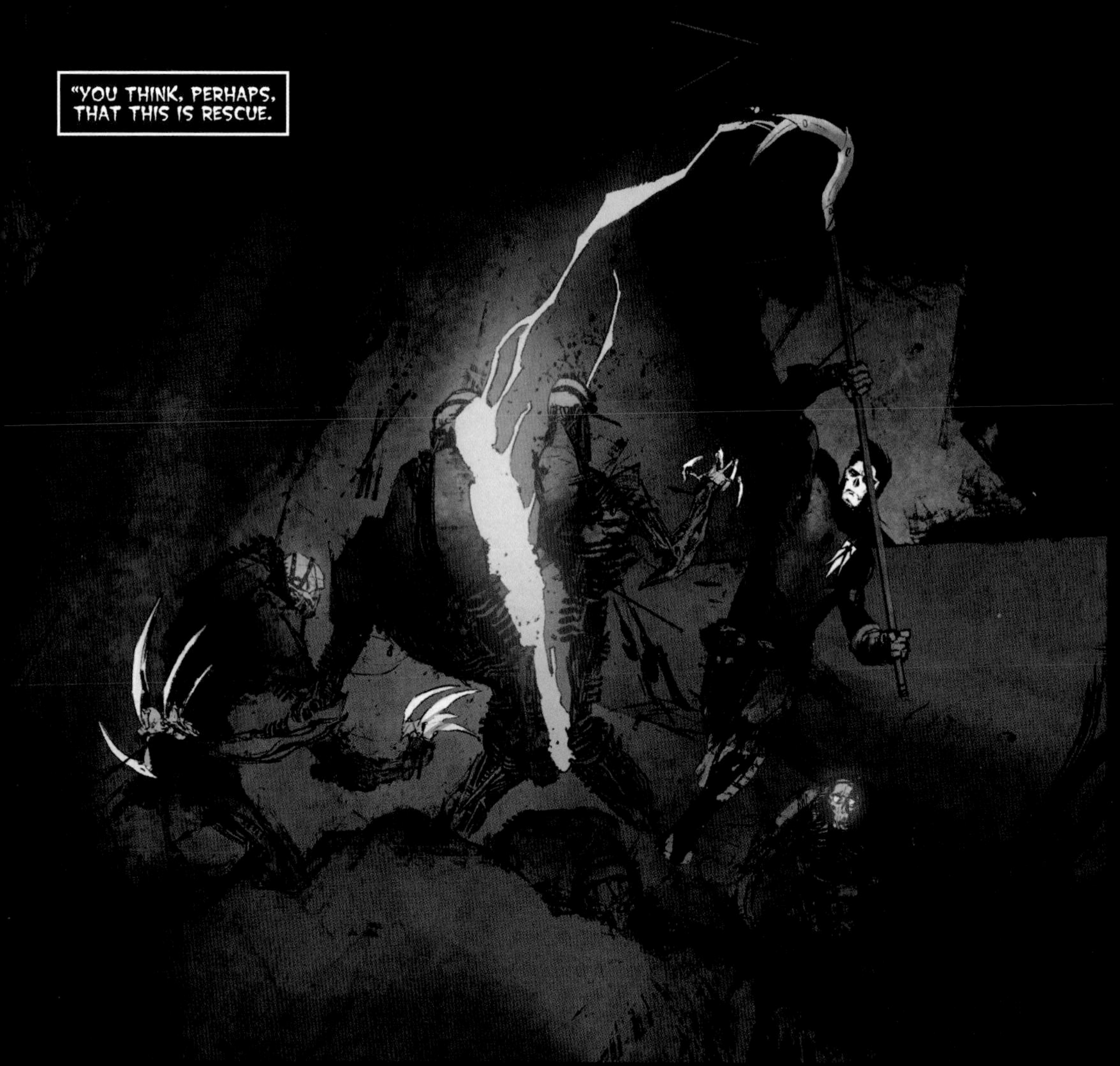
"YOU THINK, PERHAPS, THAT THIS IS RESCUE.

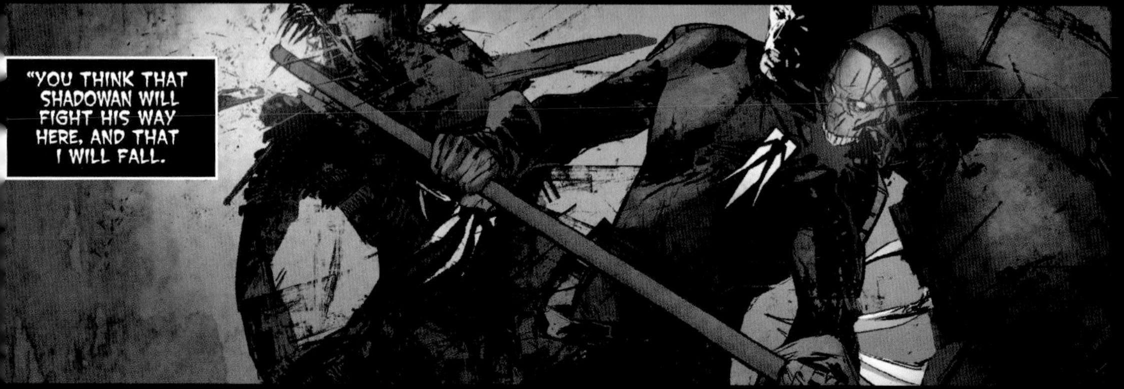
"YOU THINK THAT SHADOWAN WILL FIGHT HIS WAY HERE, AND THAT I WILL FALL.

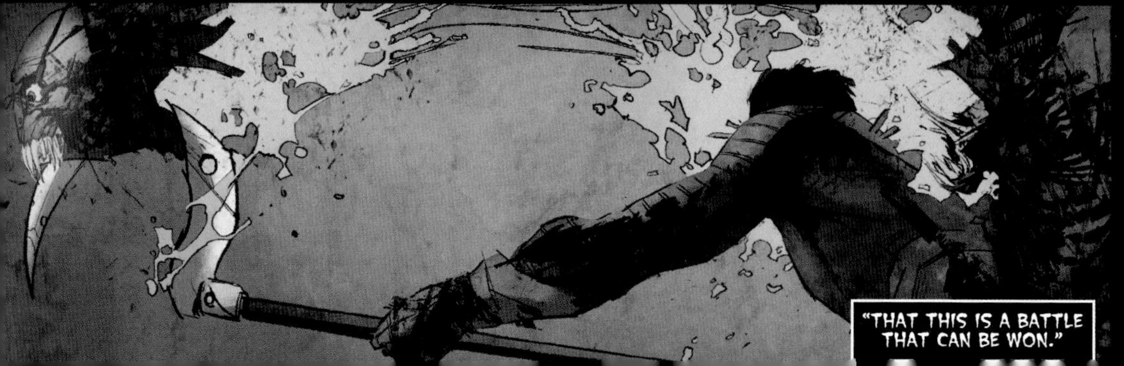
"THAT THIS IS A BATTLE THAT CAN BE WON."

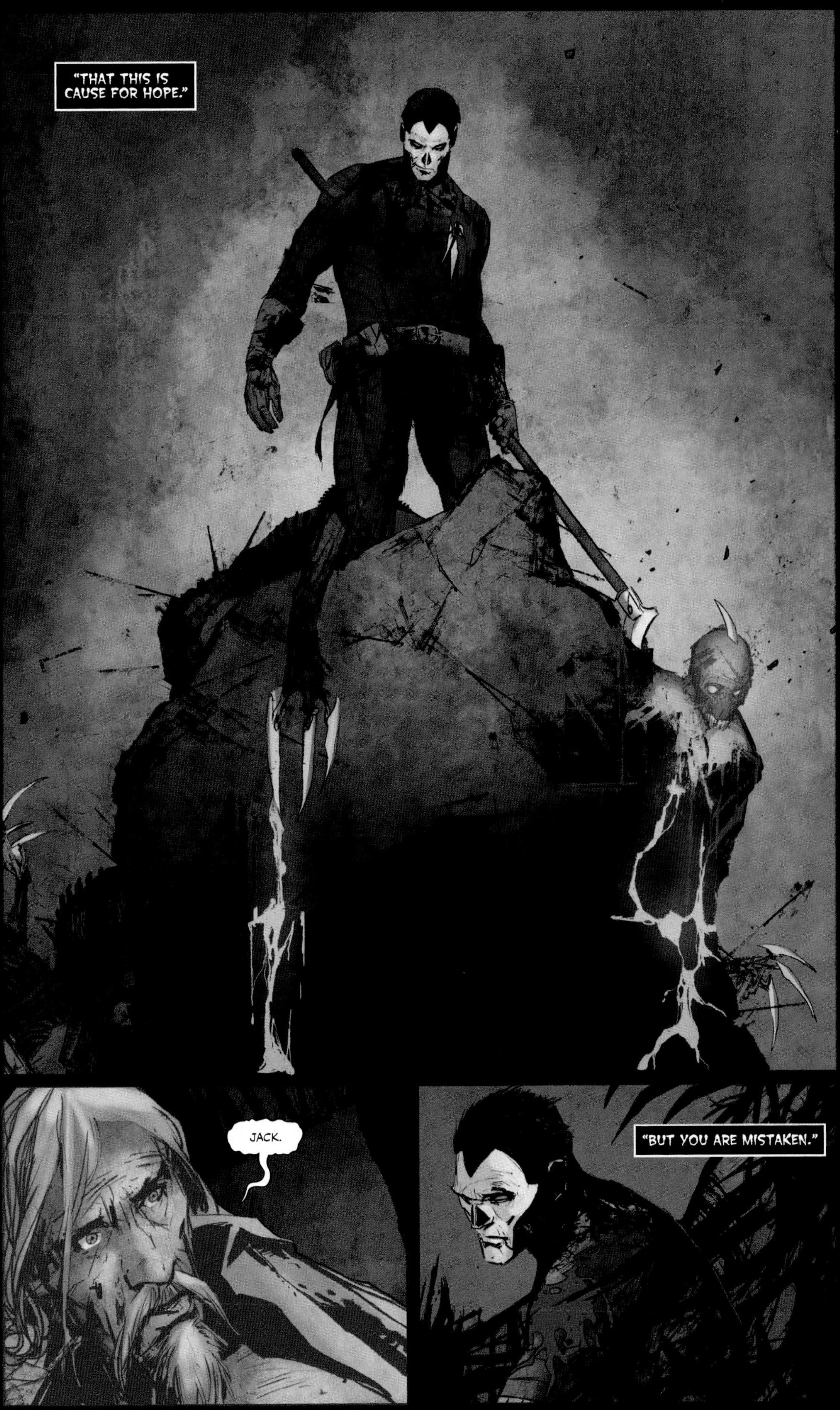
"THAT THIS IS CAUSE FOR HOPE."
JACK.
"BUT YOU ARE MISTAKEN."

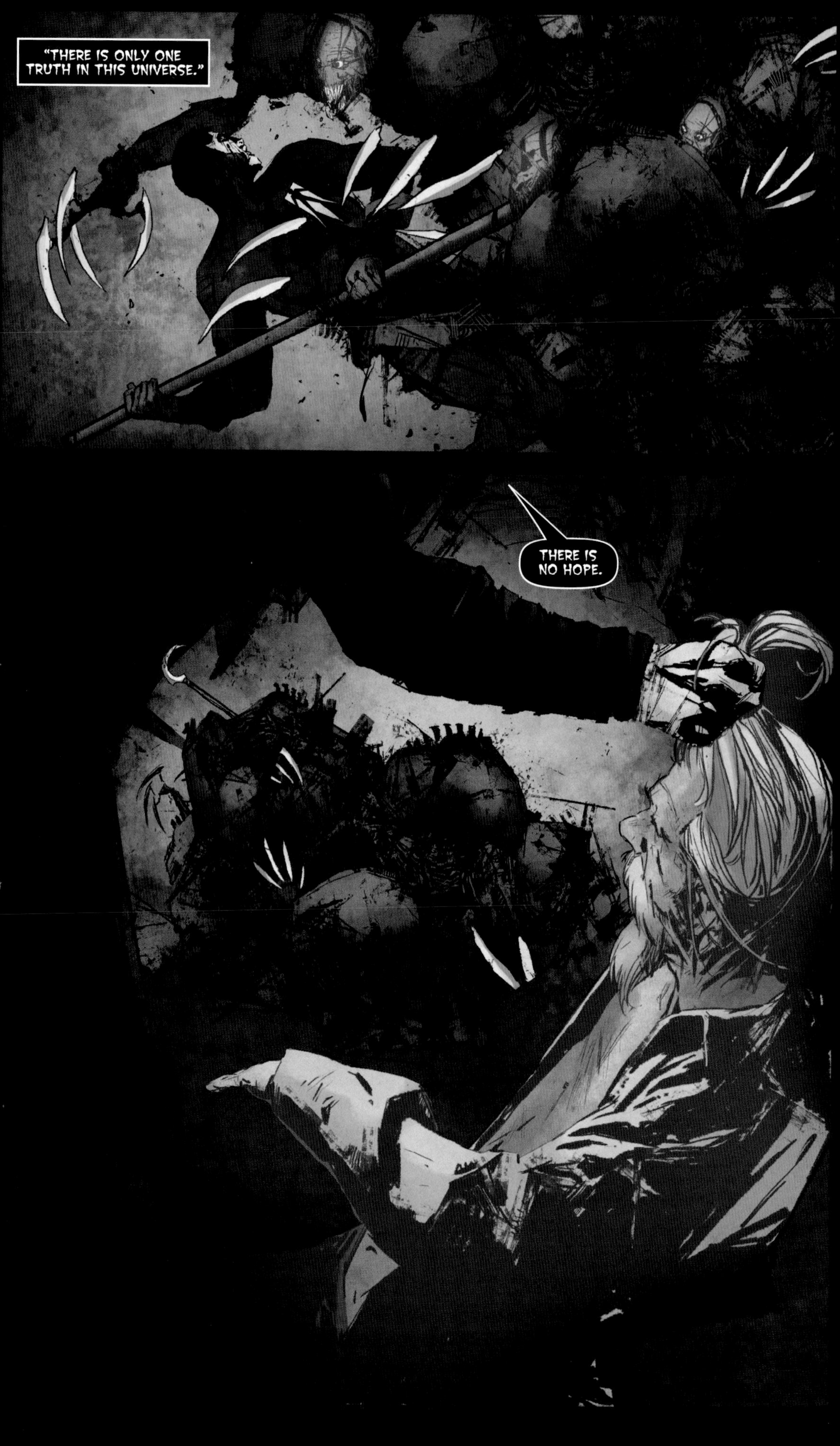
"THERE IS ONLY ONE TRUTH IN THIS UNIVERSE."
THERE IS NO HOPE.

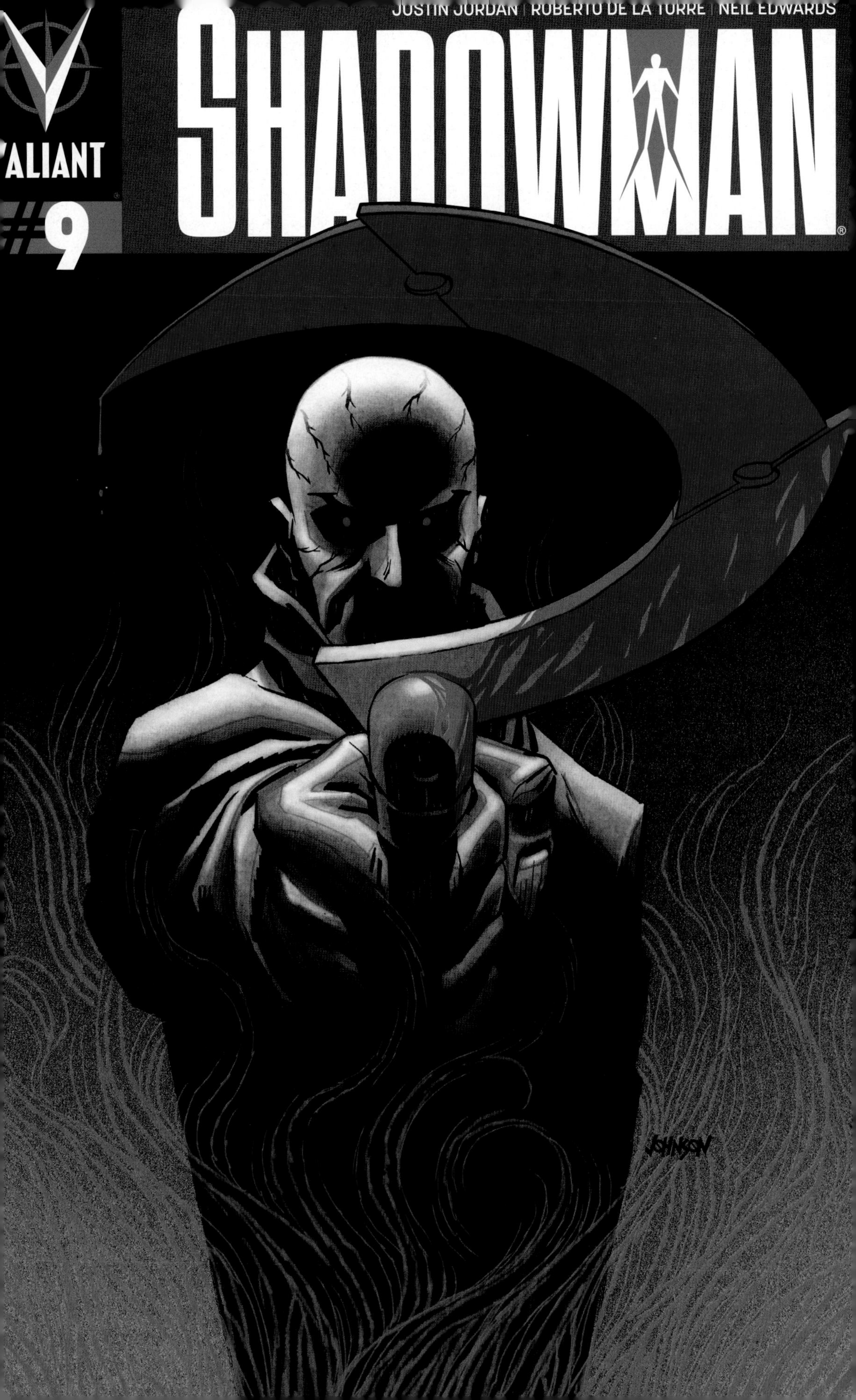
JUSTIN JORDAN | ROBERTO DE LA TORRE | NEIL EDWARDS
VALIANT
#9
SHADOWMAN
JOHNSON

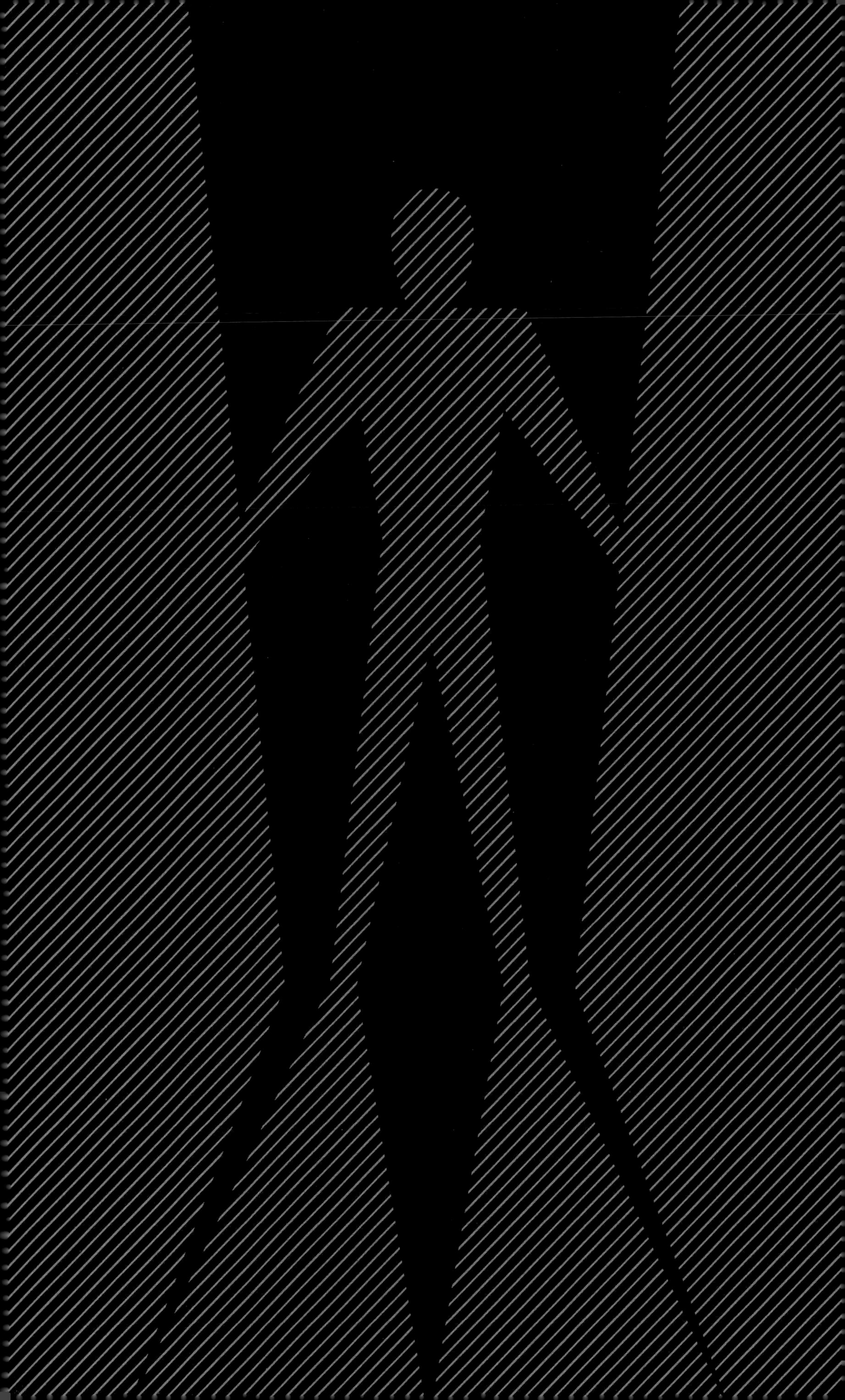

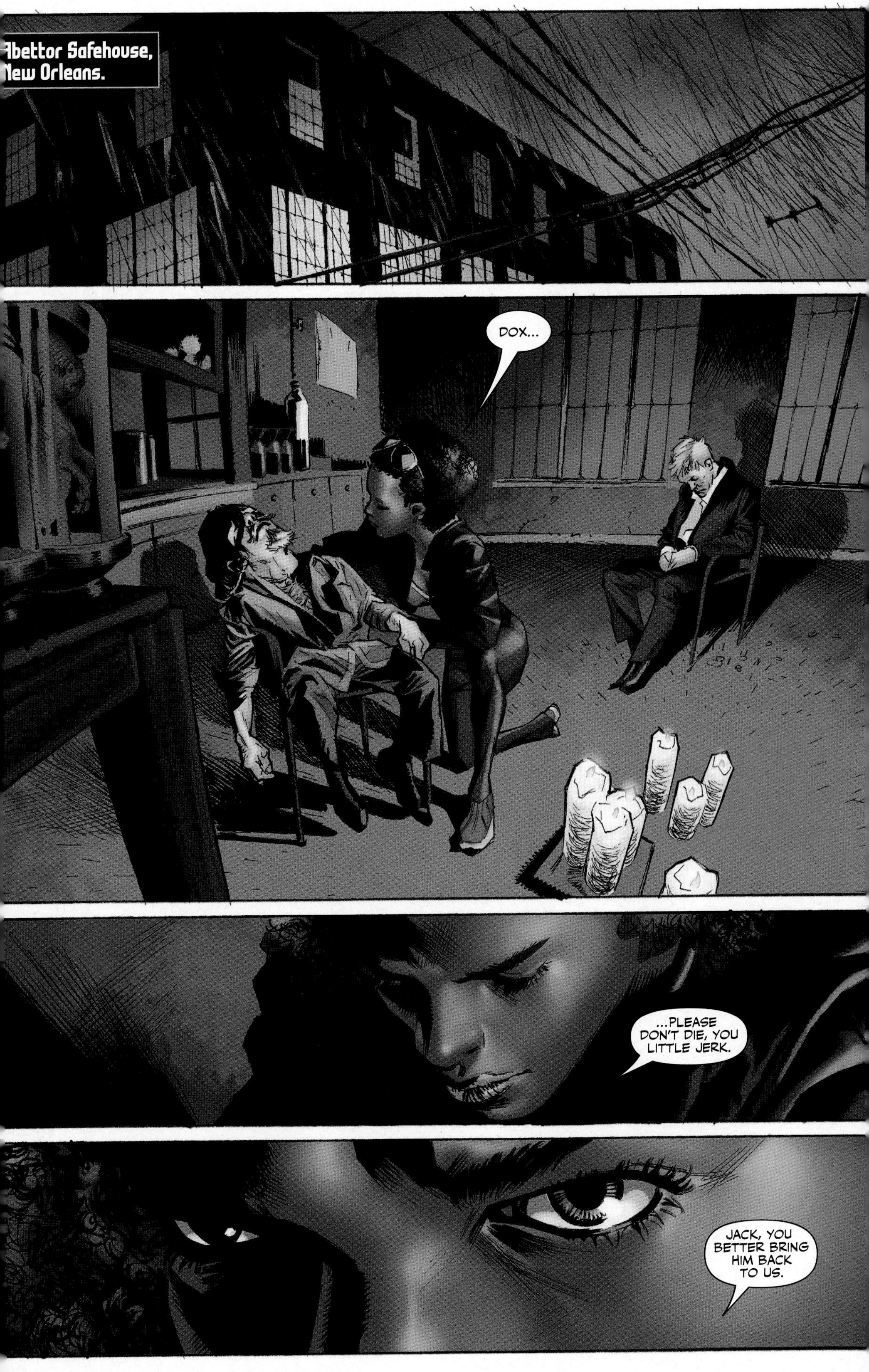
Abettor Safehouse,
New Orleans.
DOX...
...PLEASE DON'T DIE, YOU LITTLE JERK.
JACK, YOU BETTER BRING HIM BACK TO US.

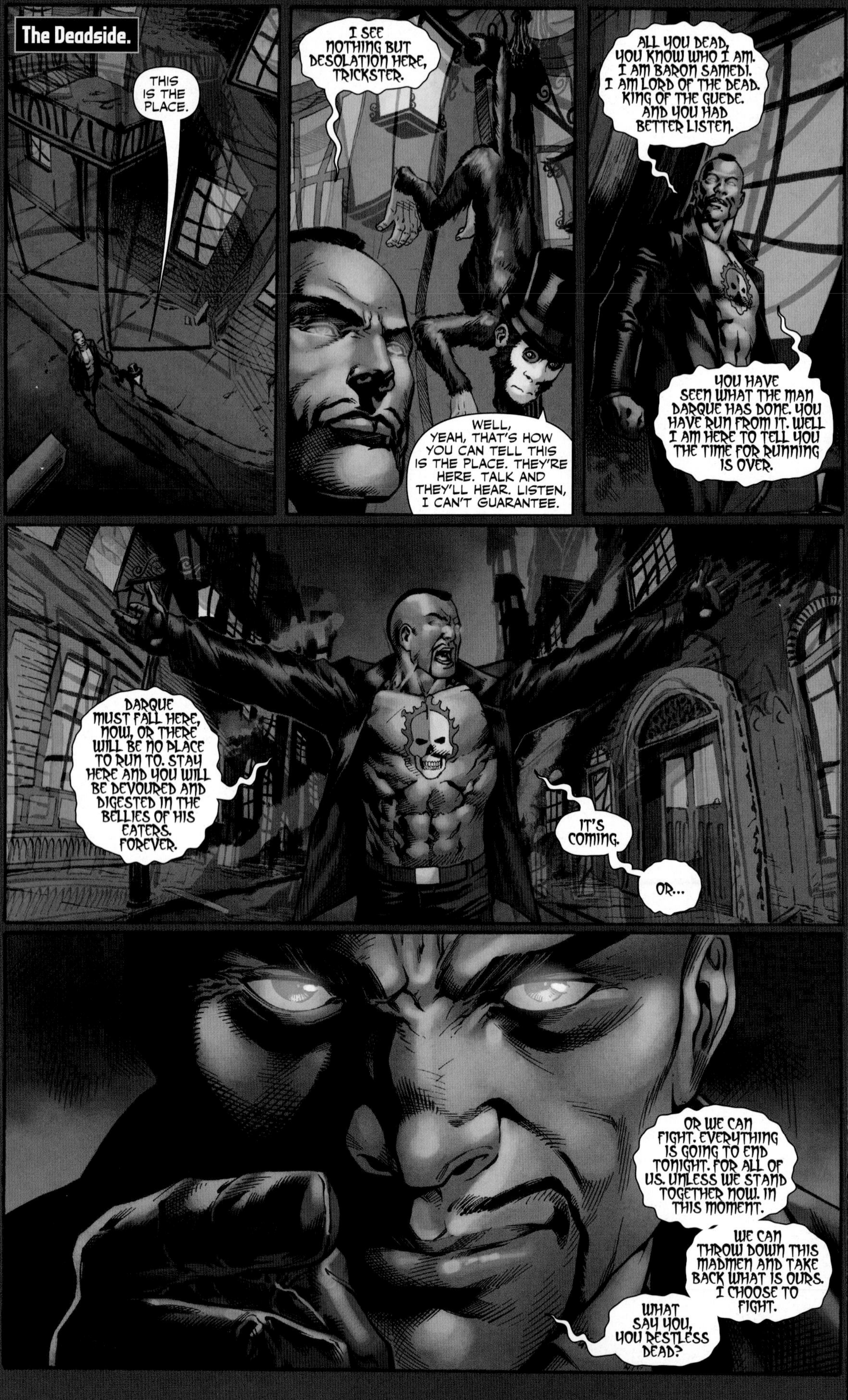
The Deadside.
THIS IS THE PLACE.
I SEE NOTHING BUT DESOLATION HERE, TRICKSTER.
WELL, YEAH, THAT'S HOW YOU CAN TELL THIS IS THE PLACE. THEY'RE HERE. TALK AND THEY'LL HEAR. LISTEN, I CAN'T GUARANTEE.
ALL YOU DEAD, YOU KNOW WHO I AM. I AM BARON SAMEDI. I AM LORD OF THE DEAD. KING OF THE GUEDE. AND YOU HAD BETTER LISTEN.
YOU HAVE SEEN WHAT THE MAN DARQUE HAS DONE. YOU HAVE RUN FROM IT. WELL I AM HERE TO TELL YOU THE TIME FOR RUNNING IS OVER.
DARQUE MUST FALL HERE, NOW, OR THERE WILL BE NO PLACE TO RUN TO. STAY HERE AND YOU WILL BE DEVOURED AND DIGESTED IN THE BELLIES OF HIS EATERS. FOREVER.
IT'S COMING.
OR...
OR WE CAN FIGHT. EVERYTHING IS GOING TO END TONIGHT. FOR ALL OF US. UNLESS WE STAND TOGETHER NOW. IN THIS MOMENT.
WE CAN THROW DOWN THIS MADMEN AND TAKE BACK WHAT IS OURS. I CHOOSE TO FIGHT.
WHAT SAY YOU, YOU RESTLESS DEAD?

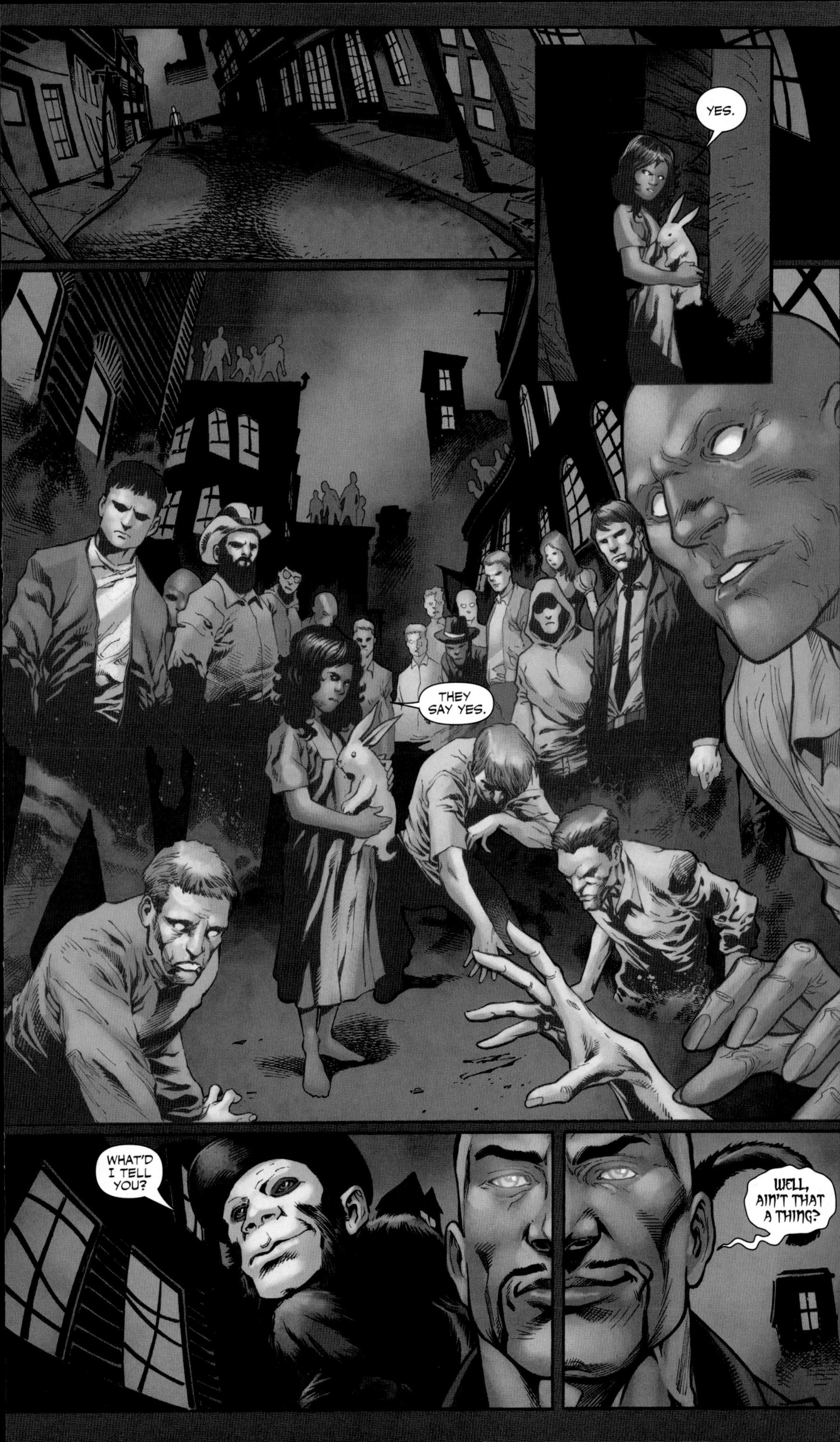
YES.
THEY SAY YES.
WHAT'D I TELL YOU?
WELL, AIN'T THAT A THING?

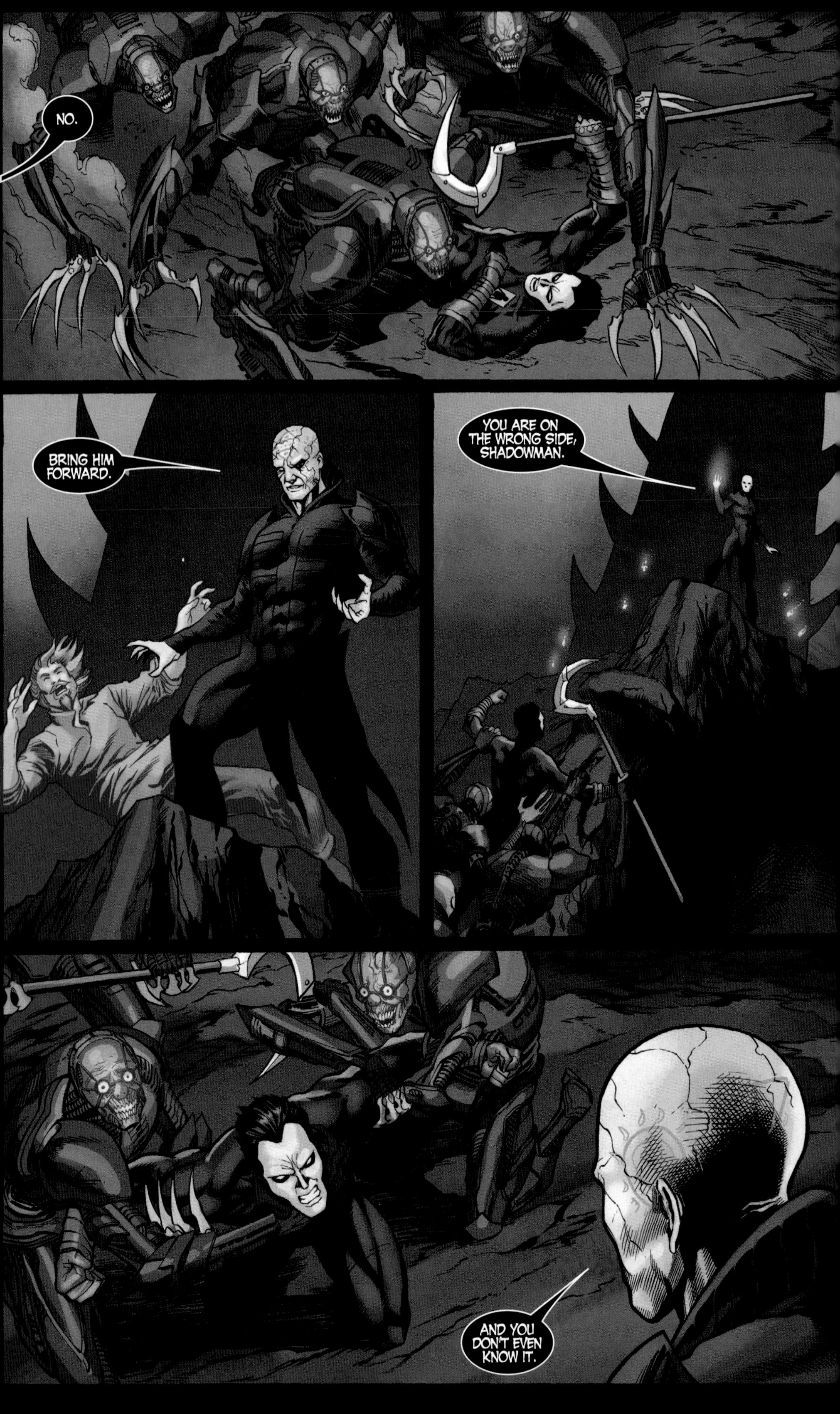
NO.
BRING HIM FORWARD.
YOU ARE ON THE WRONG SIDE, SHADOWMAN.
AND YOU DON'T EVEN KNOW IT.

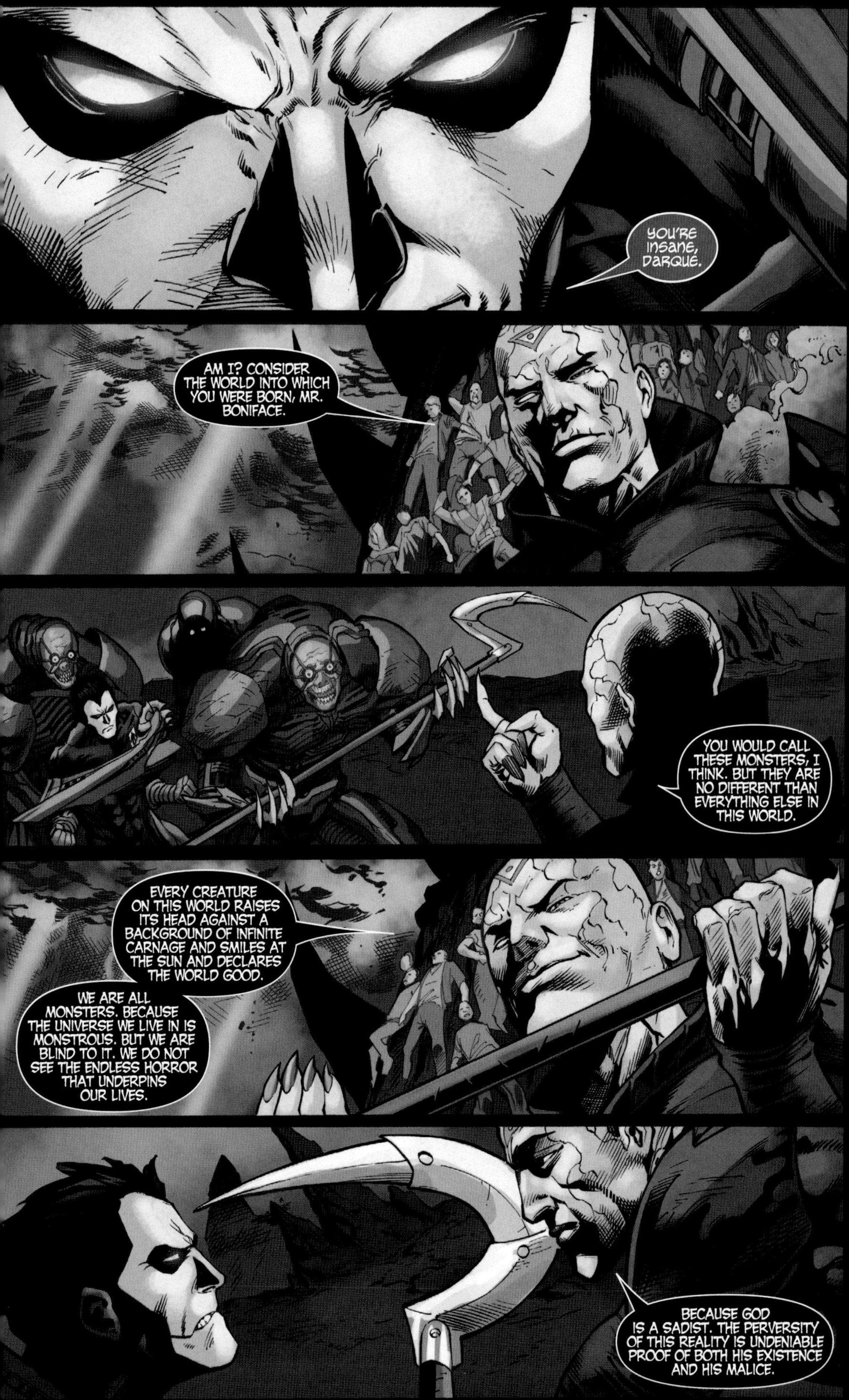
YOU'RE INSANE, DARQUE.
AM I? CONSIDER THE WORLD INTO WHICH YOU WERE BORN, MR. BONIFACE.
YOU WOULD CALL THESE MONSTERS, I THINK. BUT THEY ARE NO DIFFERENT THAN EVERYTHING ELSE IN THIS WORLD.
EVERY CREATURE ON THIS WORLD RAISES ITS HEAD AGAINST A BACKGROUND OF INFINITE CARNAGE AND SMILES AT THE SUN AND DECLARES THE WORLD GOOD.
WE ARE ALL MONSTERS. BECAUSE THE UNIVERSE WE LIVE IN IS MONSTROUS. BUT WE ARE BLIND TO IT. WE DO NOT SEE THE ENDLESS HORROR THAT UNDERPINS OUR LIVES.
BECAUSE GOD IS A SADIST. THE PERVERSITY OF THIS REALITY IS UNDENIABLE PROOF OF BOTH HIS EXISTENCE AND HIS MALICE.

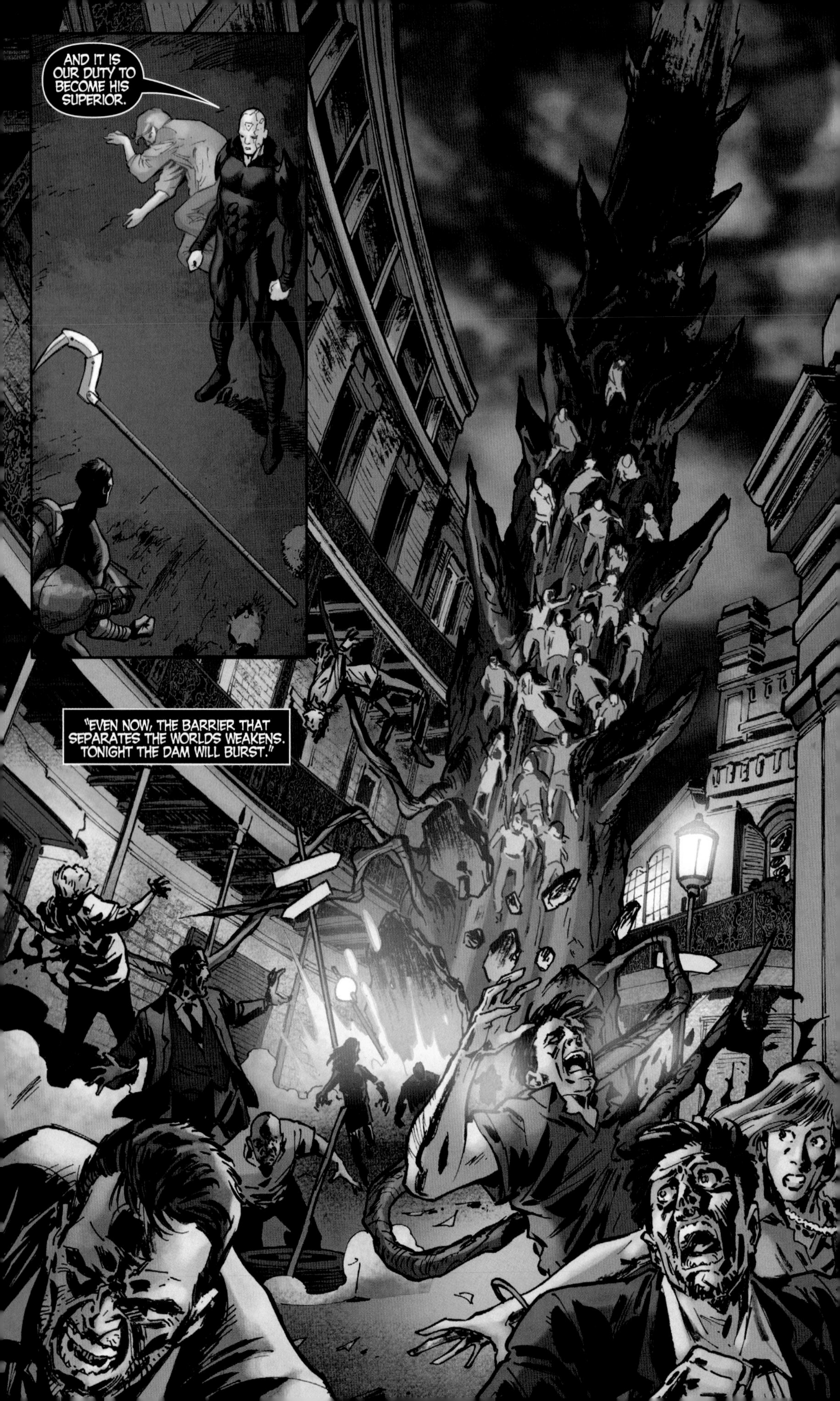

AND IT IS OUR DUTY TO BECOME HIS SUPERIOR.
"EVEN NOW, THE BARRIER THAT SEPARATES THE WORLDS WEAKENS. TONIGHT THE DAM WILL BURST."

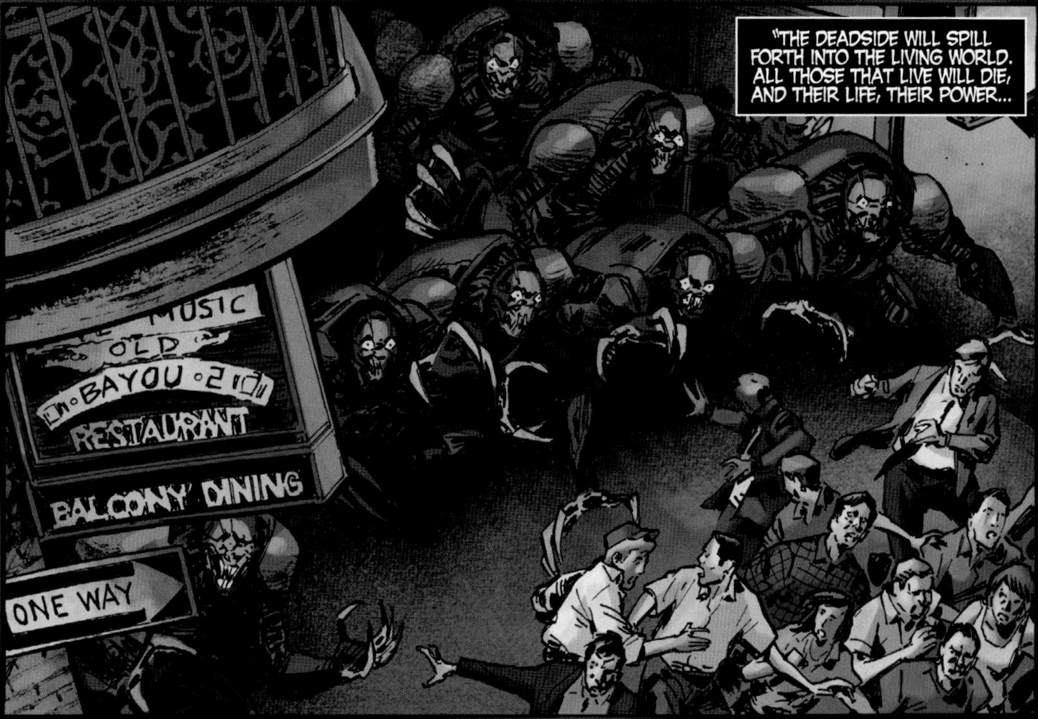
"THE DEADSIDE WILL SPILL FORTH INTO THE LIVING WORLD. ALL THOSE THAT LIVE WILL DIE, AND THEIR LIFE, THEIR POWER...
MUSIC
OLD
BAYOU
RESTAURANT
BALCONY DINING
ONE WAY

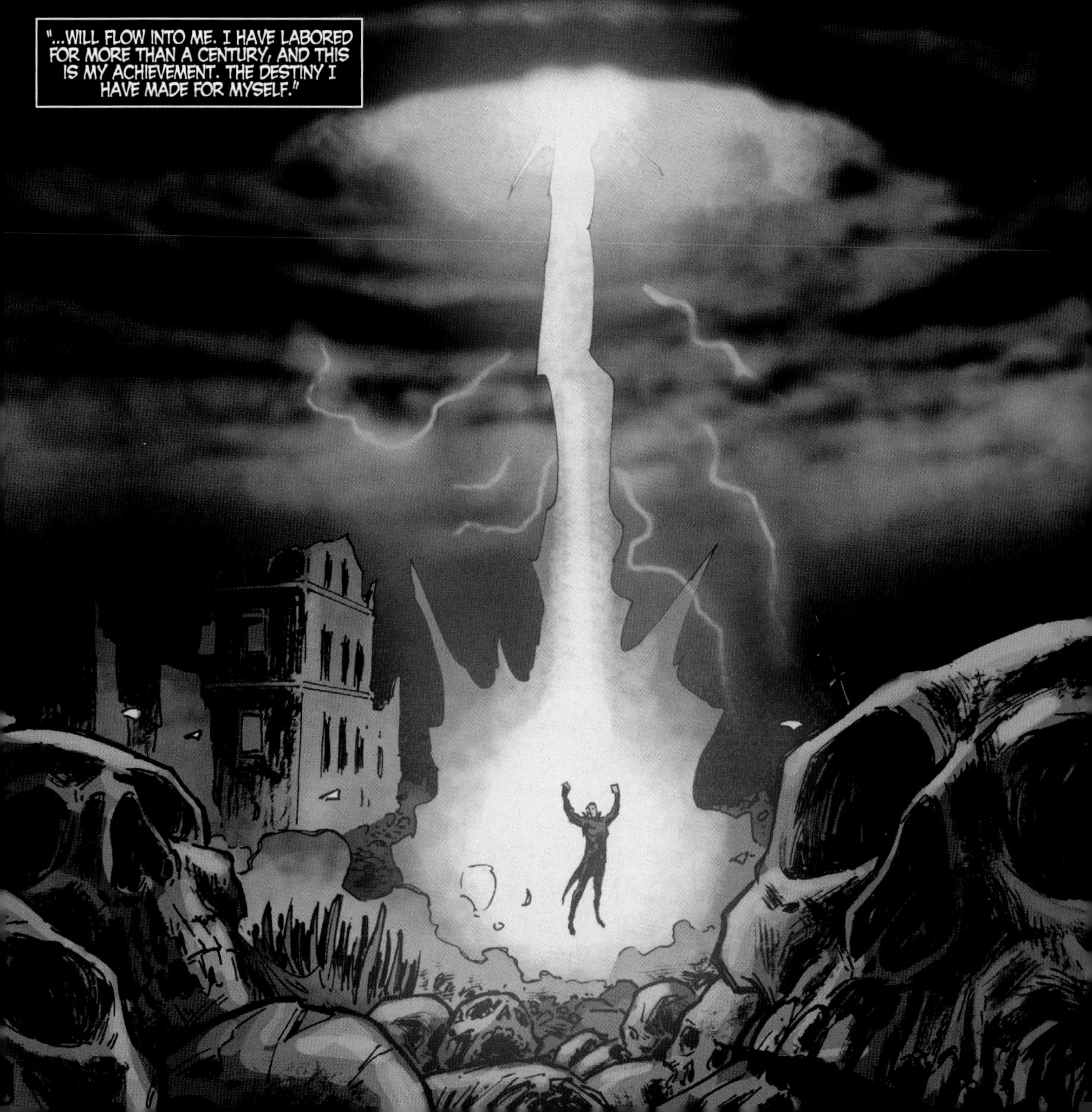
"...WILL FLOW INTO ME. I HAVE LABORED FOR MORE THAN A CENTURY, AND THIS IS MY ACHIEVEMENT. THE DESTINY I HAVE MADE FOR MYSELF."

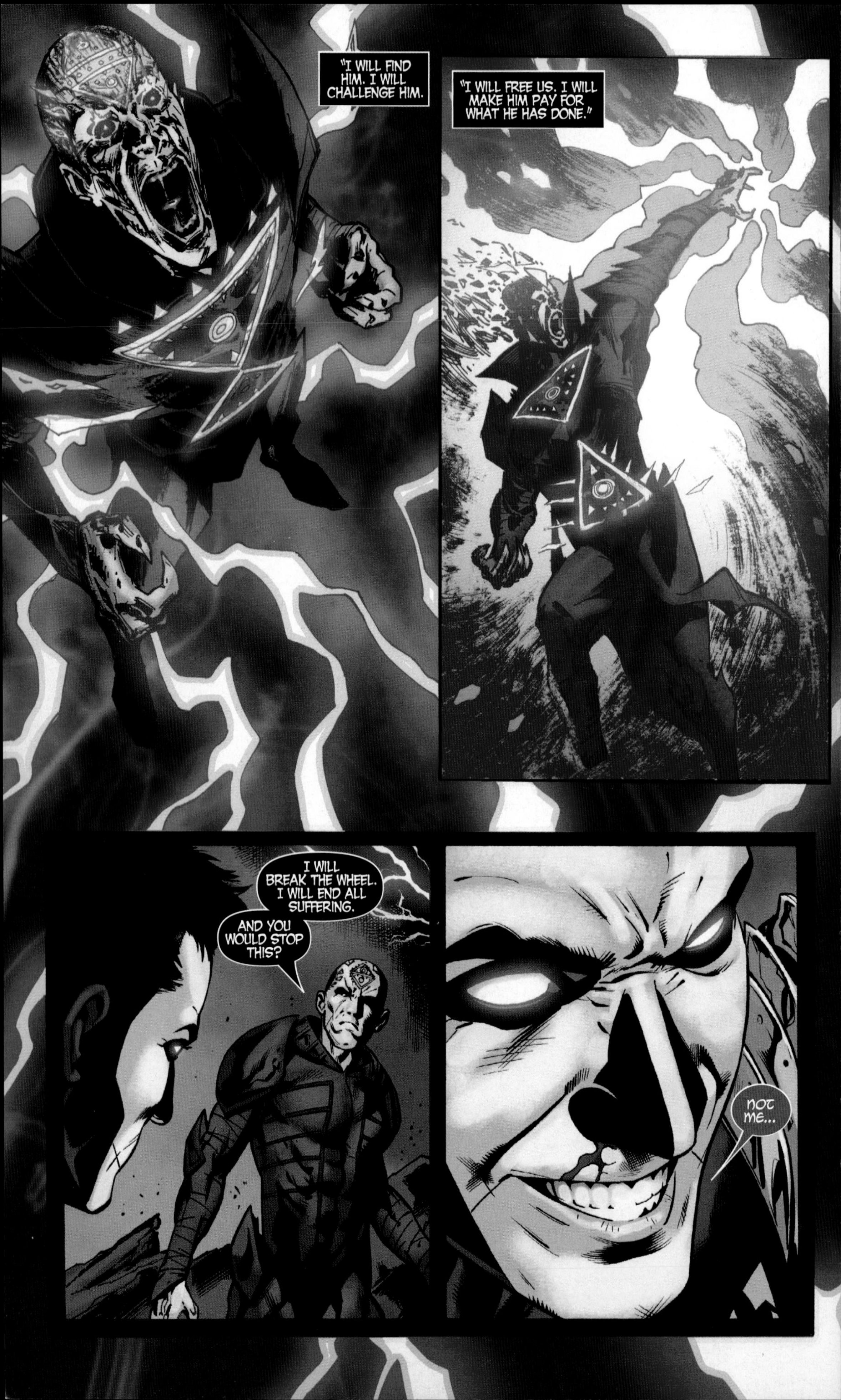
"I WILL FIND HIM. I WILL CHALLENGE HIM.
"I WILL FREE US. I WILL MAKE HIM PAY FOR WHAT HE HAS DONE."
I WILL BREAK THE WHEEL. I WILL END ALL SUFFERING.
AND YOU WOULD STOP THIS?
NOT ME...

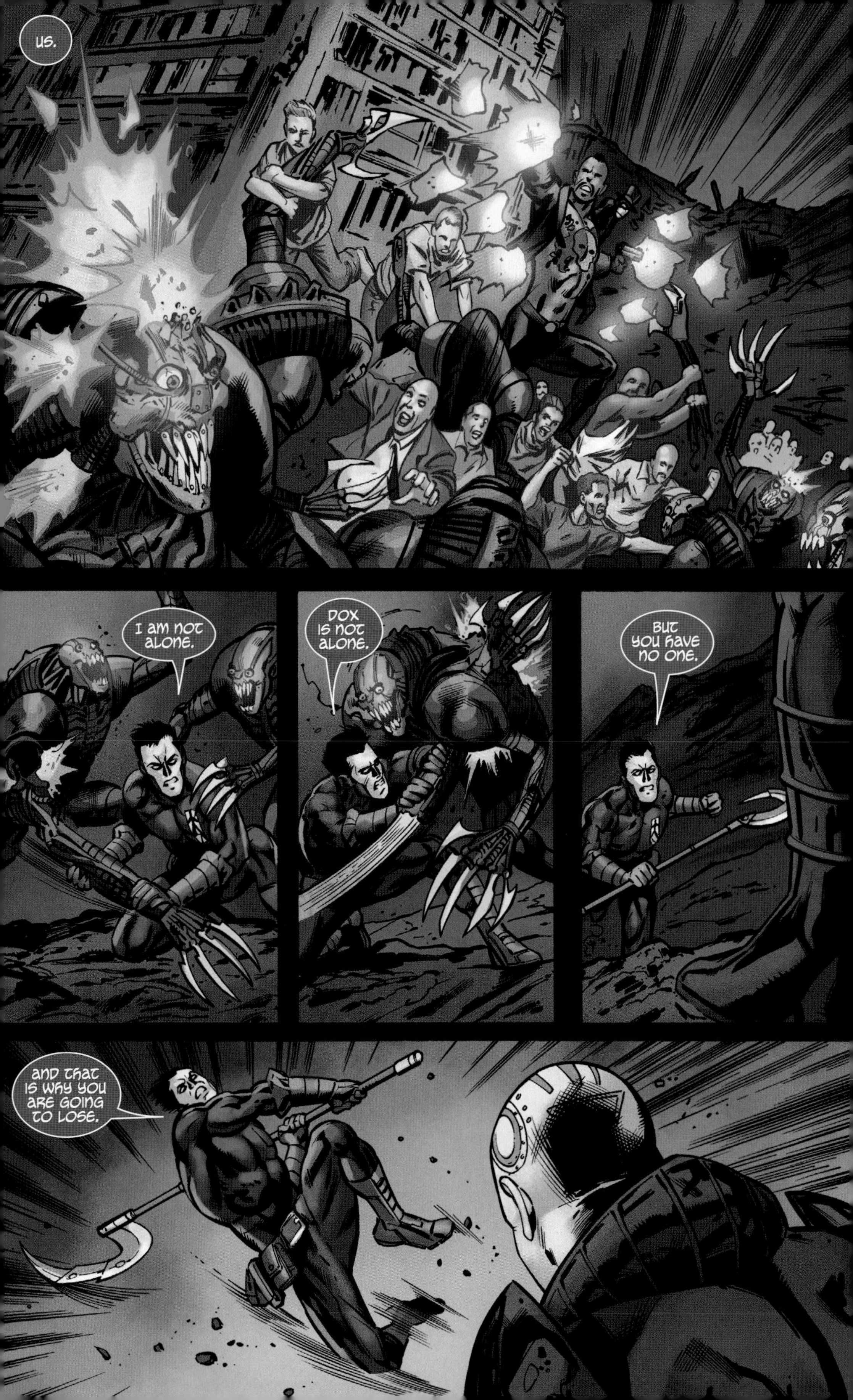
US.
I AM NOT ALONE.
DOX IS NOT ALONE.
BUT YOU HAVE NO ONE.
AND THAT IS WHY YOU ARE GOING TO LOSE.

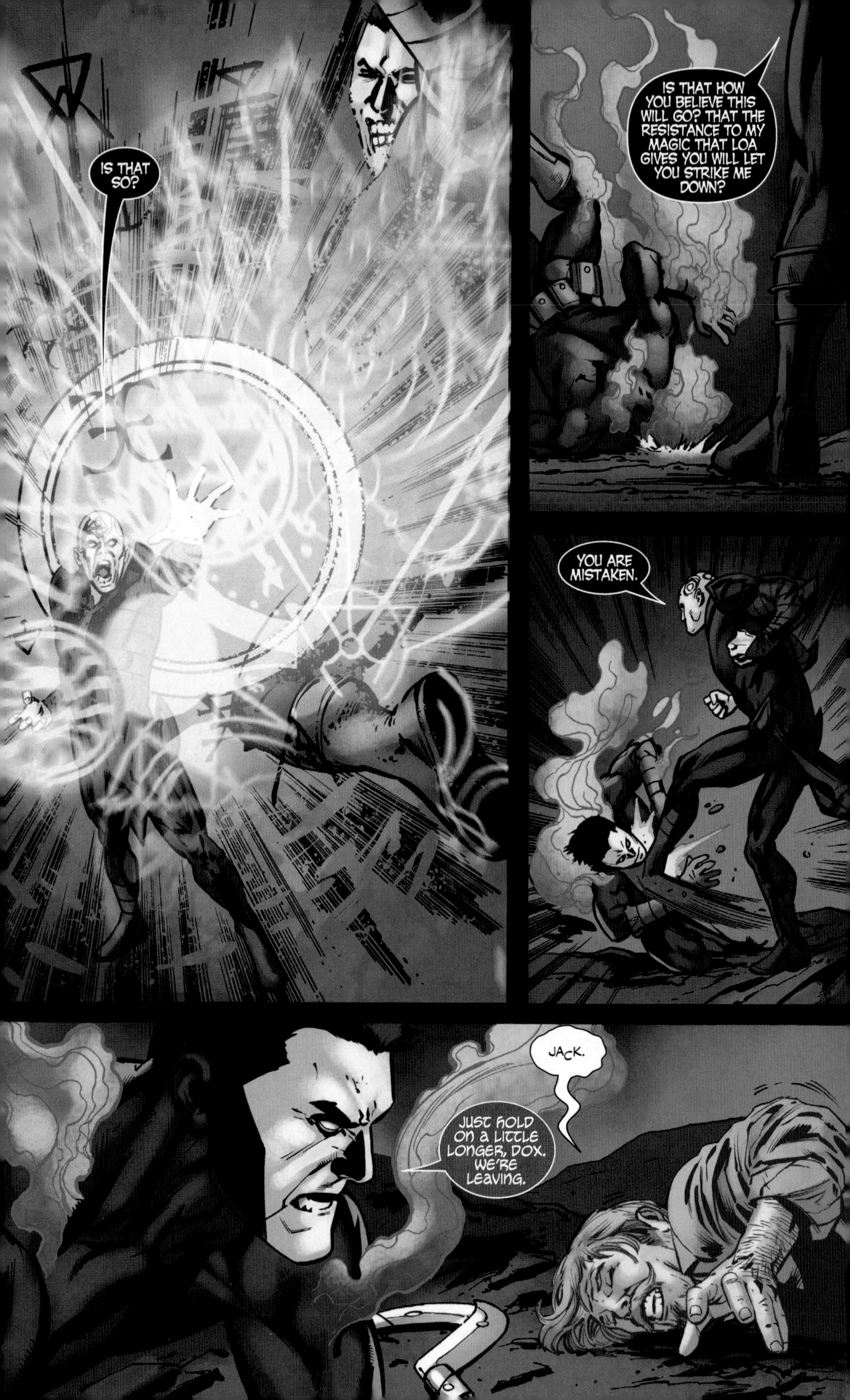
IS THAT SO?
IS THAT HOW YOU BELIEVE THIS WILL GO? THAT THE RESISTANCE TO MY MAGIC THAT LOA GIVES YOU WILL LET YOU STRIKE ME DOWN?
YOU ARE MISTAKEN.
JACK.
JUST HOLD ON A LITTLE LONGER, DOX. WE'RE LEAVING.

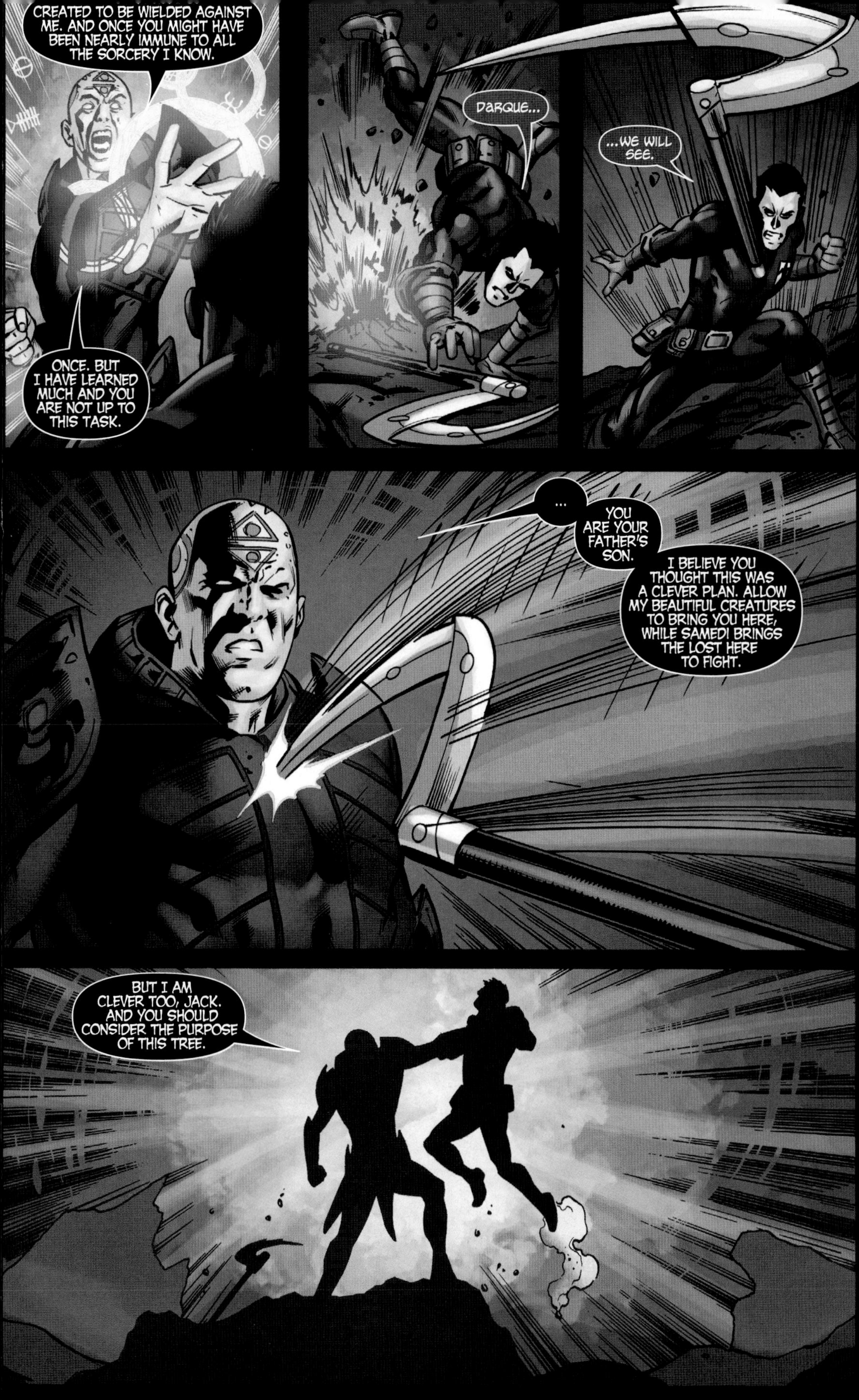
CREATED TO BE WIELDED AGAINST ME. AND ONCE YOU MIGHT HAVE BEEN NEARLY IMMUNE TO ALL THE SORCERY I KNOW.
ONCE. BUT I HAVE LEARNED MUCH AND YOU ARE NOT UP TO THIS TASK.
DARQUE...
...WE WILL SEE.
...
YOU ARE YOUR FATHER'S SON.
I BELIEVE YOU THOUGHT THIS WAS A CLEVER PLAN. ALLOW MY BEAUTIFUL CREATURES TO BRING YOU HERE, WHILE SAMEDI BRINGS THE LOST HERE TO FIGHT.
BUT I AM CLEVER TOO, JACK. AND YOU SHOULD CONSIDER THE PURPOSE OF THIS TREE.

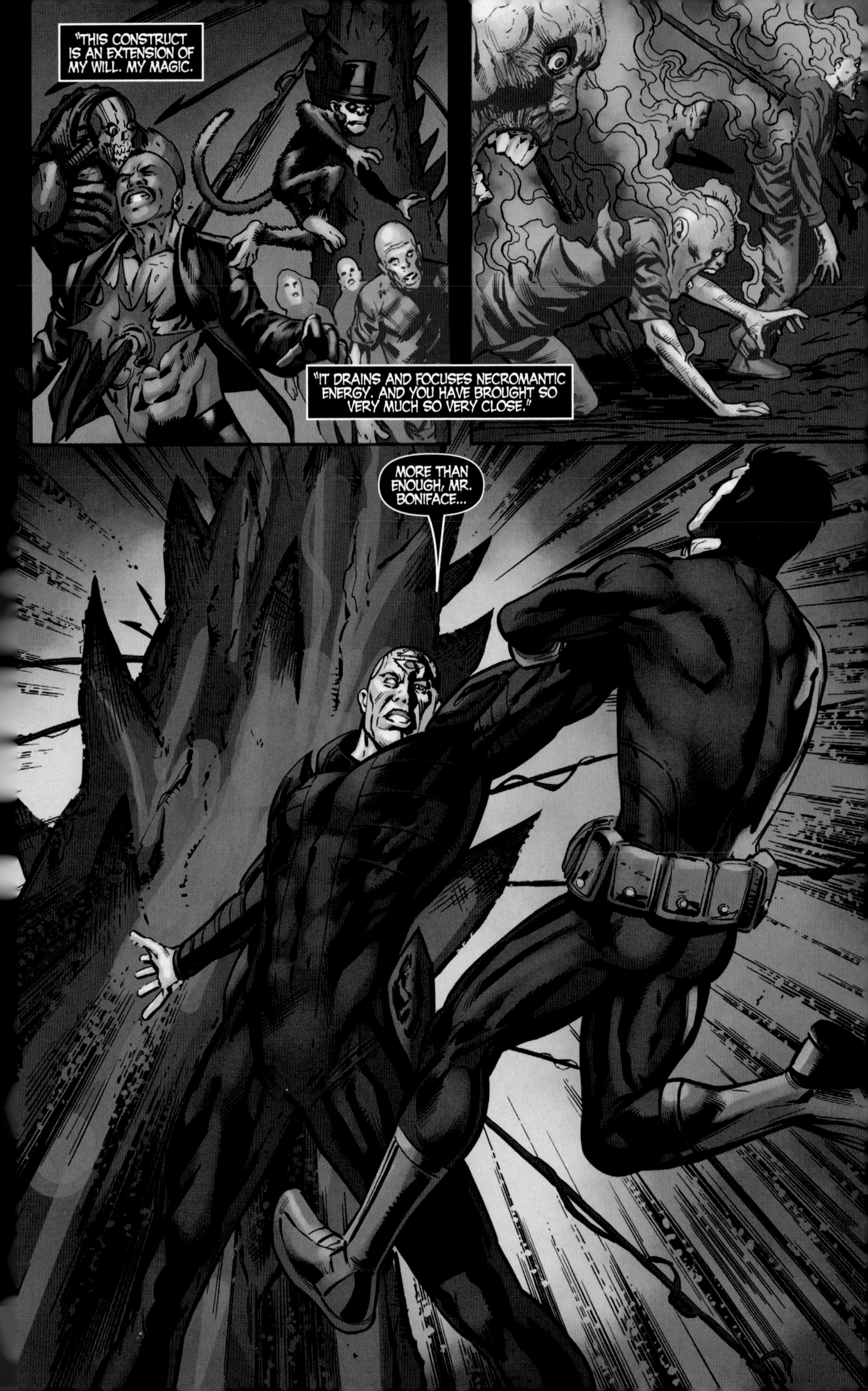
"THIS CONSTRUCT IS AN EXTENSION OF MY WILL. MY MAGIC.
"IT DRAINS AND FOCUSES NECROMANTIC ENERGY. AND YOU HAVE BROUGHT SO VERY MUCH SO VERY CLOSE."
MORE THAN ENOUGH, MR. BONIFACE...

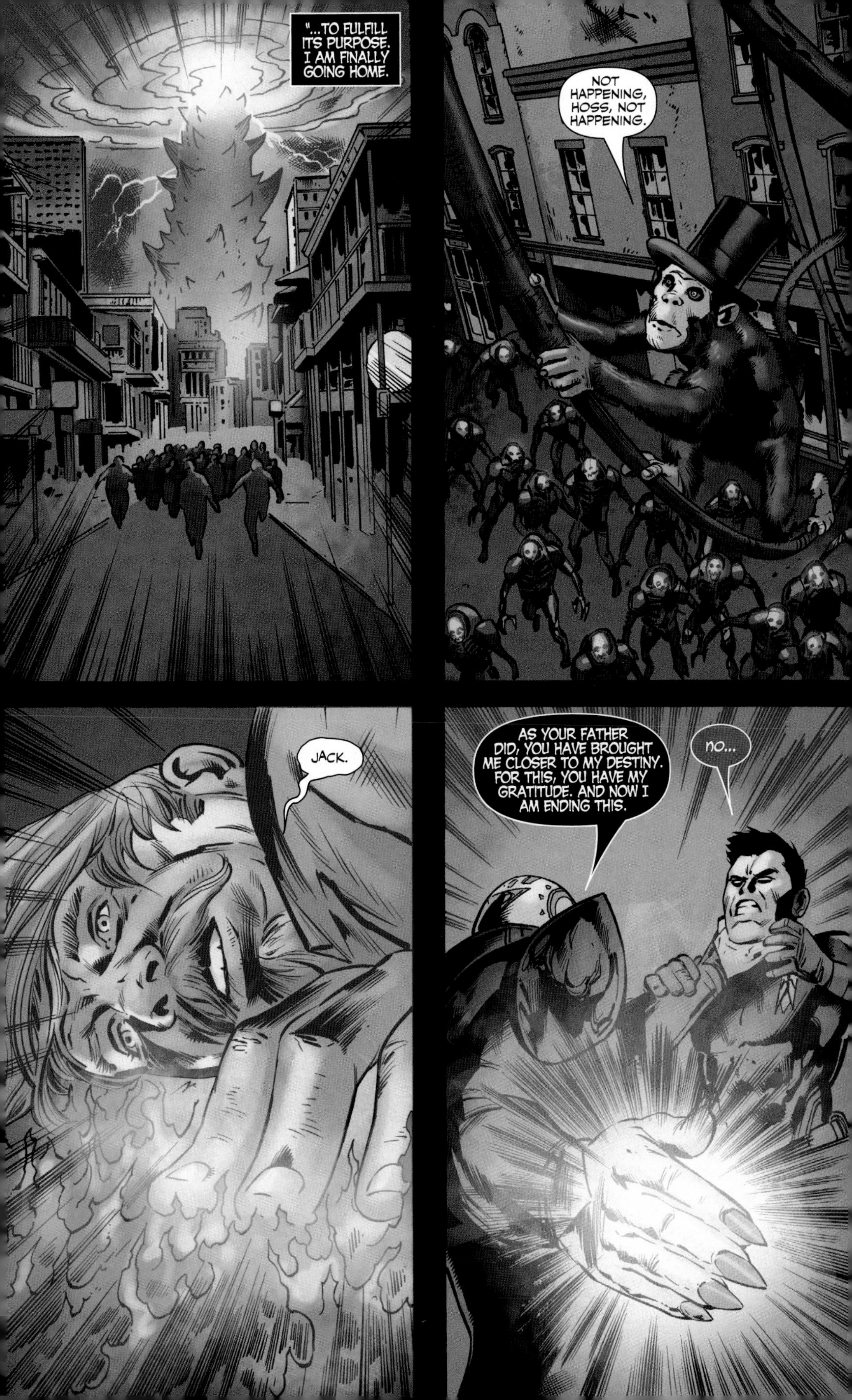
"...TO FULFILL ITS PURPOSE. I AM FINALLY GOING HOME.
NOT HAPPENING, HOSS, NOT HAPPENING.
JACK.
AS YOUR FATHER DID, YOU HAVE BROUGHT ME CLOSER TO MY DESTINY. FOR THIS, YOU HAVE MY GRATITUDE. AND NOW I AM ENDING THIS.
no...

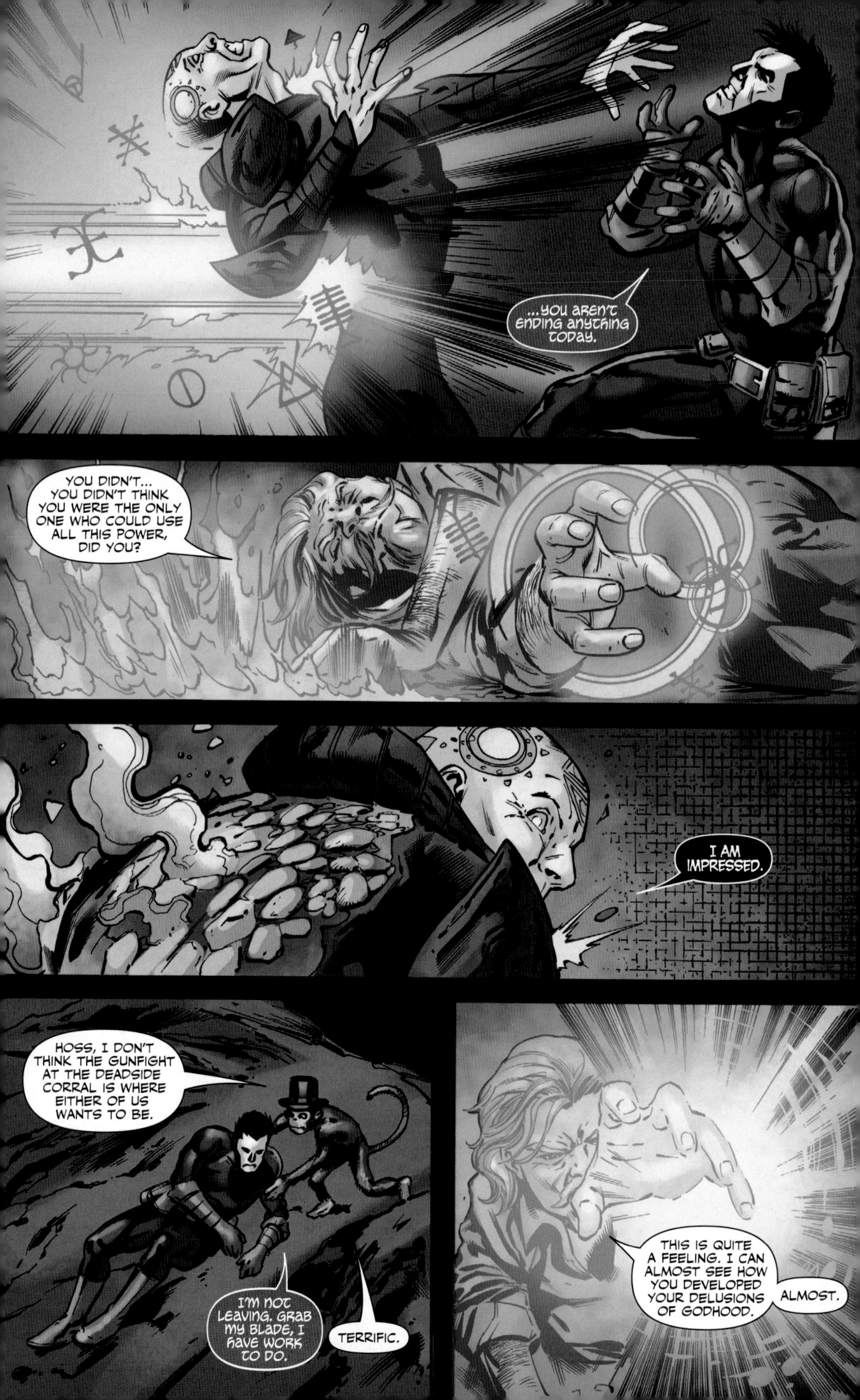
...YOU AREN'T ENDING ANYTHING TODAY.
YOU DIDN'T... YOU DIDN'T THINK YOU WERE THE ONLY ONE WHO COULD USE ALL THIS POWER, DID YOU?
I AM IMPRESSED.
HOSS, I DON'T THINK THE GUNFIGHT AT THE DEADSIDE CORRAL IS WHERE EITHER OF US WANTS TO BE.
I'M NOT LEAVING. GRAB MY BLADE, I HAVE WORK TO DO.
TERRIFIC.
THIS IS QUITE A FEELING. I CAN ALMOST SEE HOW YOU DEVELOPED YOUR DELUSIONS OF GODHOOD.
ALMOST.

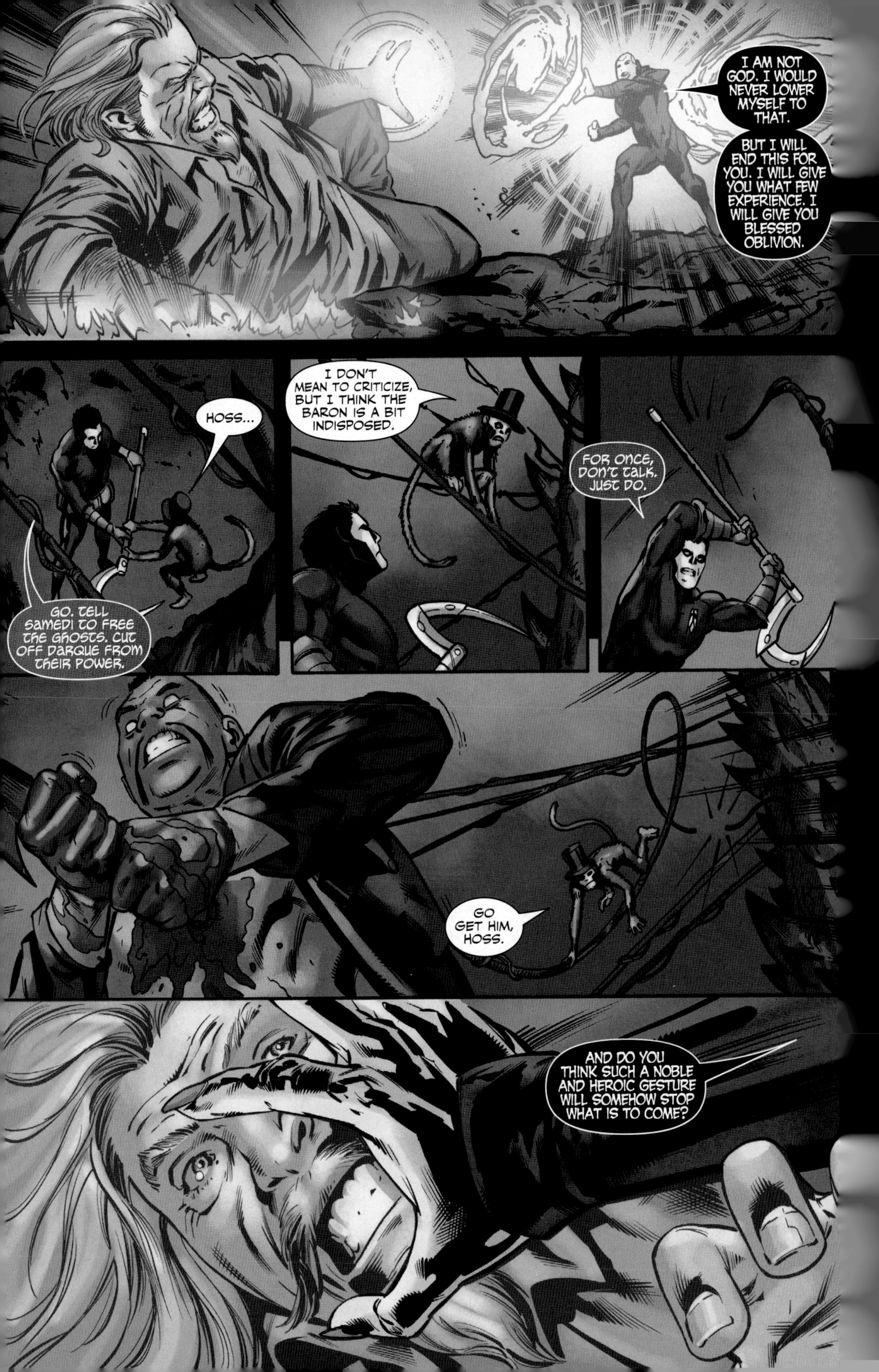
I AM NOT GOD. I WOULD NEVER LOWER MYSELF TO THAT.
BUT I WILL END THIS FOR YOU. I WILL GIVE YOU WHAT FEW EXPERIENCE. I WILL GIVE YOU BLESSED OBLIVION.
HOSS...
GO. TELL SAMEDI TO FREE THE GHOSTS. CUT OFF DARQUE FROM THEIR POWER.
I DON'T MEAN TO CRITICIZE, BUT I THINK THE BARON IS A BIT INDISPOSED.
FOR ONCE, DON'T TALK. JUST DO.
GO GET HIM, HOSS.
AND DO YOU THINK SUCH A NOBLE AND HEROIC GESTURE WILL SOMEHOW STOP WHAT IS TO COME?

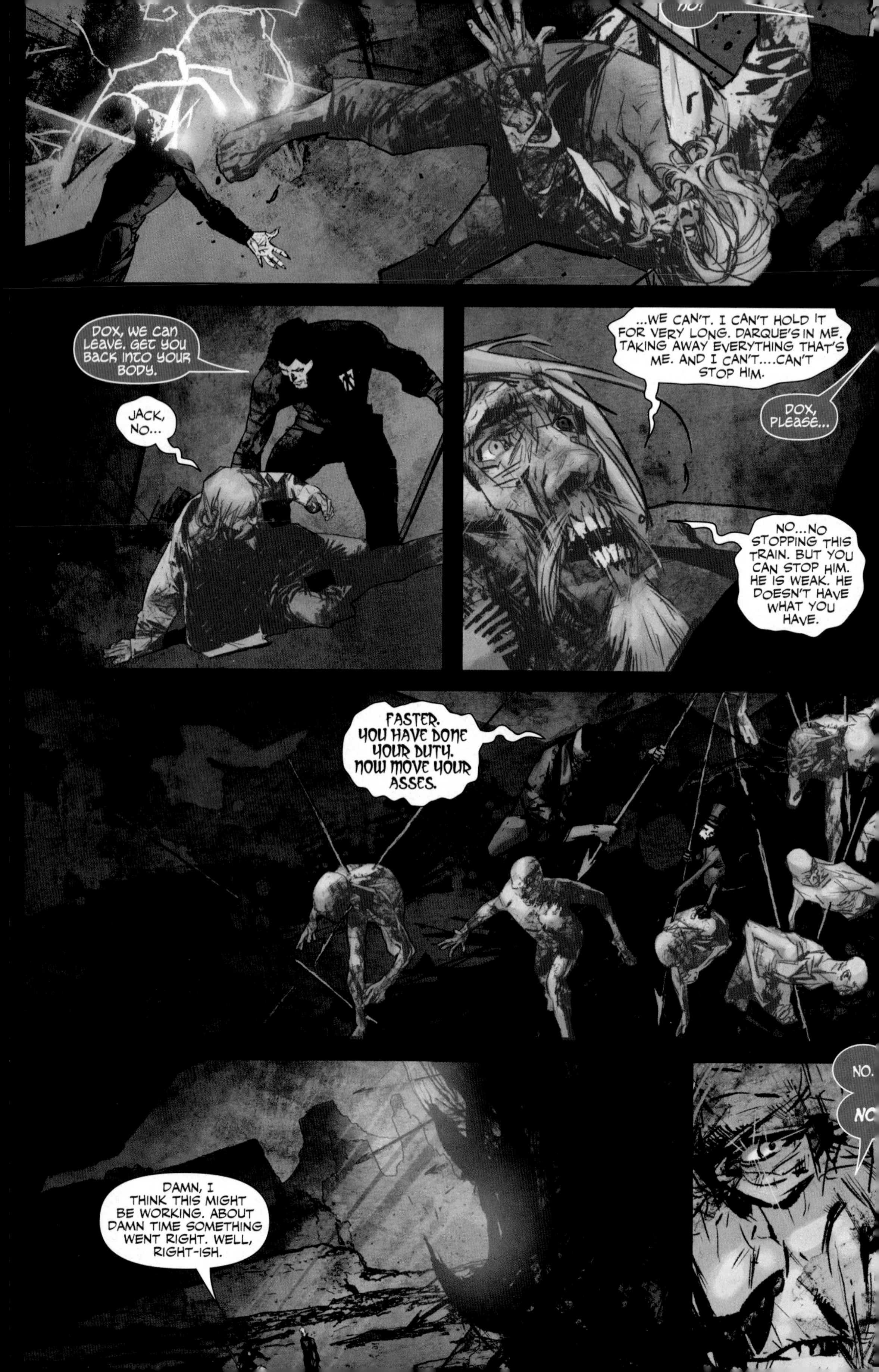
NO!
DOX, WE CAN LEAVE. GET YOU BACK INTO YOUR BODY.
JACK, NO...
...WE CAN'T. I CAN'T HOLD IT FOR VERY LONG. DARQUE'S IN ME. TAKING AWAY EVERYTHING THAT'S ME. AND I CAN'T....CAN'T STOP HIM.
DOX, PLEASE...
NO...NO STOPPING THIS TRAIN. BUT YOU CAN STOP HIM. HE IS WEAK. HE DOESN'T HAVE WHAT YOU HAVE.
FASTER. YOU HAVE DONE YOUR DUTY. NOW MOVE YOUR ASSES.
DAMN, I THINK THIS MIGHT BE WORKING. ABOUT DAMN TIME SOMETHING WENT RIGHT. WELL, RIGHT-ISH.
NO.

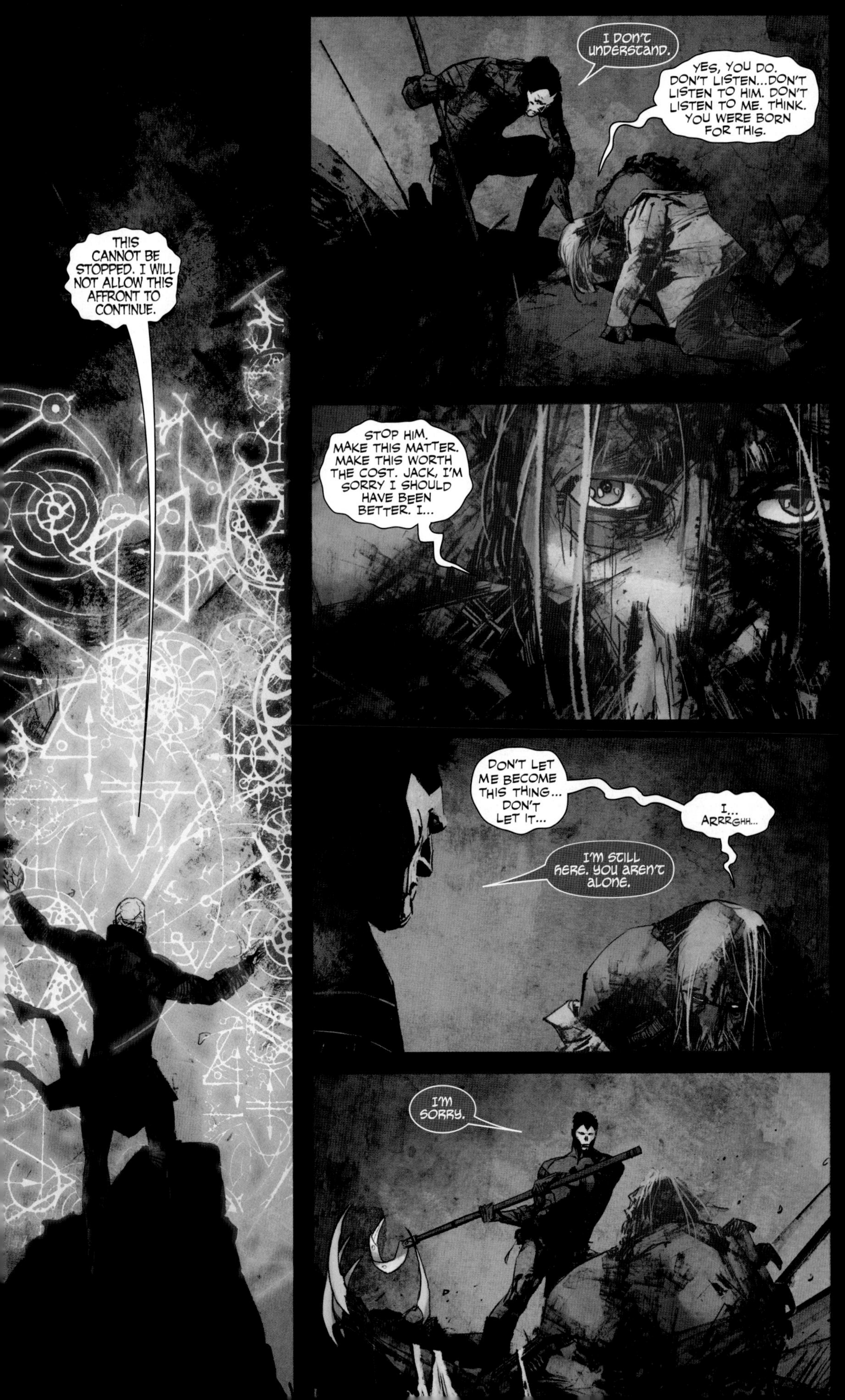
THIS CANNOT BE STOPPED. I WILL NOT ALLOW THIS AFFRONT TO CONTINUE.
I DON'T UNDERSTAND.
YES, YOU DO. DON'T LISTEN...DON'T LISTEN TO HIM. DON'T LISTEN TO ME. THINK. YOU WERE BORN FOR THIS.
STOP HIM. MAKE THIS MATTER. MAKE THIS WORTH THE COST. JACK, I'M SORRY I SHOULD HAVE BEEN BETTER. I...
DON'T LET ME BECOME THIS THING... DON'T LET IT...
I... ARRRGHH...
I'M STILL HERE. YOU AREN'T ALONE.
I'M SORRY.

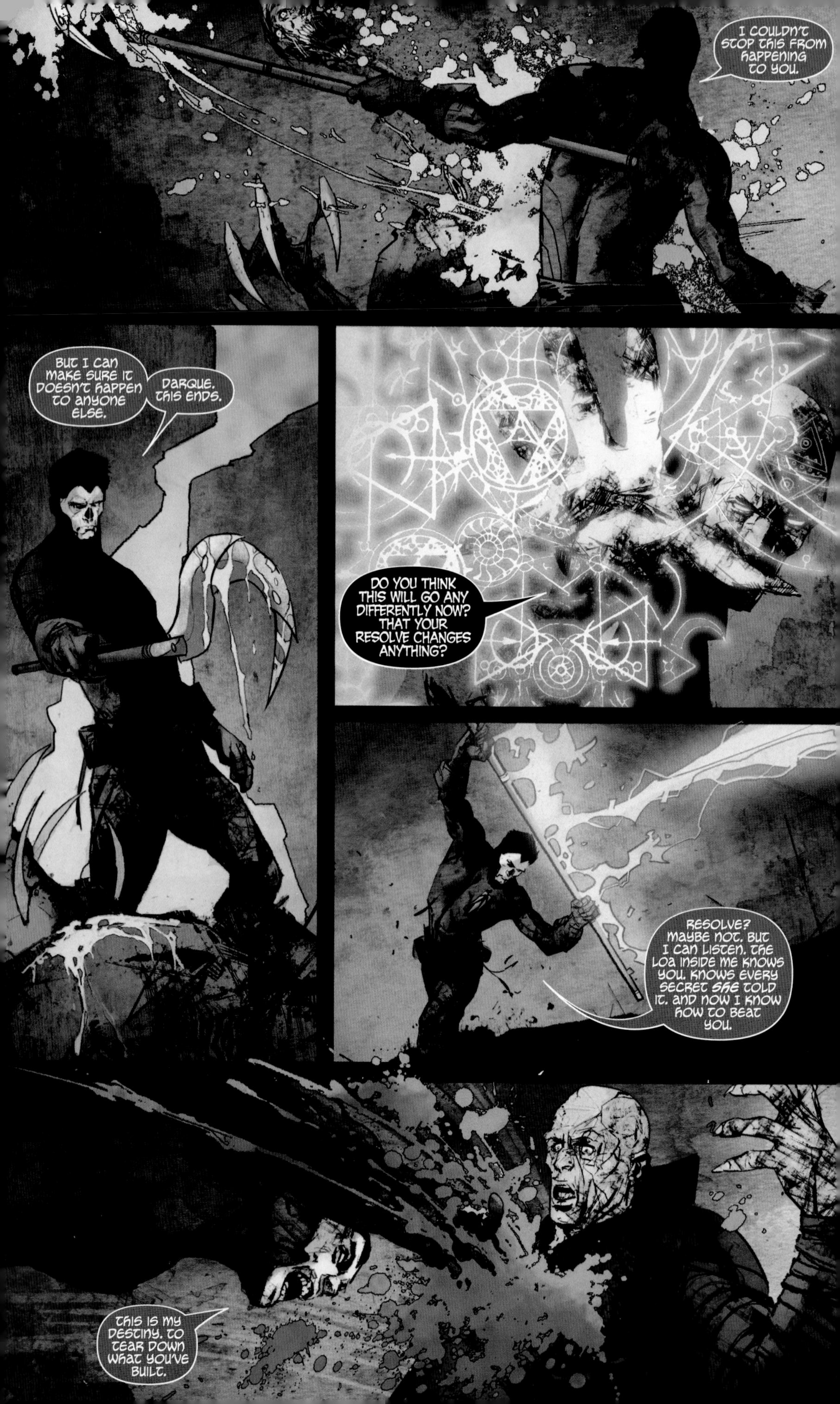
I COULDN'T STOP THIS FROM HAPPENING TO YOU.
BUT I CAN MAKE SURE IT DOESN'T HAPPEN TO ANYONE ELSE.
DARQUE. THIS ENDS.
DO YOU THINK THIS WILL GO ANY DIFFERENTLY NOW? THAT YOUR RESOLVE CHANGES ANYTHING?
RESOLVE? MAYBE NOT. BUT I CAN LISTEN. THE LOA INSIDE ME KNOWS YOU. KNOWS EVERY SECRET SHE TOLD IT. AND NOW I KNOW HOW TO BEAT YOU.
THIS IS MY DESTINY. TO TEAR DOWN WHAT YOU'VE BUILT.

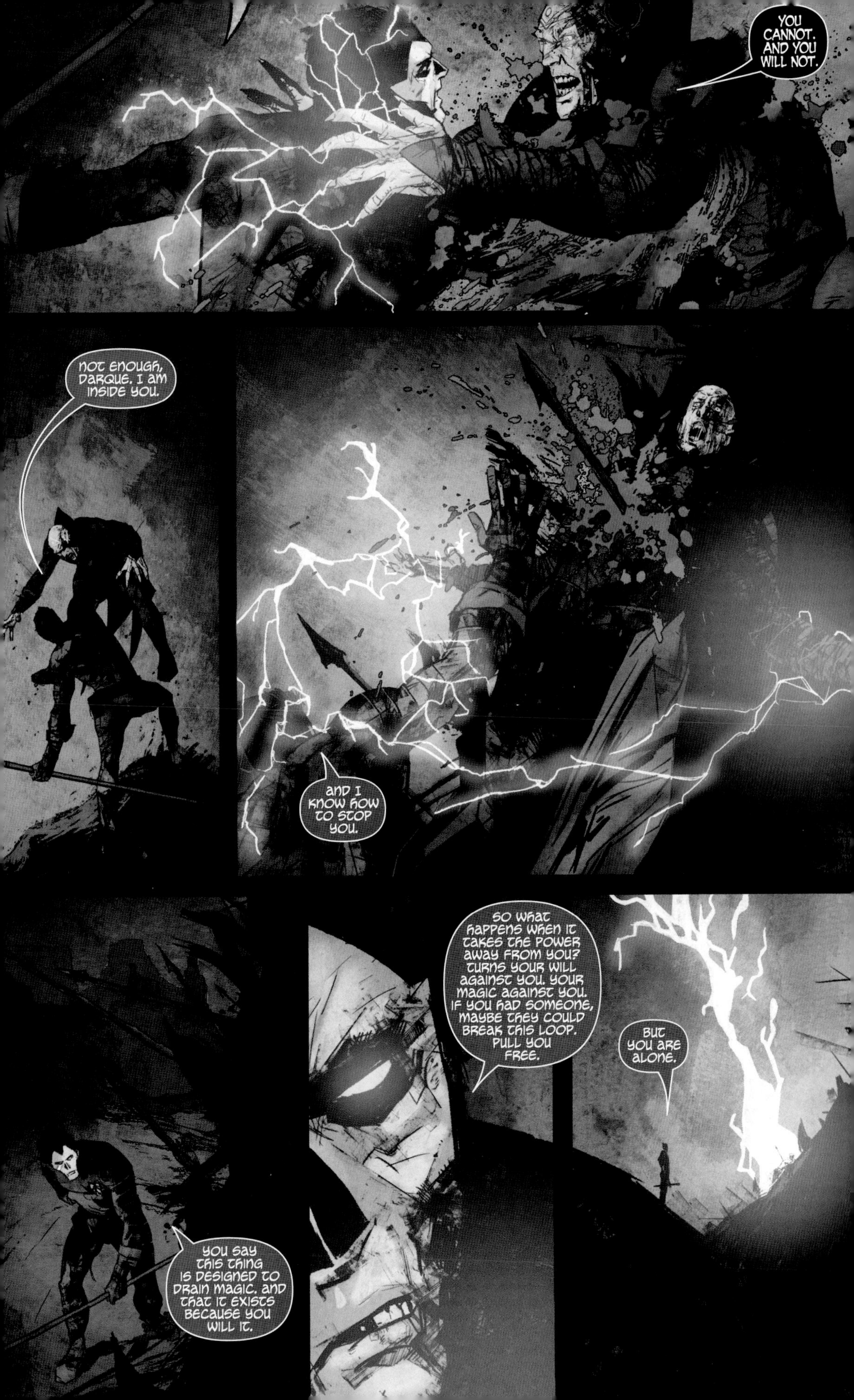
YOU CANNOT. AND YOU WILL NOT.
NOT ENOUGH, DARQUE. I AM INSIDE YOU.
AND I KNOW HOW TO STOP YOU.
YOU SAY THIS THING IS DESIGNED TO DRAIN MAGIC. AND THAT IT EXISTS BECAUSE YOU WILL IT.
SO WHAT HAPPENS WHEN IT TAKES THE POWER AWAY FROM YOU? TURNS YOUR WILL AGAINST YOU. YOUR MAGIC AGAINST YOU. IF YOU HAD SOMEONE, MAYBE THEY COULD BREAK THIS LOOP. PULL YOU FREE.
BUT YOU ARE ALONE.

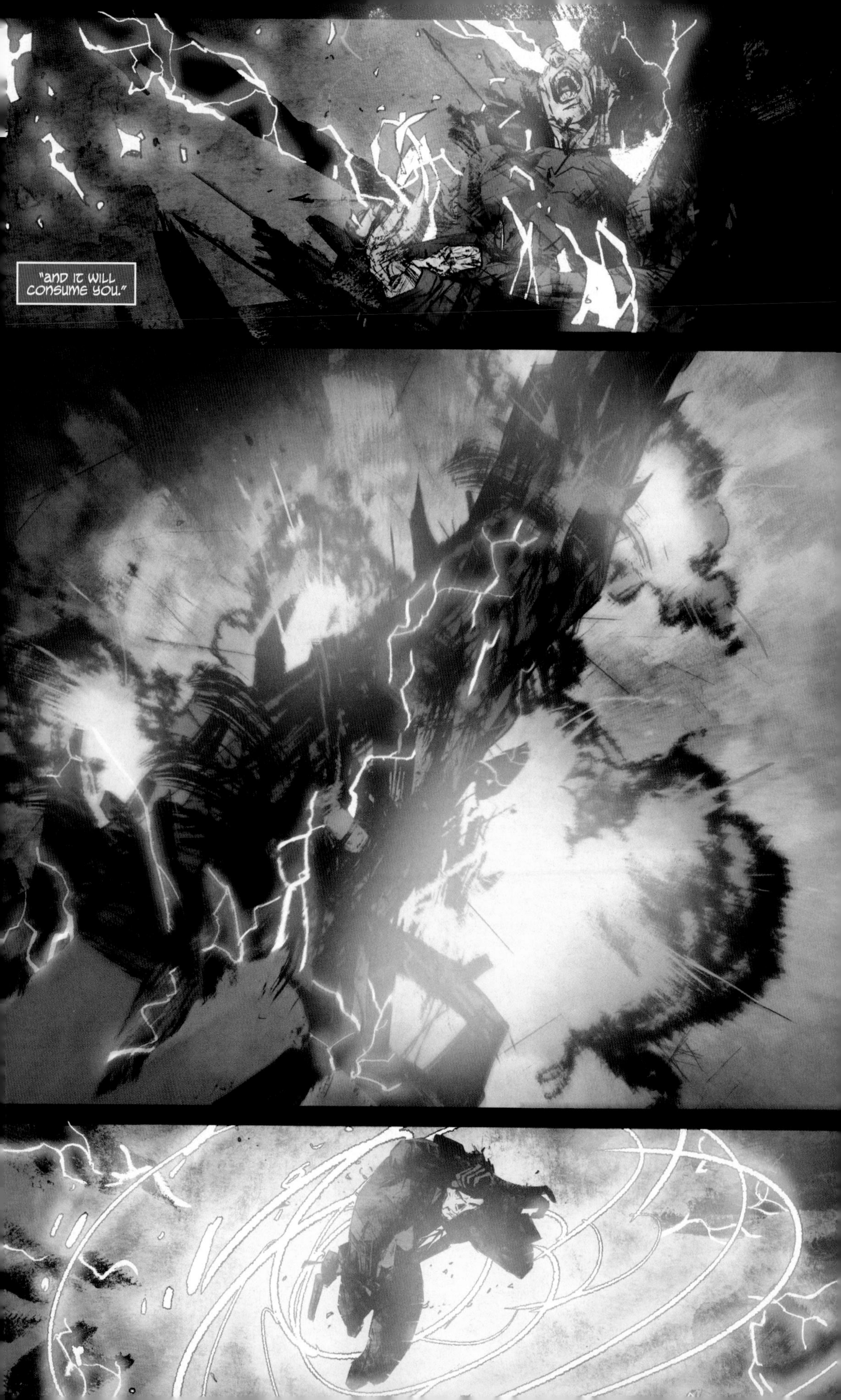
"AND IT WILL CONSUME YOU."

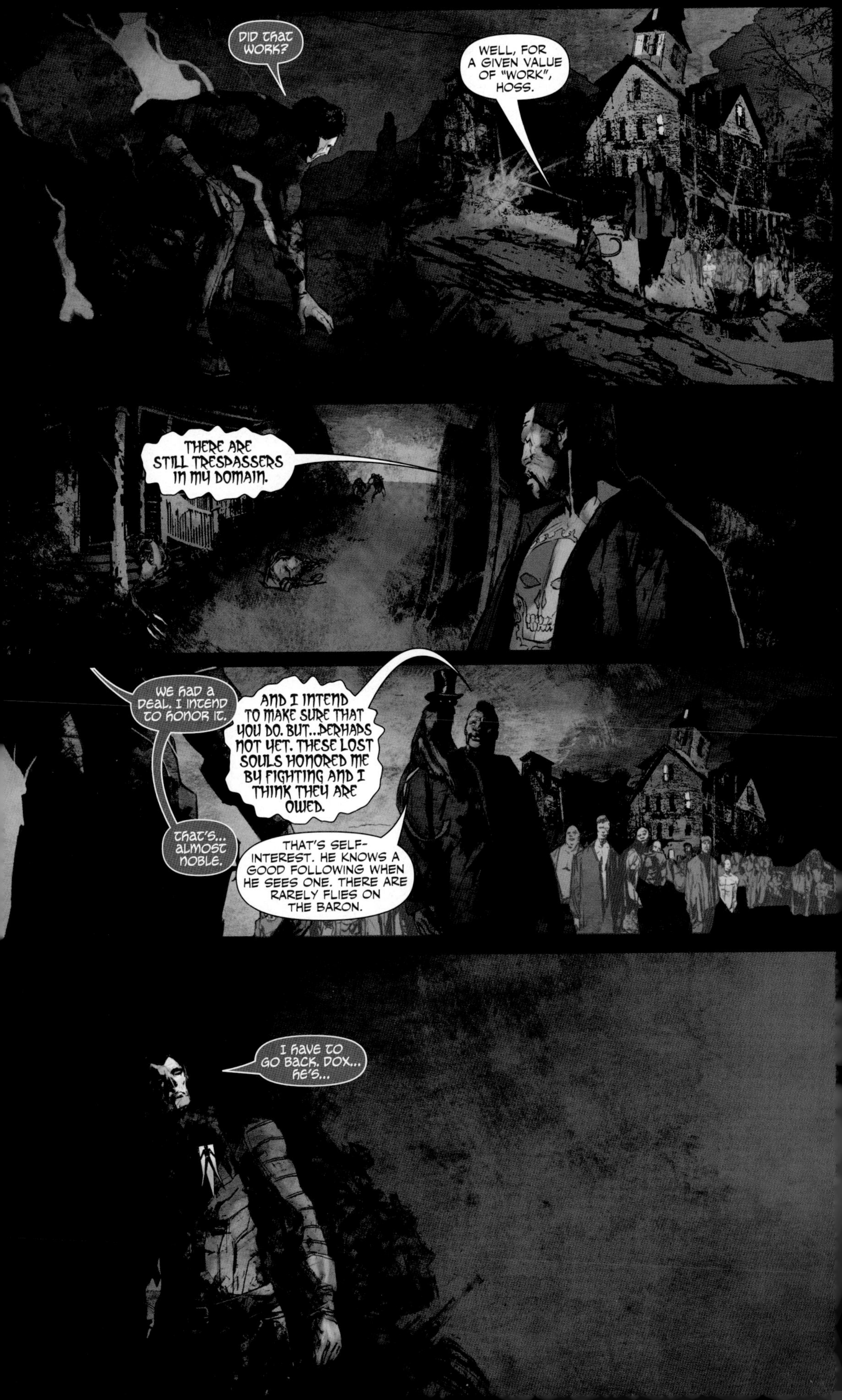

DID THAT WORK?
WELL, FOR A GIVEN VALUE OF "WORK", HOSS.
THERE ARE STILL TRESPASSERS IN MY DOMAIN.
WE HAD A DEAL. I INTEND TO HONOR IT.
AND I INTEND TO MAKE SURE THAT YOU DO. BUT...PERHAPS NOT YET. THESE LOST SOULS HONORED ME BY FIGHTING AND I THINK THEY ARE OWED.
THAT'S... ALMOST NOBLE.
THAT'S SELF-INTEREST. HE KNOWS A GOOD FOLLOWING WHEN HE SEES ONE. THERE ARE RARELY FLIES ON THE BARON.
I HAVE TO GO BACK, DOX... HE'S...

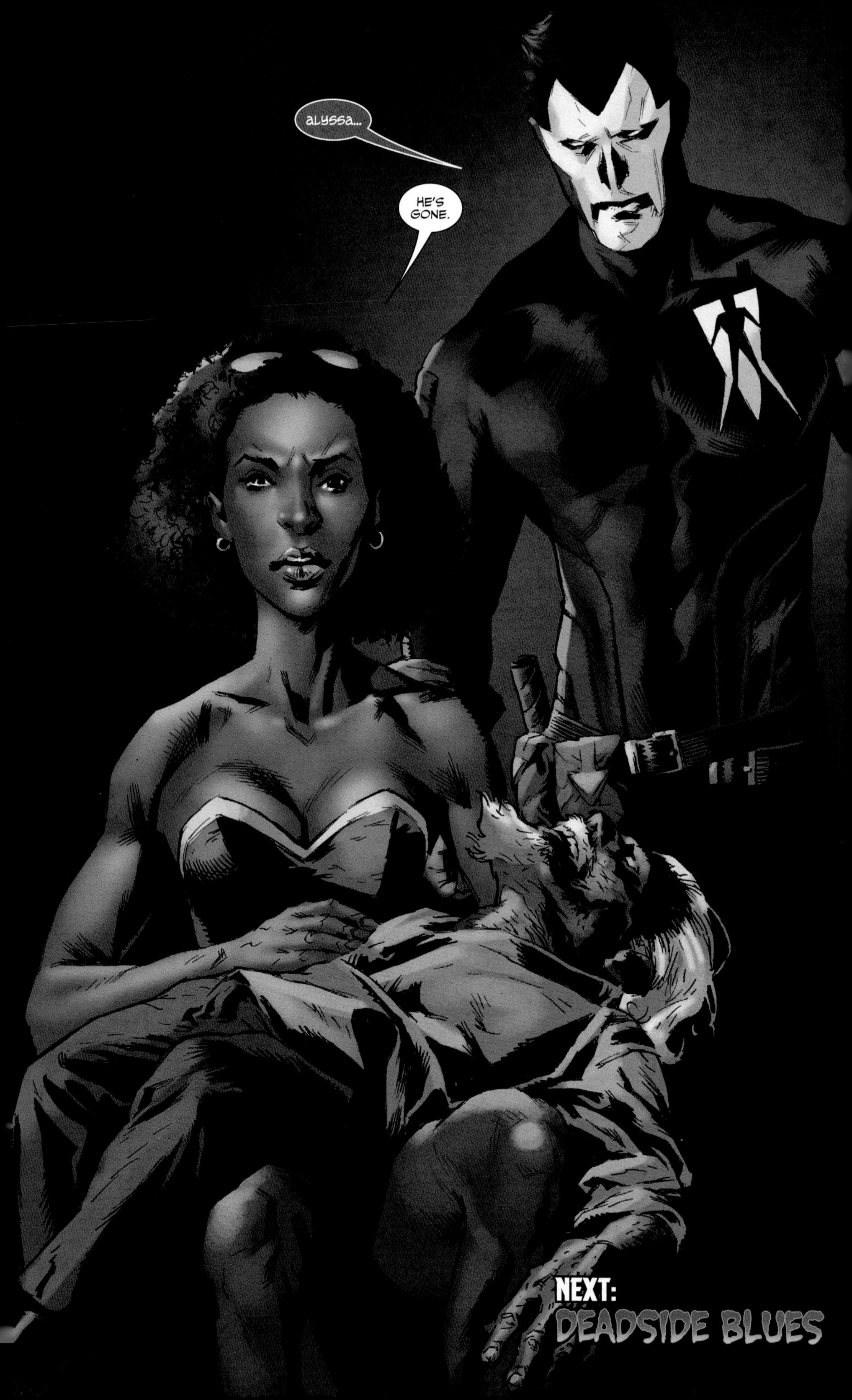
aLyssa...
HE'S GONE.
NEXT:
DEADSIDE BLUES

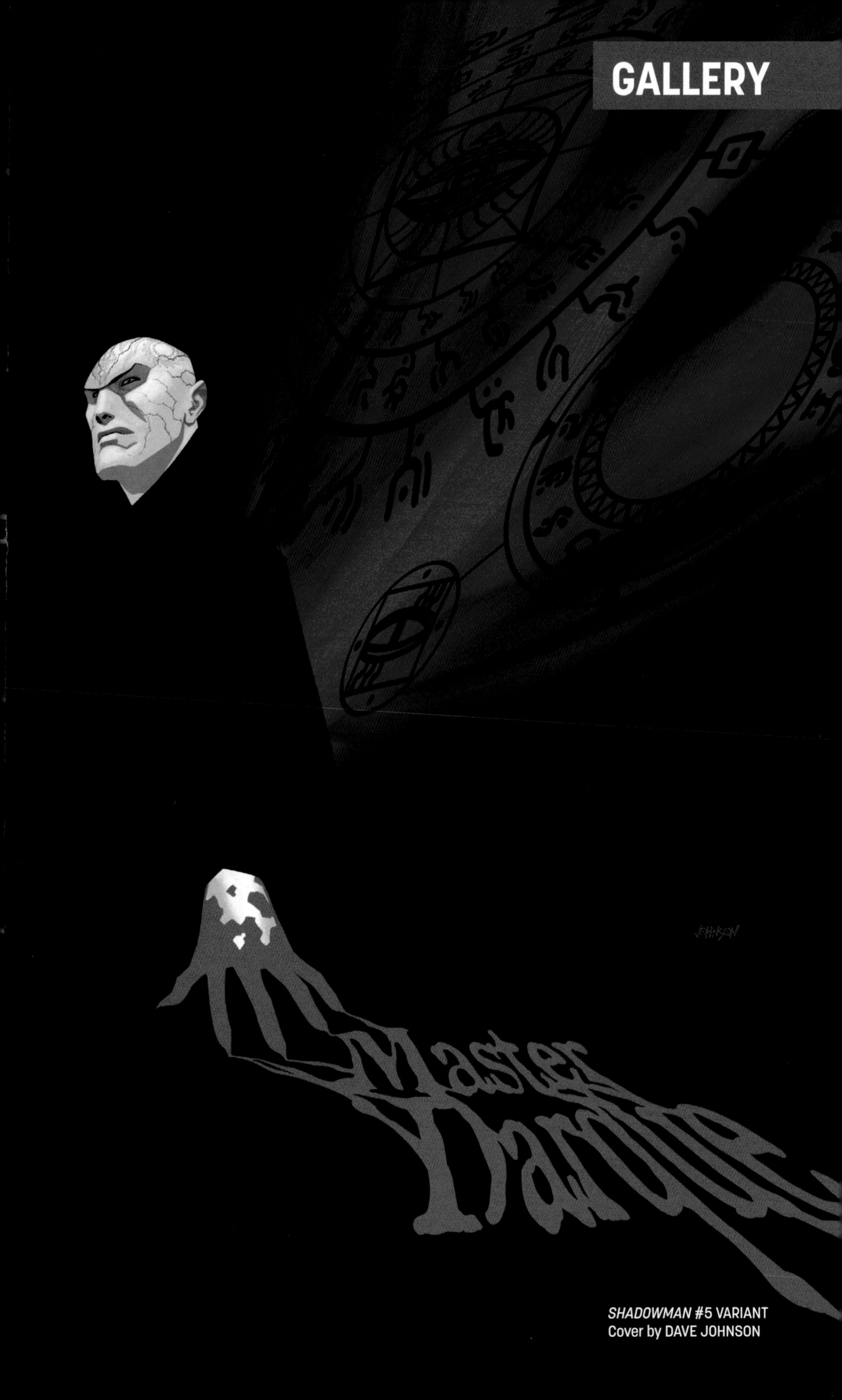
JOHNSON
Master Darque

SHADOWMAN #5 VARIANT
Cover by DAVE JOHNSON

SHADOWMAN #5 VARIANT
Cover by RAFAEL GRAMPÁ

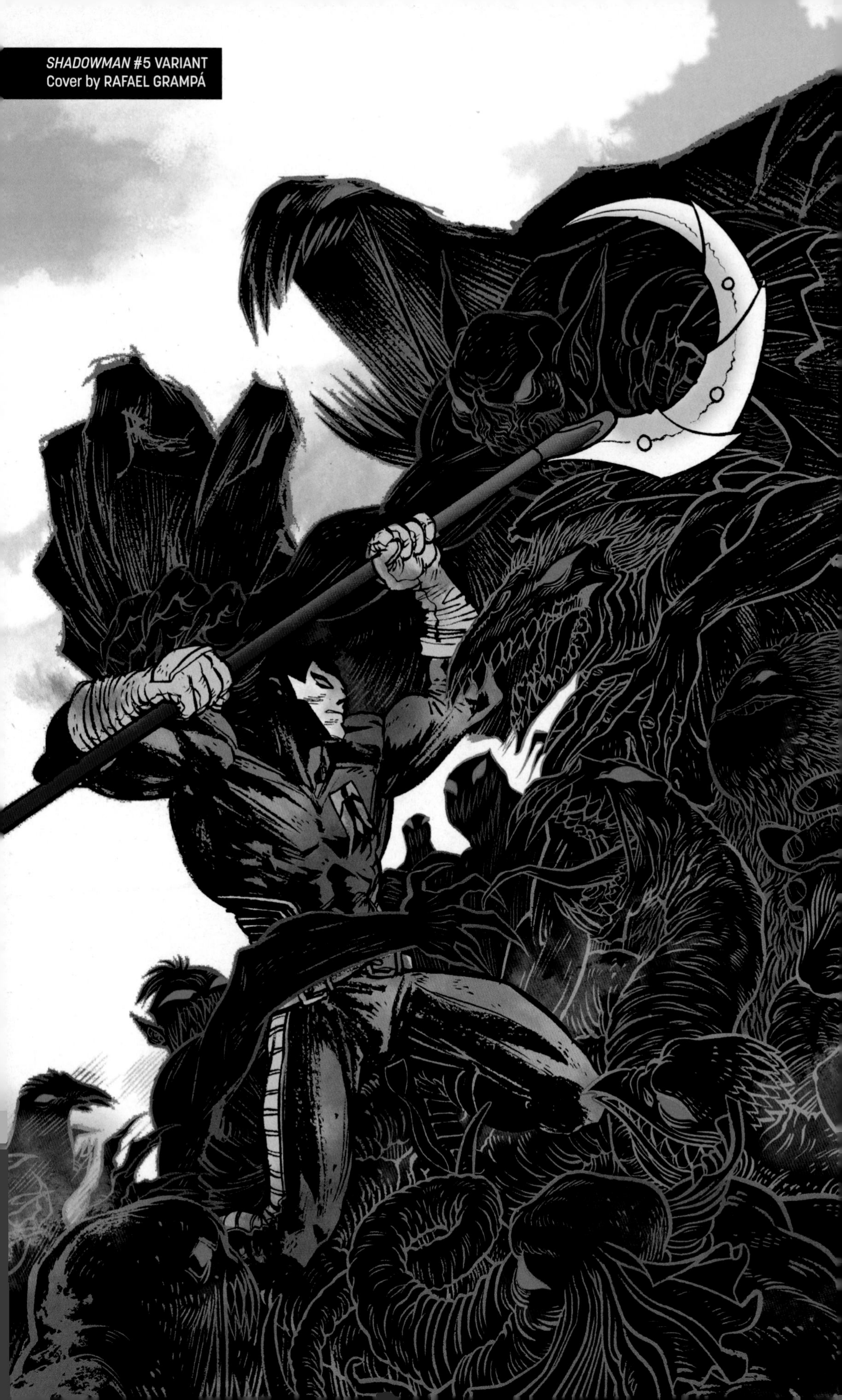

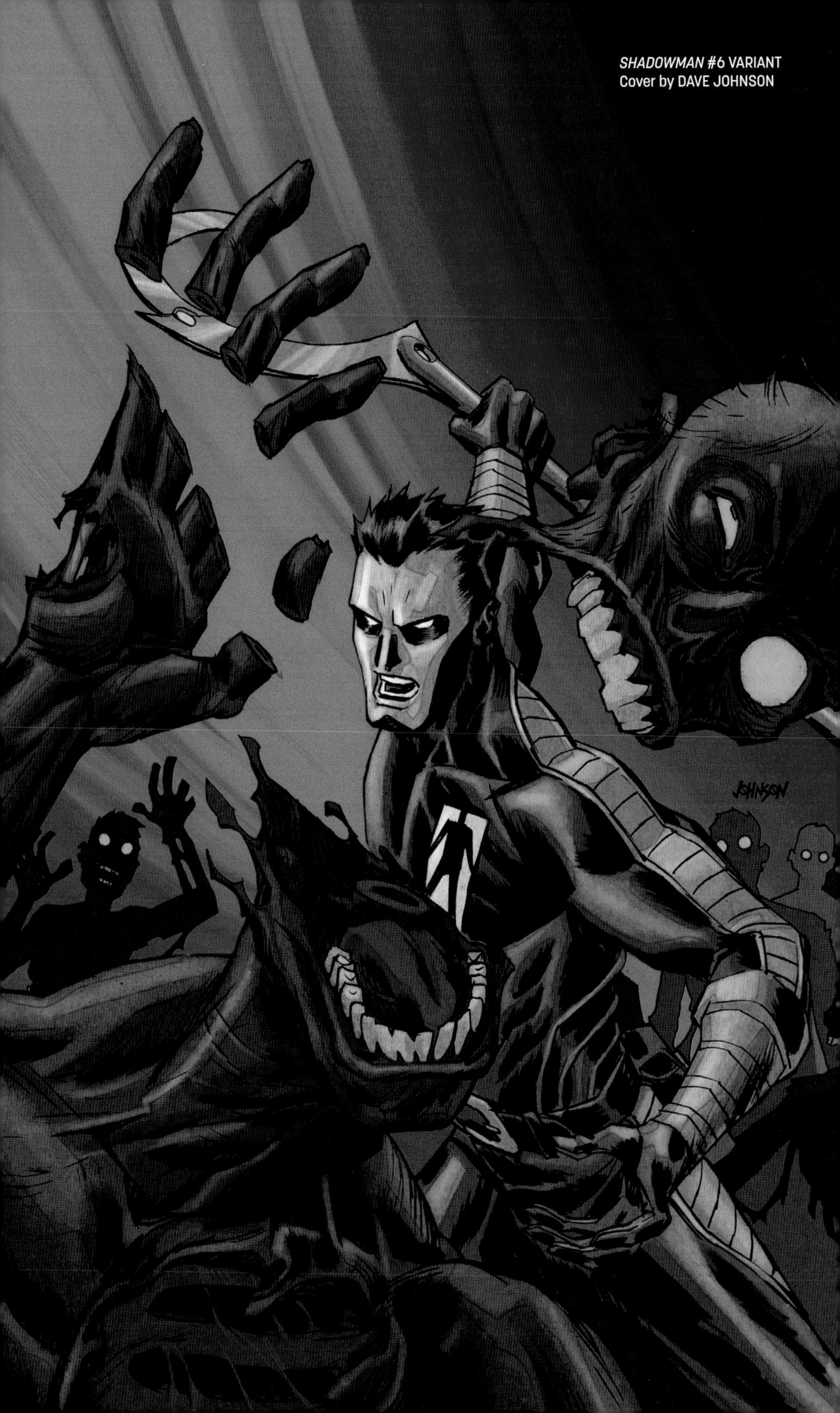
JOHNSON
SHADOWMAN #6 VARIANT
Cover by DAVE JOHNSON

SHADOWMAN #6 COVER
Pencils and inks by PATRICK ZIRCHER

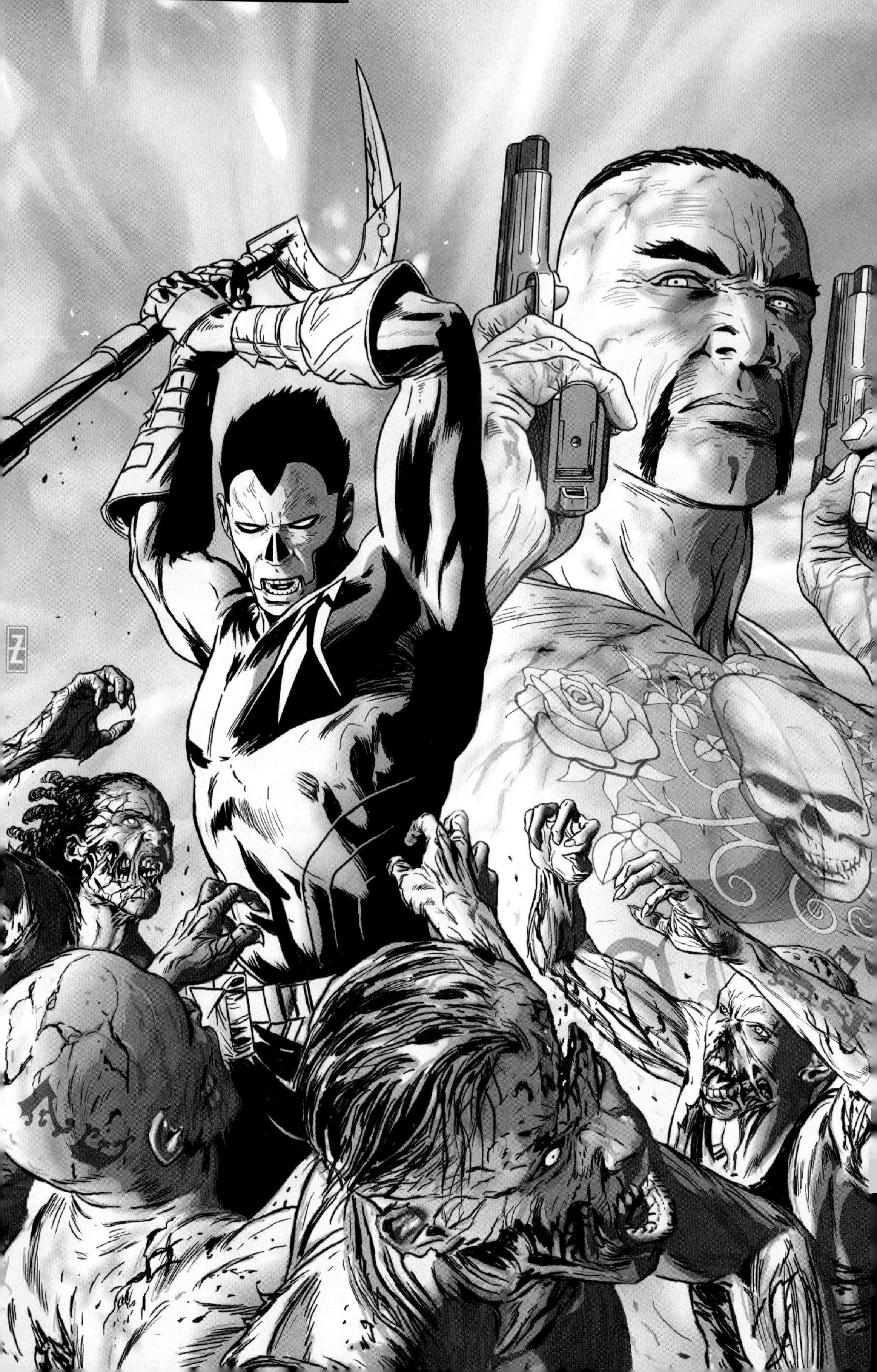

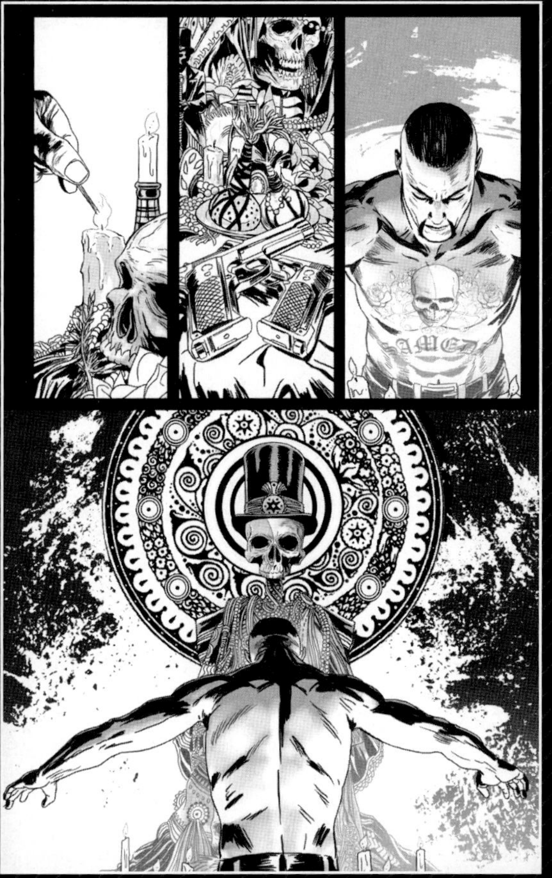

Shadowman #6, p.1
Pencils and inks by PATRICK ZIRCHER

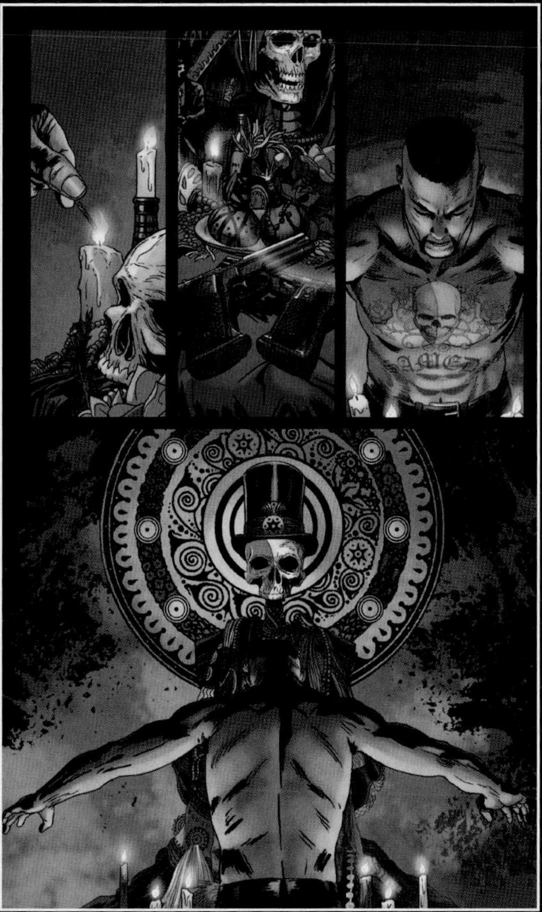

Shadowman #6, p.1
Colors by BRIAN REBER

Shadowman #6, p. 2
Pencils and inks by PATRICK ZIRCHER

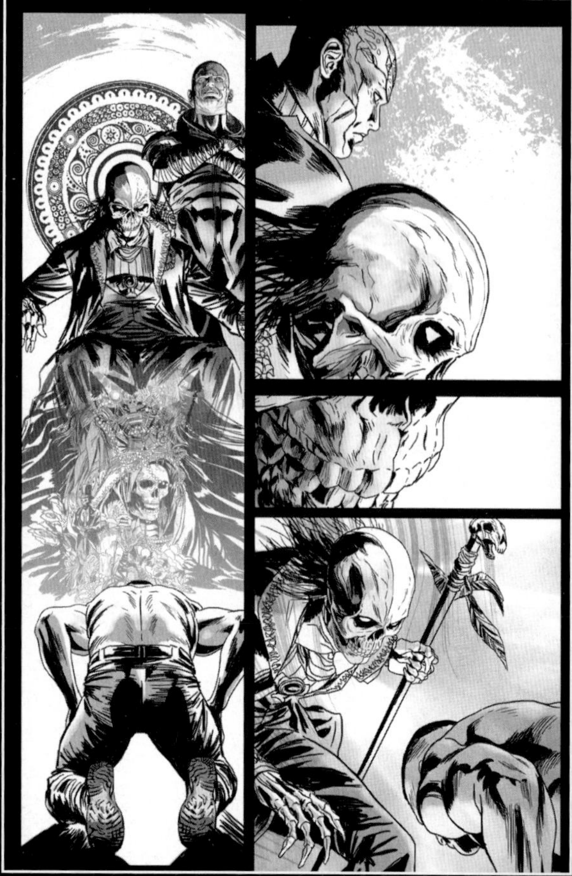

Shadowman #6, p. 2
Colors by BRIAN REBER

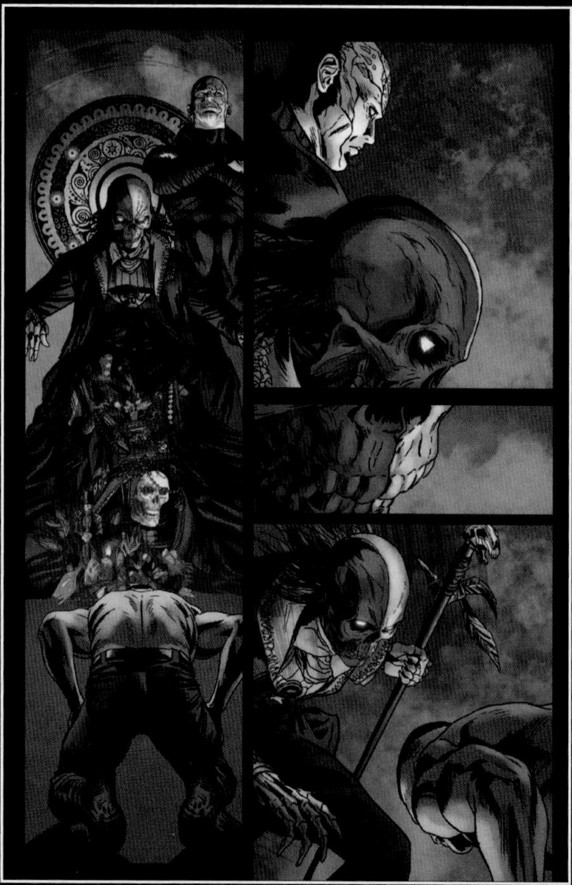

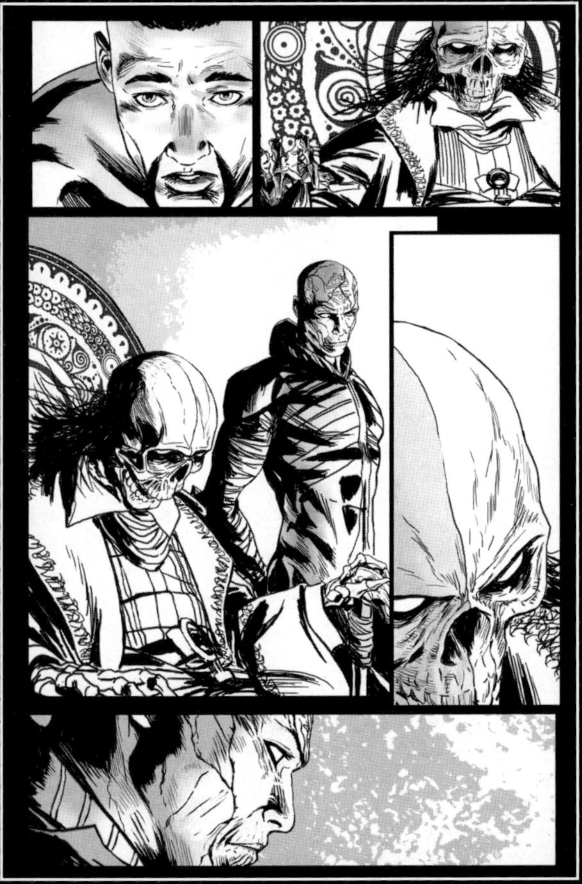

Shadowman #6, p. 3
Pencils and inks by PATRICK ZIRCHER

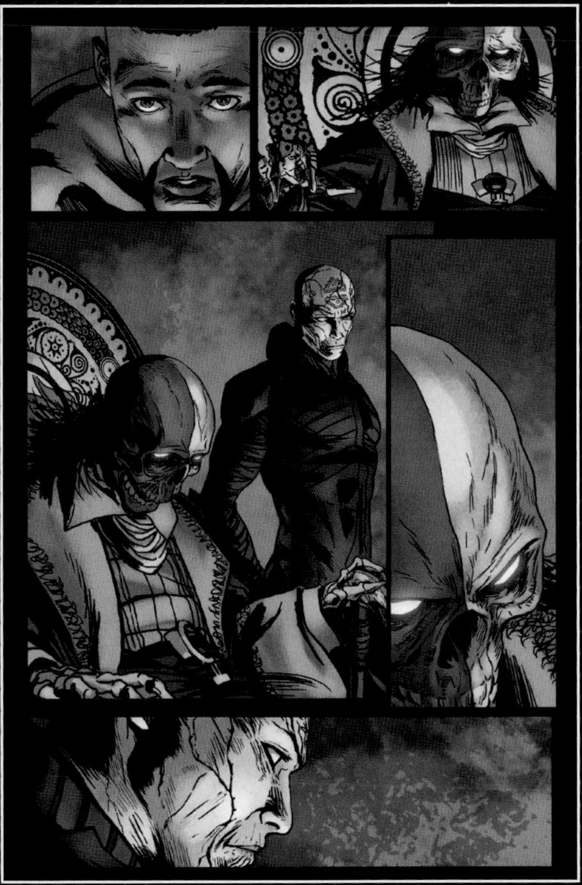

Shadowman #6, p. 3
Colors by BRIAN REBER

Shadowman #6, p. 4
Pencils and inks by PATRICK ZIRCHER

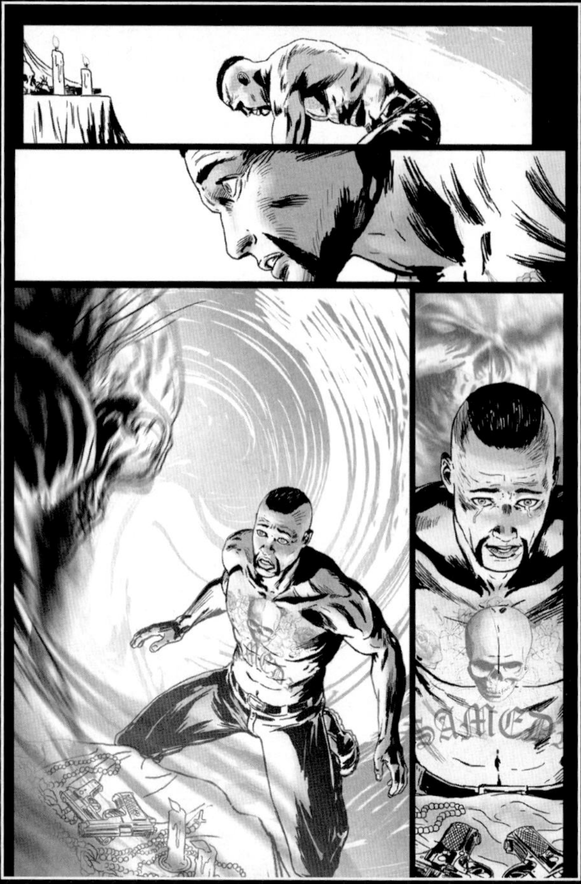

Shadowman #6, p. 4
Colors by BRIAN REBER

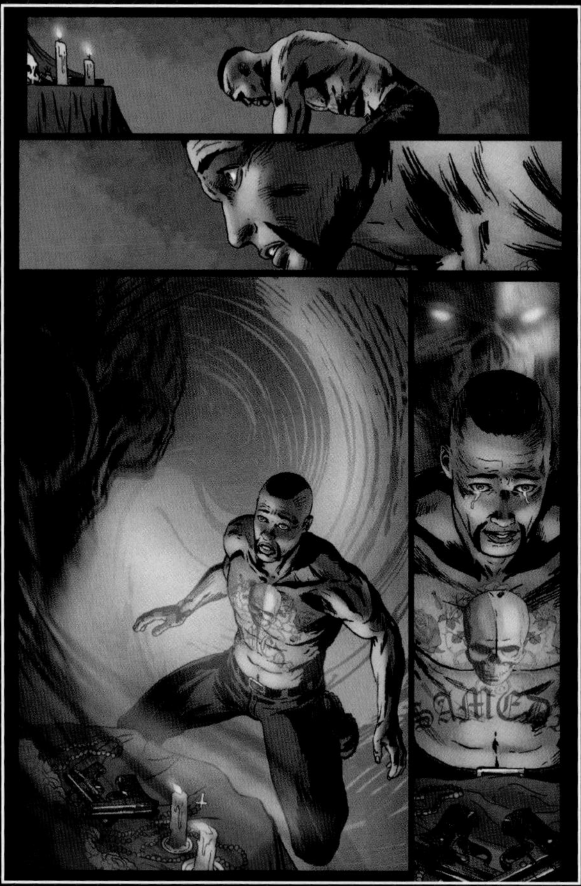

SHADOWMAN #7 COVER
Pencils and inks by PATRICK ZIRCHER

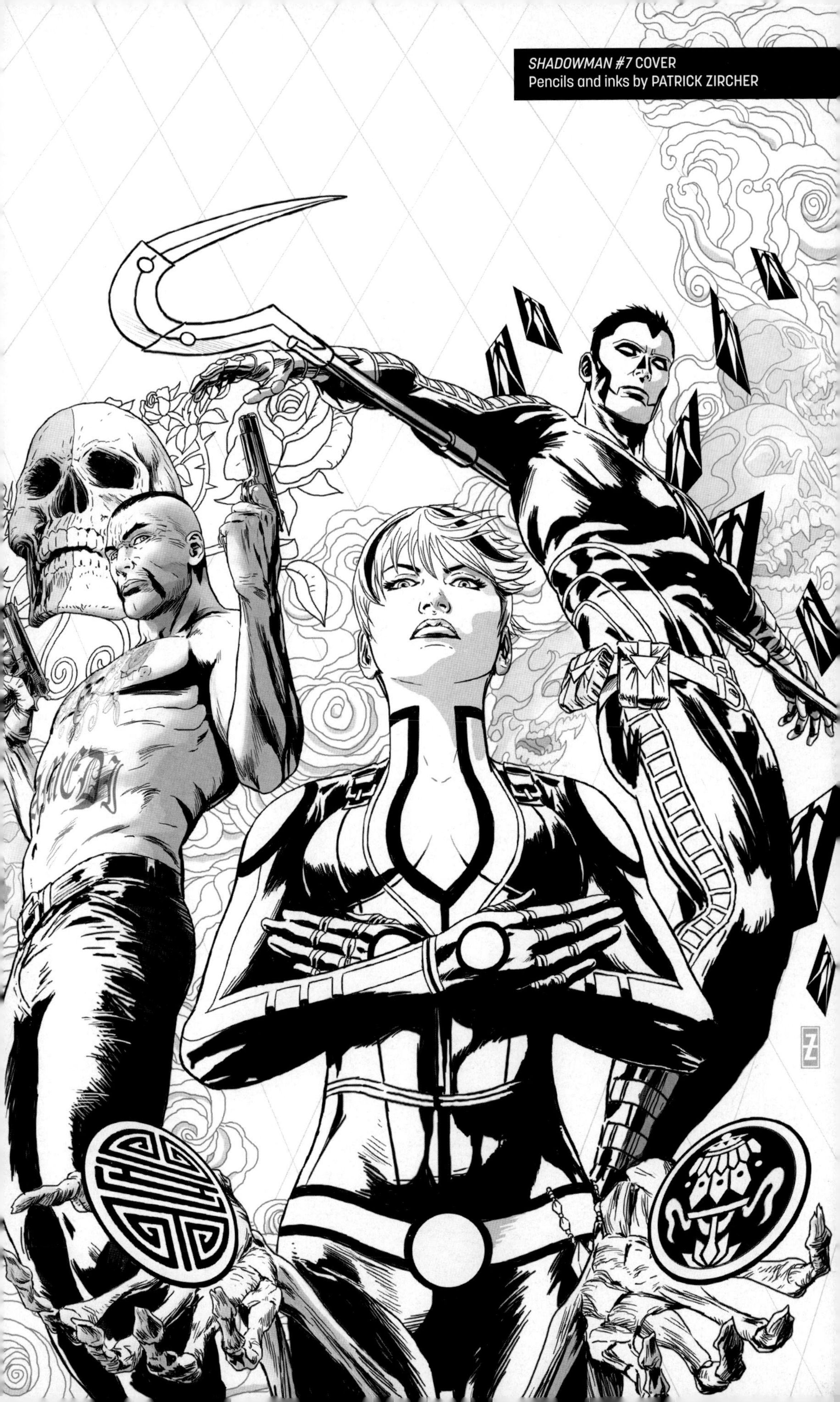

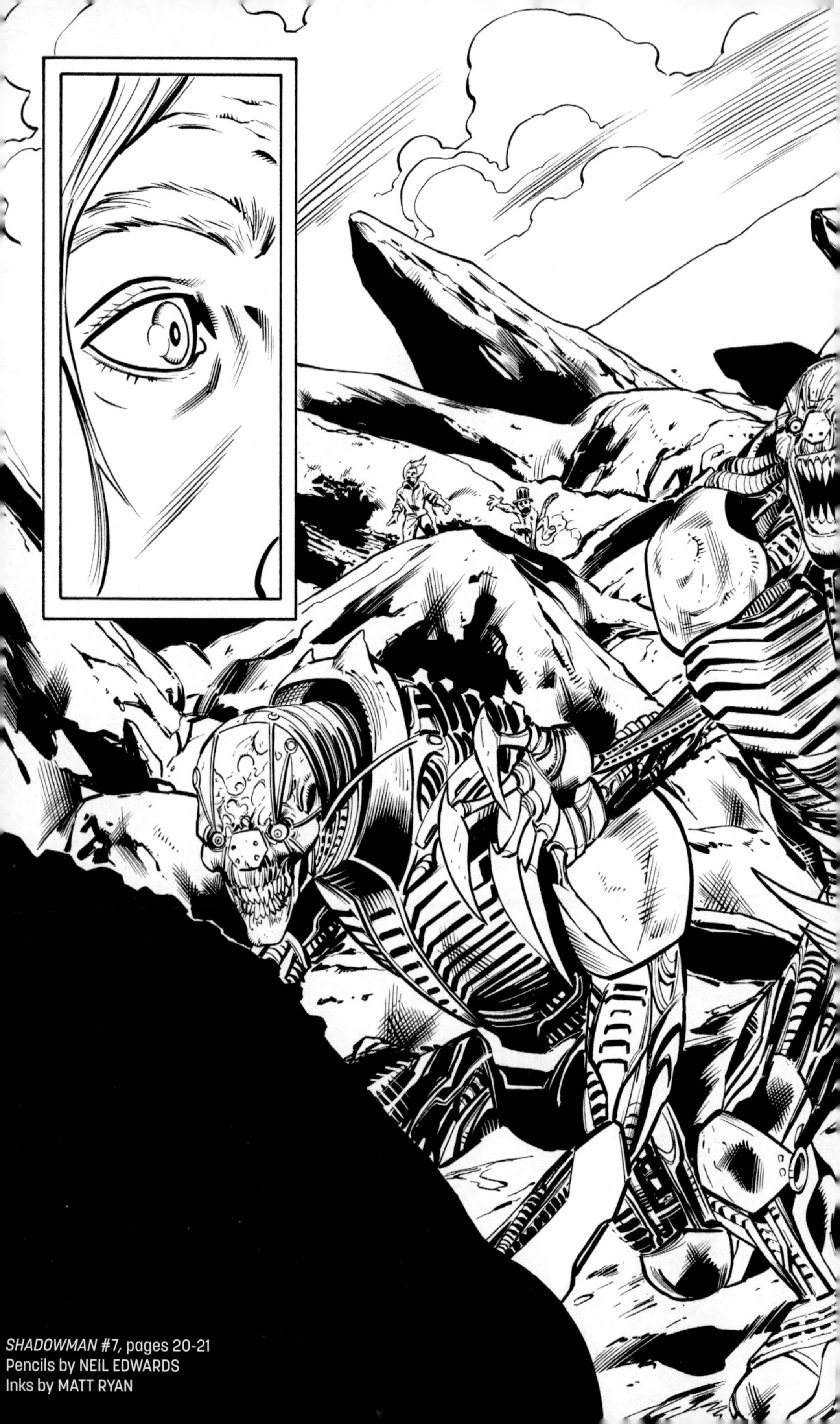

SHADOWMAN #7, pages 20-21
Pencils by NEIL EDWARDS
Inks by MATT RYAN

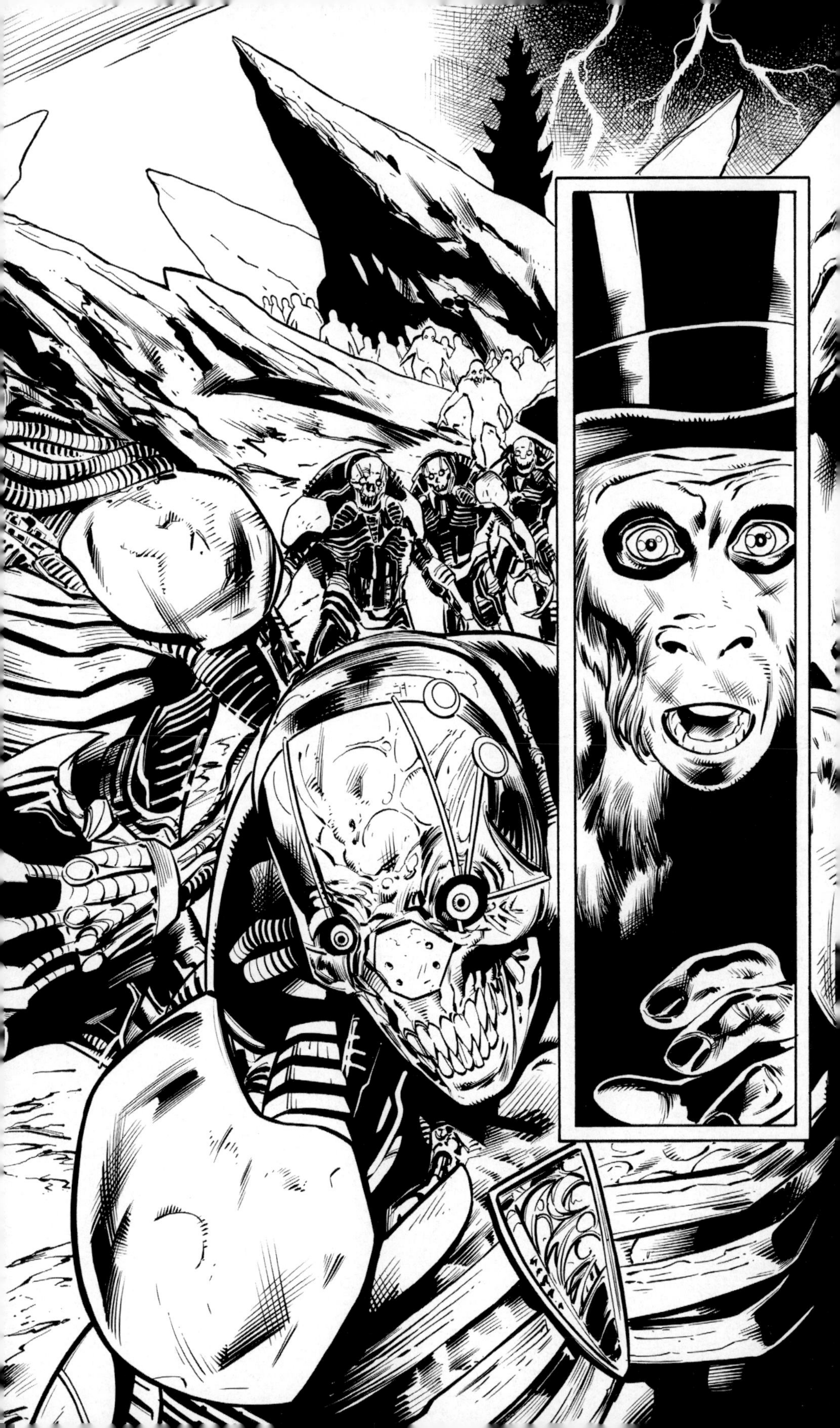

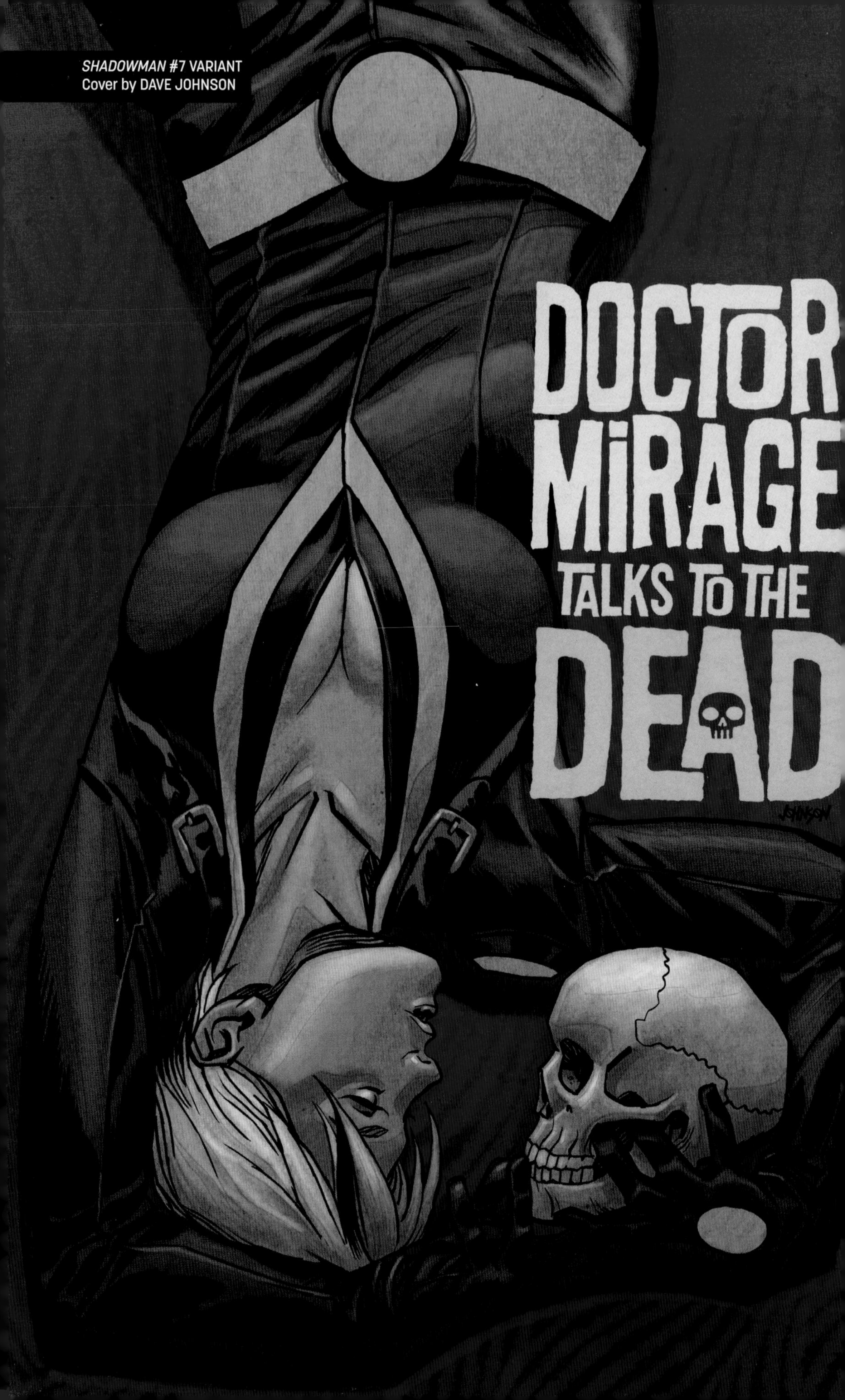
DOCTOR
MiRAGE
TALKS TO THE
DEAD
JOHNSON

SHADOWMAN #7 VARIANT
Cover by DAVE JOHNSON

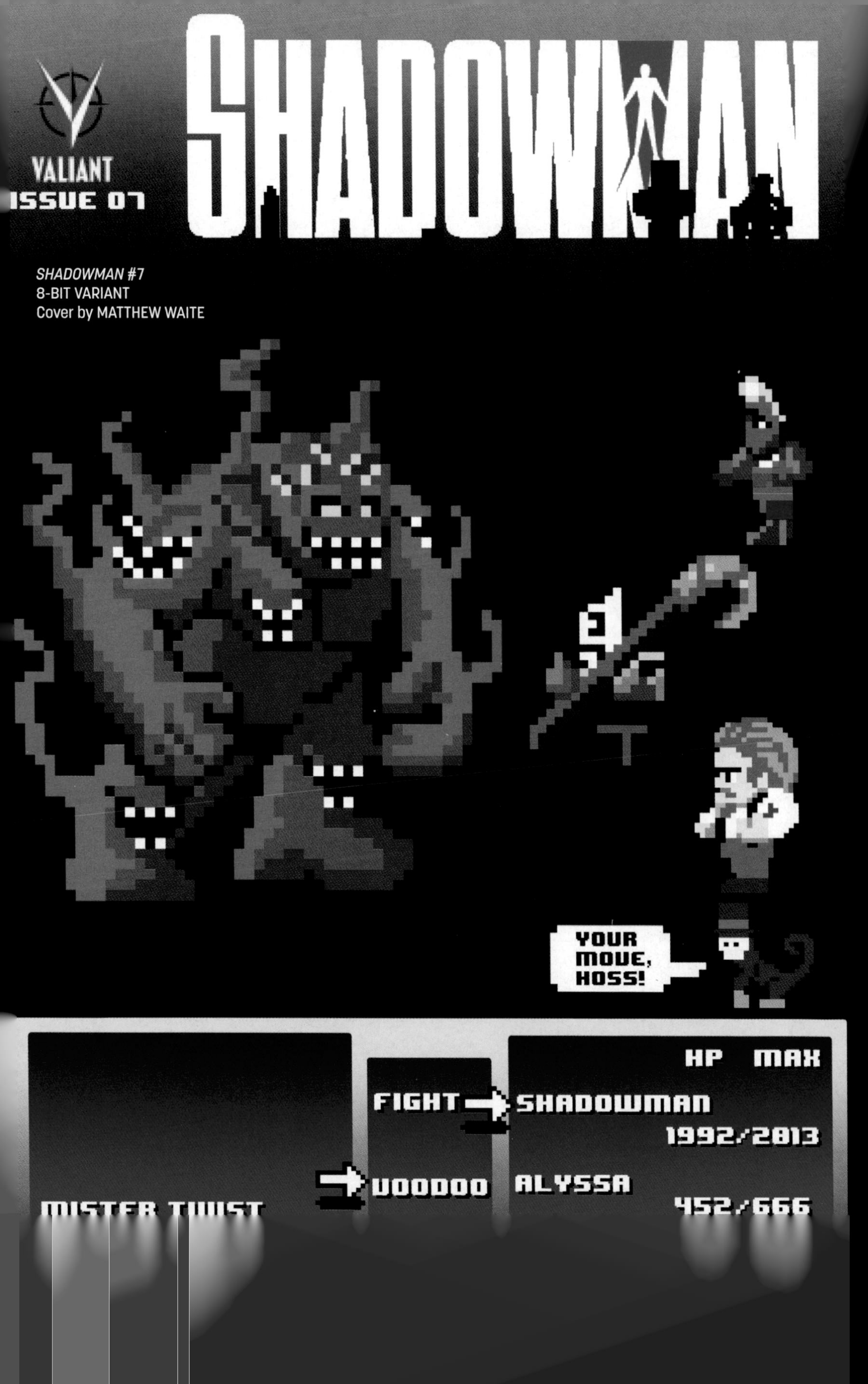
VALIANT
ISSUE 07
SHADOWMAN
YOUR MOVE, HOSS!
HP MAX
FIGHT
SHADOWMAN
1992/2013
VOODOO
ALYSSA
452/666
MISTER TWIST
SHADOWMAN #7
8-BIT VARIANT
Cover by MATTHEW WAITE

Shadowman #8, p. 13
Pencils by NEIL EDWARDS
Inks by MATT RYAN

Shadowman #8, p. 15
Pencils by NEIL EDWARDS
Inks by MATT RYAN

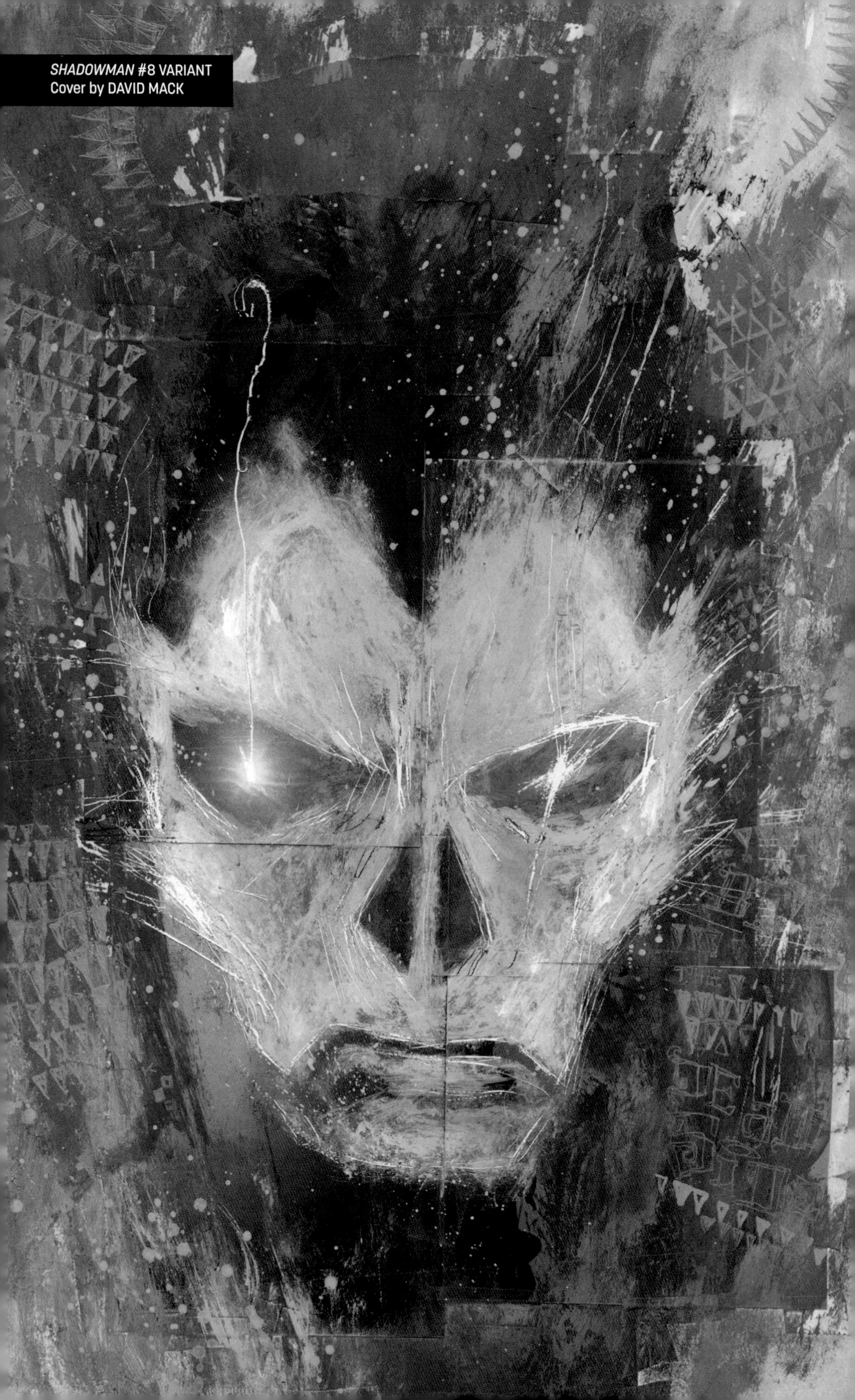

SHADOWMAN #8 VARIANT
Cover by DAVID MACK

SHADOWMAN #8 COVER
Pencils and inks by PATRICK ZIRCHER

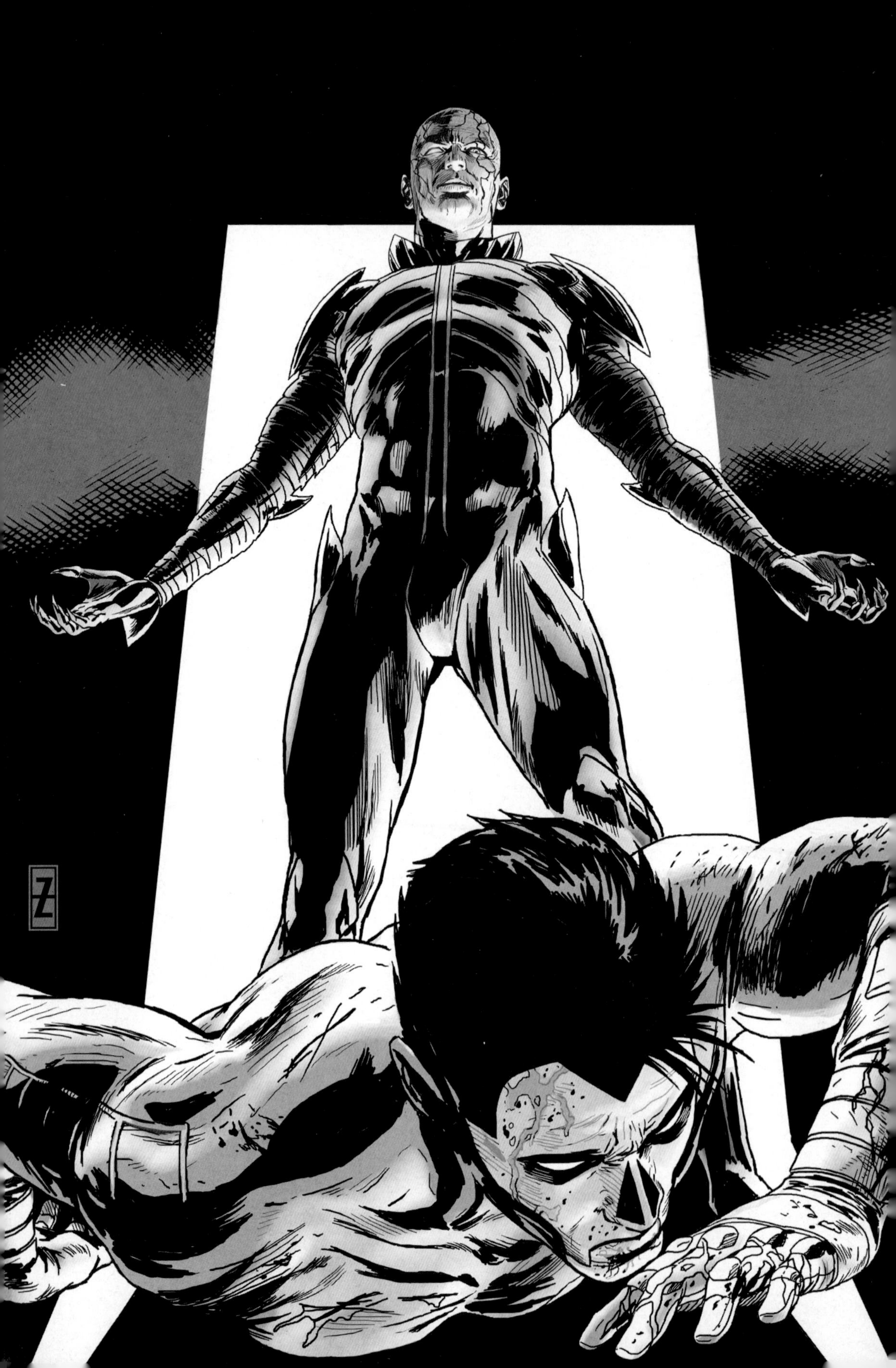

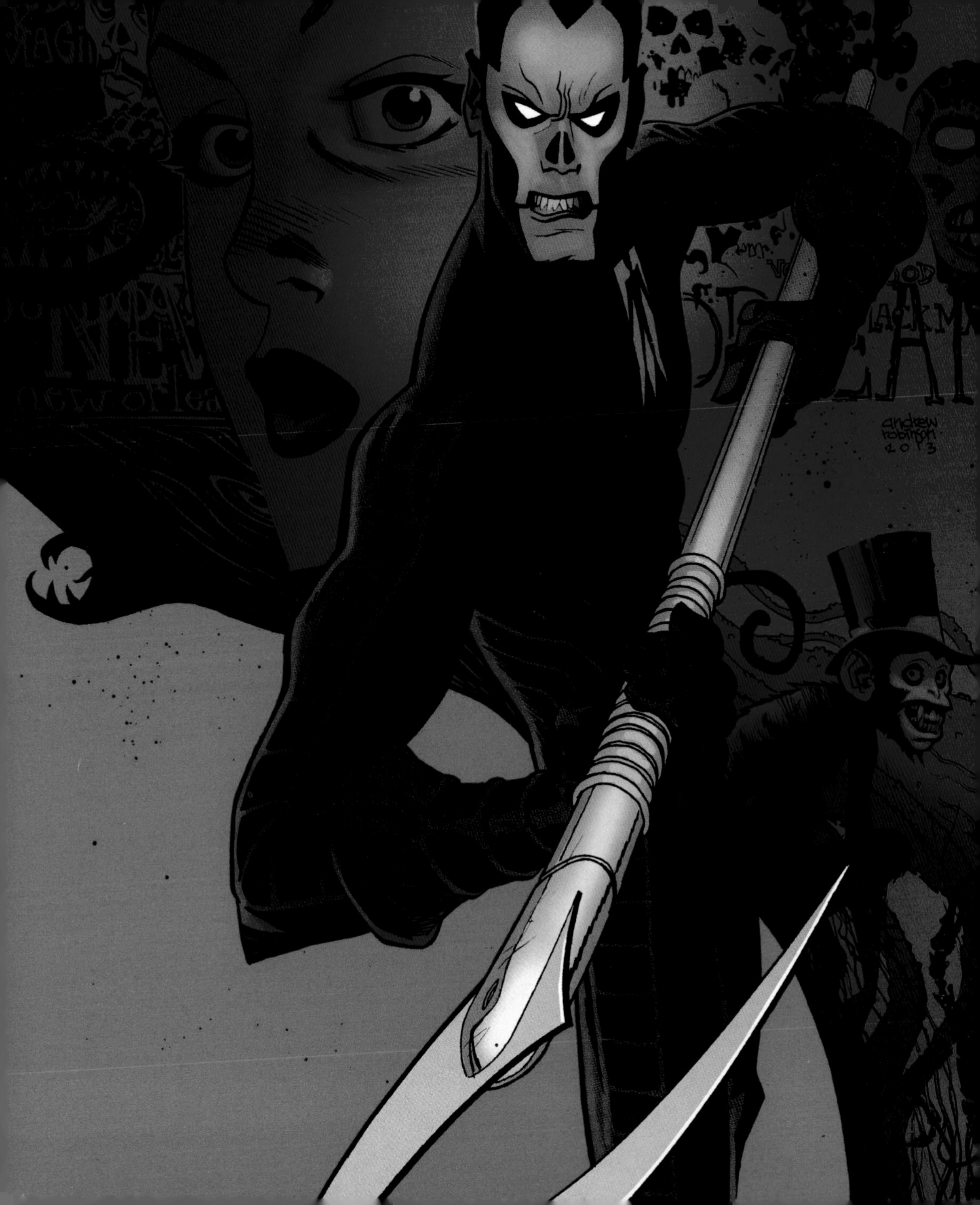
andrew robinson 2013

VALIANT MASTERS

A NEW LINE OF DELUXE HARDCOVERS COLLECTING THE ORIGINAL ADVENTURES OF VALIANT'S GREATEST HEROES FOR THE FIRST TIME ANYWHERE! FEATURING CLASSIC WORK BY SOME OF COMICS' MOST ACCLAIMED TALENTS.

KEVIN VANHOOK | DON PERLIN
VALIANT
BLOOD OF THE MACHINE
BLOODSHOT
VALIANT MASTERS
"Bloodshot reigns supreme as one of the best characters ever created."
- Ain't It Cool News

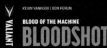

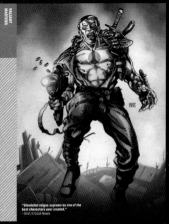

VALIANT MASTERS: BLOODSHOT VOL. 1: BLOOD OF THE MACHINE

Written by KEVIN VANHOOK
Art by DON PERLIN
Cover by BARRY WINDSOR-SMITH

- Collecting **BLOODSHOT #1-8 (1993)** and an all-new, in-continuity story from the original **BLOODSHOT** creative team of **Kevin VanHook**, **Don Perlin**, and **Bob Wiacek** available only in this volume
- Featuring Bloodshot's first solo mission in the Valiant Universe and appearances by **Ninjak**, the **Eternal Warrior** and **Rai**

HARDCOVER
ISBN: 978-0-9796409-3-3

MARK A. MORETTI | JOE QUESADA | JIMMY PALMIOTTI
VALIANT
BLACK WATER
NINJAK
VALIANT MASTERS
"Groundbreaking art and epic characters... [Valiant] set comics on its ears..."
- Ain't It Cool News

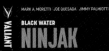

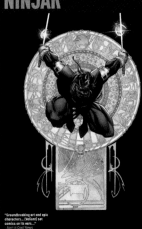

VALIANT MASTERS: NINJAK VOL. 1: BLACK WATER

Written by MARK MORETTI
Art by JOE QUESADA & MARK MORETTI
Cover by JOE QUESADA

- Collecting **NINJAK #1-6 and #0-00 (1994)** with covers, interiors, and rarely seen process art by best-selling artist and creator **Joe Quesada**
- Featuring the complete origin of Valiant's original stealth operative and appearances by **X-O Manowar** and **Bloodshot**

HARDCOVER
ISBN: 978-0-9796409-7-1

JIM SHOOTER | STEVE ENGLEHART | BOB HALL | DAVID LAPHAM | STEVE DITKO
VALIANT
SPIRITS WITHIN
SHADOWMAN
VALIANT MASTERS

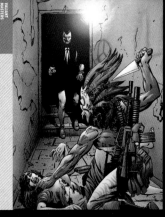

VALIANT MASTERS: SHADOWMAN VOL. 1: SPIRITS WITHIN

Written by STEVE ENGLEHART, BOB HALL, BOB LAYTON, JIM SHOOTER and MORE
Art by STEVE DITKO, BOB HALL, DAVID LAPHAM, DON PERLIN and MORE
Cover by DAVID LAPHAM

- Collecting **SHADOWMAN #0-7 (1992)** and material from **DARQUE PASSAGES #1 (1994)** with an all-new new introduction by visionary Shadowman writer/artist **Bob Hall**
- The first-ever deluxe hardcover collection to feature the origin and debut solo adventures of Shadowman in the original Valiant Universe!

HARDCOVER
ISBN: 978-1-939346-01-8

VALIANT®

EXPLORE THE VALIANT UNIVERSE

X-O MANOWAR VOL. 1:
BY THE SWORD
Written by ROBERT VENDITTI
Art by CARY NORD
Collecting X-O MANOWAR #1-4
TRADE PAPERBACK

X-O MANOWAR VOL. 2:
ENTER NINJAK
Written by ROBERT VENDITTI
Art by LEE GARBETT
Collecting X-O MANOWAR #5-8
TRADE PAPERBACK

HARBINGER VOL. 1: OMEGA RISING
Written by JOSHUA DYSART
Art by KHARI EVANS &
LEWIS LAROSA
Collecting HARBINGER #1-5
TRADE PAPERBACK

HARBINGER VOL. 2: RENEGADES
Written by JOSHUA DYSART
Art by PHIL BRIONES, MATTHEW CLARK,
KHARI EVANS, LEE GARBETT, BARRY KITSON
and PERE PEREZ
Collecting HARBINGER #6-10
TRADE PAPERBACK

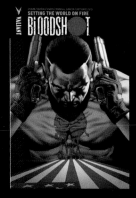

BLOODSHOT VOL. 1:
SETTING THE WORLD ON FIRE
Written by DUANE SWIERCZYNSKI
Art by MANUEL GARCIA & ARTURO LOZZI
Collecting BLOODSHOT #1-4
TRADE PAPERBACK

BLOODSHOT VOL. 2:
THE RISE & THE FALL
Written by DUANE SWIERCZYNSKI
Art by MANUEL GARCIA & ARTURO LOZZI
Collecting BLOODSHOT #5-9
TRADE PAPERBACK

ARCHER & ARMSTRONG VOL. 1:
THE MICHELANGELO CODE
Written by FRED VAN LENTE
Art by CLAYTON HENRY
Collecting ARCHER &
ARMSTRONG #1-4
TRADE PAPERBACK

ARCHER & ARMSTRONG VOL. 2:
WRATH OF THE ETERNAL WARRIOR
Written by FRED VAN LENTE
Art by EMANUELA LUPACCHINO
Collecting ARCHER &
ARMSTRONG #5-9
TRADE PAPERBACK

SHADOWMAN VOL. 1: BIRTH RITES
Written by JUSTIN JORDAN &
PATRICK ZIRCHER
Art by PATRICK ZIRCHER
Collecting SHADOWMAN #1-4
TRADE PAPERBACK

SHADOWMAN

VOLUME THREE: DEADSIDE BLUES

THE SECRET ORIGIN OF ALL SHADOWMEN, PAST AND PRESENT...

Long ago, in the antebellum South, Master Darque's evil spawned the one thing that could stop him: the Shadowman. Now, for the very first time, discover how the dark roots of Darques' depravity has intertwined with Shadowman for more than a century and the betrayal that forged them both in this collection of acclaimed tales from some of comics brightest talents.

Collecting SHADOWMAN #0 and SHADOWMAN #10-12, join Harvey Award-nominated writer Justin Jordan (*The Strange Talent of Luther Strode*) and an all-star cast of visionary creators - including Ales Kot (*Suicide Squad*), Christopher Sebela (*Captain Marvel*), Miguel Sepulveda (*Red Lanterns*), Mico Suayan (*The Punisher*), Jim Zub (*Skullkickers*), and more - for an unadulterated look inside the secret world of New Orleans' nocturnal guardian.

TRADE PAPERBACK
ISBN: 978-1-939346-16-2

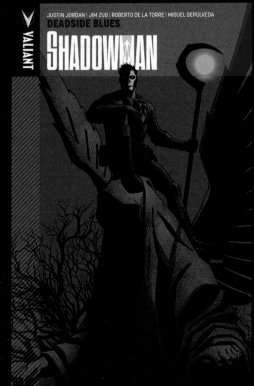

JUSTIN JORDAN | JIM ZUB | ROBERTO DE LA TORRE | MIGUEL SEPULVEDA
DEADSIDE BLUES
SHADOWMAN